How to Become a Miracle-Worker with Your Life

Steps to Use the Almighty Ancient Technique
of Ho'oponopono

How to Become a Miracle-Worker with Your Life

Steps to Use the Almighty Ancient Technique
of Ho'oponopono

Dr. Bruno Roque Cignacco (PhD)

BOOKS

Winchester, UK
Washington, USA

JOHN HUNT PUBLISHING

First published by O-Books, 2015
O-Books is an imprint of John Hunt Publishing Ltd., 3 East St., Alresford,
Hampshire SO24 9EE, UK
office@jhpbooks.com
www.johnhuntpublishing.com
www.o-books.com

For distributor details and how to order please visit the 'Ordering' section on our website.

ISBN: 978 1 78535 121 1
Library of Congress Control Number: 2015936394

A CIP catalogue record for this book is available from the British Library.

Design: Lee Nash

UK: Printed and bound by CPI Group (UK) Ltd, Croydon, CR0 4YY
Printed in North America by CPI GPS partners

We operate a distinctive and ethical publishing philosophy in all
areas of our business, from our global network of authors to
production and worldwide distribution.

CONTENTS

Acknowledgements

This book is dedicated to the memory of my Mother who was the person who first introduced me to the metaphysical principles which have deeply influenced this book. This text is also dedicated to the memory of my Uncle Hugo Francesconi, for his continuous support and faith in me.

I am also deeply grateful to:

– Fayola Saunders, a very sweet and special person in my life who showed great enthusiasm in reviewing the manuscript.
– My Father, my Sister, my Niece and my Godson.
– My Friends.
– My Clients.
– The people working for John Hunt Publishing for their significant support during the publishing process.

You were born with wings. Why prefer to crawl through life?
– Rumi

Prologue I

When the artist paints a painting, you can look at it and say, "Ah, the artist was in a certain frame of mind," or, "Look at the dull colors and the dreary landscape," or, "Look at the wild colors and the fantastic forms," or, "See, there is no form, and yet there is marvelous vitality." And so are each of you artists, and you create the world that you know. And when you look at the world, you know that you can say, "Look, this is what I have created." And if you do not like what you see, then there is no point in ripping apart the painting, or ripping apart the framework of your life. Instead, you change your pigments. And in this case, your pigments are your thoughts and your imagination. And then you change your painting.
– Seth

Before introducing this book, I would like to tell you a real story that happened some years ago. This tale is about a medic called Dr. Ihaleakala Hew Len who is a well-renowned Hawaiian psychologist. At first when I read about this, I thought that the whole story was fabricated or it was just a popular legend. Nevertheless I progressively discovered that the entire story was true.

In the past Dr. Len began working at the forensic unit of a mental hospital in Hawaii, more specifically in the psychiatric department. The ward in which Dr. Len worked was full of mentally ill criminals. Many people imprisoned wore restraints on their wrists or ankles, and were kept in total seclusion.

When Dr. Len arrived at the hospital for the first time, he was informed that some patients had attacked other people. Some members of the personnel working there quit their jobs because they truly believed it was very dangerous. Before starting work, Dr. Len clearly stated that when working there he wanted to apply his special methodology to deal with the inmates.

1

When working at the hospital Dr. Len used a non-traditional method over many months in a silent but disciplined manner. At the ward, he became well known for having cured many inmates. When he was asked about this, Dr. Len admitted that he never saw the prisoners personally. Dr. Len never prescribed any medication either. The question that you must be surely asking yourself is: *"How did Dr. Len cure those inmates if he did not even have any direct contact with them?"*

In an interview Dr. Len commented that one of the things he did over the months when working at his post was to look at the patients' medical records. He also commented that every working day while he was reading the inmates' files he asked himself: *"What is going on in me that I manifest this?"* He posed that question to himself in order to know which dark traits (or negative emotions, such as revenge, hatred, etc.) were going on in his life which made him responsible for manifesting those dangerous people in the ward.

From this particular perspective, Dr. Len considered that he was personally responsible for everything going on in his life, even the current state of the inmates. He also said that he continually said these phrases: *"I am sorry"*, *"I love you"*, *"Please forgive me"* and *"Thank you."* These four sentences are related to an ancient Hawaiian technique called Ho'oponopono. He explained that the continual repetition of those sentences has a healing effect. With the repetition of these four phrases Dr. Len said that he was cleaning his own subconscious negative memories, which implied his detrimental judgments, attitudes and beliefs about those prisoners. As Dr. Len used this special technique most of the inmates became progressively cured.

Over time, when Dr. Len was working at the ward, the prisoners were unshackled and some new in-ward and off-ward activities were introduced in that workplace. As he continued using this special technique the staff working at the prison could hold medical conversations with the inmates safely, something unimaginable in the past.

Questions you might be asking yourself right now are: *"How could this happen?", "Did Dr. Len use a kind of magic?"* or *"How did Dr. Len, by repeating these four sentences ("I am sorry", "I love you", "Please forgive me", "Thank you"), cure these inmates?"* When asked about this, this professional said that he had subconscious memories which were shared with these prisoners. These inmates turned up in his life because his own subconscious memories manifested that situation.

Dr. Len explained that, by repeating the Ho'oponopono's sentences (*"I am sorry", "Please forgive me", "I love you"* and *"Thank you"*), he progressively cleaned his own negative subconscious mind of past data, which included the memories connecting him with those perilous inmates. As a consequence, most of the inmates recovered completely.

After a while, the entire prison was closed down because it became totally unnecessary. This story might appear difficult to believe. Nonetheless, all over this book you will see that the cleaning technique used by Dr. Len is extremely powerful because it is very real.

Prologue II

Ho'oponopono is a simple way to arriving at unity, inner space and returning to harmony. Ho'oponopono implies solving a problem from the ground up and applying the solution to useful ends. It expresses the deep need to live once again in harmony with oneself and with humanity, nature and God.

– Ulrich Dupree

With the upsurge of the New Age trend, there are several techniques, some of them widely promoted, that you can use for your personal evolution. These worthy instruments can help you to improve your life in different dimensions such as prosperity, health, relationships, career, and others.

You might have tried some of these tools (for example: visualization, affirmations, etc.), and at least temporarily benefited from them. However, you might also have had some doubts about the real scope and duration of the positive effects of these very methods. You could also have felt that most of these tools seem to deal only with the consequences of your difficulties, and not with their causes.

If this was your experience, you might have wondered whether there was a method with a different perspective on personal transformation, with more longstanding effects, a tool which could eradicate your problems straightforwardly from their causes and for good.

Over the different chapters and appendices of this book a powerful technique called Ho'oponopono will be explained. This tool has real alchemic power because it removes the problematic situations in your life from their root, instead of temporarily fixing them. From this perspective, the main cause of all the difficulties in your life are memories or past programming you hold on your subconscious level.

Even though you cannot realize the presence of these subconscious programs, at least directly, you can notice some of their effects, which are your negative life circumstances. In many cases you deal with the same difficulties (consequences) again and again because their origin (or cause) is your subconscious programs.

Albert Einstein once said, *"There are only two ways to live your life. One is as though nothing is a miracle. The other one is as though everything is a miracle."* With the frequent use of Ho'oponopono, your whole life will be turned into a miracle because this technique will help you transmute discordant conditions into harmonious ones.

Besides, when you clean your subconscious mind from its limiting memories, you will also be reconnected to the unbounded ocean of wisdom and love, which is called the Divine. This divine source will provide you with useful guidance and loving support to make your life progress in all dimensions. With the divine support you will fully harness your inner resources to evolve endlessly.

The Divine is not different from you; in fact, it is the essence of all that you are. The main religions in the world agree on the fact you are the likeness and image of Divinity. In accordance to this, Dr. Len wisely states that: *"this lifetime is truly a gift from the Divine... we are carbon copies of this pure perfect source."*

Ho'oponopono is not another tool that comes in vogue; it is not a quick-fix remedy either. Even though many scholars cannot scientifically explain the positive effects of the use of this technique, its value cannot be deprecated. There is much anecdotal evidence about the overwhelming power of this tool all over the world. Its effectiveness has been displayed in various fields, such as: healing of health conditions and increases in abundance, among others.

If you are, like most people, harassed by umpteen difficulties, there is good news for you. Your problems can be considered as prized opportunities to test the power of the Ho'oponopono technique. If you truly want to improve your life, you must give this tool a try.

Some masters called Ho'oponopono a *"miracle-maker tool."* Siegel states that: *"a true miracle is often defined as an event that defies the laws of nature"* and also as *"God's redirections from which something good would come."* In accordance to this definition, the frequent application of Ho'oponopono will bring about positive occurrences in life, which are unlikely to be explained with logical arguments.

In order to see the effects of this wonderful technique, you must follow all the specific guidelines thoroughly described in this book. The use of this tool will not actually take a lot of effort. When you do Ho'oponopono you are in contact with Divine energy, and Divinity never uses the hard way; everything occurs smoothly and at ease. From this perspective, all resources you need at any moment are provided in the most adequate fashion.

Ho'oponopono just requires that you periodically say four sentences (*"I am sorry"*, *"Please forgive me"*, *"I love you"* and *"Thank you"*). If you apply this technique with consistency, you will surely see tangible results, when least expected. Sometimes your problems will be solved in a heartbeat; other times they will take a longer time.

Ho'oponopono is not only a simple tool but also a flexible one. Once you understand the basics of this tool, you can morph it and use your own version of it. This text contains a wealth of knowledge on it and can certainly be considered as an over-arching manual about these topics. The different chapters of this book will delineate the main principles underpinning this tool, a thorough analysis of the four Ho'oponopono sentences and countless practical and easy-to-apply exercises, among other topics.

It is advisable to read the whole book, at least once, before putting this knowledge into practice. Once again do not let these words wrap you in a layer of doubt. It behooves you to test this ancient technique; this is the only way for it to actually work for you.

Section I

Essence and Principles of Ho'oponopono

This section sets out the main traits and principles of this ancient technique.

Chapter 1

Essence of Ho'oponopono

Canst thou not minister to a mind diseased;
Pluck from the memory a rooted sorrow;
Raze out the written troubles of the brain,
and with sweet oblivious antidote
Cleanse the stuff'd bossom of that perilous staff which weighs
upon the heart?
– William Shakespeare, Macbeth

1. Origin of the word "Ho'oponopono"

You are a special piece of work, noble in reason, infinite in faculties,
express and admirable in form and moving, like an angel in action,
like a god in apprehension.
– Og Mandino

The etymology of this tool's name is quite revealing by itself.
When the word "Ho'oponopono" is broken down, the first part
Ho'o means *"to perform"*, *"to make"*, *"to carry out"* or *"to make it
happen."* On the other side, *pono* has several meanings such as
"good", *"virtuous"*, *"correct"*, *"moral"*, *"proper"*, *"right"*, *"adequate"*,
"orderly", *"aligned"* or *"true in essence."*

The word *pono* is used twice (*ponopono*) in the name of this
technique in order to emphasize its meaning. Lee states: *"If it is
good, if it is in balance, if it is right, if it helps, if it is righteous, if it
corrects, if it is responsible, if it is caring, if it is humble, if it is peaceful,
if it honors, it is pono."*

In short, the overall meaning of Ho'oponopono is *"to correct"*,
"to make things in the right fashion", *"to mend mistakes"*, *"to repair"*
or *"to rectify things."* It is a very effective tool to fix all things that

you dislike in your life. You use this technique to correct any errors by deleting the memories held on your subconscious level. These subconscious programs are being replayed constantly, without you even noticing them, and hinder your connection with the Divine. As said in the second Prologue, these subconscious memories are the only cause of all the negative circumstances in your life. These programs do not allow you to receive any inspirational guidance from the Divine.

Ho'oponopono is actually a technique to resolve all your problems. Every time you experience a problem, there are subconscious memories playing out in your mind which are creating this very difficulty.

This tool was originally applied by the indigenous Hawaiian shamans called *kahunas* to solve conflicts among members of the local communities. In that sense, DeNoyelles states that: *"Ho'oponopono is an ancient... healing art of reconciliation and forgiveness that's been used for centuries to support, correct, restore, and maintain harmonious relationships between people, Nature and Spirit."* You will find more details about the traditional way of doing Ho'oponopono in Appendix C. During the last few years this powerful tool has become well-known worldwide; its benefits are enjoyed in different latitudes far beyond the tiny archipelago in the Pacific Ocean where it saw its origins.

2. Characteristics of this technique

Ho'oponopono is a distinctive transformative tool. Some of the main characteristics of this technique are:

a) Simplicity and effortlessness
For some people, the straightforwardness of this potent technique is quite shocking. Despite its simple way of use, this tool is very effective. In order to do Ho'oponopono you only have to say four sentences (*"I am sorry"*, *"Please forgive me"*, *"I love you"* and *"Thank you"*) as frequently as possible. The effectiveness of this technique

11

lays on its consistent and determined use over time.

This tool is totally within your grasp and it can be applied everywhere and on any occasion, which makes this tool very flexible. You don't have to perform any complicated rituals to see tangible results. Some say you do not have to believe in the effectiveness of this technique to enjoy its positive effects.

This technique is based on the principle of effortlessness. In order to transmute your life circumstances, you don't need to struggle or work hard. With this technique all your negative life circumstances will be transmuted naturally.

When you use this tool, you must fully accept your adverse life situations to clean your subconscious memories originating them. You should take full responsibility and realize your subconscious programs are the only cause of all your life circumstances.

This tool should be used regularly because you have umpteen subconscious memories which need to be deleted. When you do Ho'oponopono you delete past memories incorporated in your subconscious mind a long time ago and also recently. In your daily life, you are constantly incorporating, most of the time unwittingly, new subconscious memories. This makes Ho'oponopono a non-stop process, a continual process.

b) Based on love, forgiveness and gratitude
One of the four Ho'oponopono sentences is "I am sorry." This means that you are repentant for your mistakes; you recognize them and want to do things better. You also realize that these mistakes made you temporarily disconnected from the Divine.

From the Ho'oponopono perspective repentance is acknowledgement and confession of your wrongdoings in a guiltless and humble manner. When you are truly repentant you can take responsibility for your life. This attitude allows you to remove your subconscious memories, which create all circumstances in your life.

The second phrase is "Please forgive me." When you repeat

these words, you are looking for reconciliation with your own being. With this sentence you seek forgiveness for having held subconscious memories. You are not in denial any longer because you admit that your subconscious programs manifested all your life circumstances.

By asking for forgiveness you also release any grievance, tension, grudge or resentment tying you to the past. You also open your heart in a compassionate manner to heal all emotional wounds with unconditional love. When you frequently use the phrase "Please forgive me" you want to remove your past programming, which is the source of all pain in your life. You also realize that even though you are fallible, your pure essence is seamless and you can do things correctly from now on.

Another Ho'oponopono sentence is "I love you." With these words you can connect with a high vibratory state such as love, which is the most expansive and harmonizing energy that exists. Love enlivens everything in the Universe. Every time you experience the energy of love, you are connected to Divinity and also focused on your divine core.

When you say "I love you" frequently you express your love to your memories to dissolve them. These subconscious programs give you the chance to delete them, and restore your connection to Divinity. Love allows you to go beyond appearances to dwell in your unpolluted true nature.

Many religious masters have wisely stated: *"Love your foes."* Your subconscious programs are actually your enemies. When you do Ho'oponopono you embrace these enemies with the energy of love to diffuse them.

The fourth sentence you must repeat when doing Ho'oponopono is *"Thank you."* It is said that whenever you are thankful, you appreciate all good things around you. All states of fear, guilt, and self-punishment are gracefully cast behind when you are appreciative, because you focus only on the positive. When you say *"Thank you"* you also express your gratitude for going through the cleaning process of your subconscious memories.

When you are appreciative you can also accept your mistakes with no reservation. With a thankful attitude you are more prone to make things right, which implies removing your subconscious memories. Forgiveness is the best gift you can give yourself; it sets you free from your subconscious programs, but also free to receive divine inspiration.

c) Wide application

Ho'oponopono can be applied by any person, regardless of their age, nationality, occupation or gender. This tool is not related to any religion or cult. This technique is of great value to solve both big problems and very small ones and it can improve your life in all dimensions: health problems (mental, spiritual, emotional or physical), financial predicaments, career failure and relational disagreements, among others.

Satyam says that this tool can be applied to overcoming limiting beliefs, solving problems of anxiety, curing physical symptoms, fixing conflicting relationships, purifying unhealthy places or objects, and also tackling the end of certain life cycles (such as: divorce, bankruptcy, bereavement, etc.). The use of this tool has an overarching application.

Another point to highlight is the long-lasting effects of Ho'oponopono. This cleaning tool is focused on releasing or cleaning your past programming. All negative situations are manifested in your life because of programs playing out on your subconscious level. When you utilize this technique you remove the root of your problems. As a consequence of this, your difficulties tend to disappear naturally.

d) Partnership with Divinity

Every time you use Ho'oponopono your subconscious memories are being erased with the assistance of Divinity. The Divine (or any other name that you want to use) is the main source of unconditional love and peacefulness. Divinity is always willing to help you remove your subconscious programming. All people can access this radiant energy, which is all-merciful, compassionate and forgiving and transformative. All you have to do is claim it by applying Ho'oponopono. The Divine is where you naturally belong to, so your true nature is pure, unpolluted and seamless. Your subconscious negative memories are temporarily interfering in your natural connection with your divine essence.

When you practice Ho'oponopono, you are dealing with the most powerful energy ever conceived because you are in partnership with Divinity. Any error can be easily rectified when you request the Divine to do so by doing Ho'oponopono.

When you delete your subconscious programs you arrive at a state called *zero point*, where there are no subconscious memories. At this state you are more prone to receive divine inspirational messages.

In performing this ancient technique you can return to your essential state of purity and equilibrium, in which you are essentially a perfect replica of the Divine. In this state you are being driven only by divine directions, instead of being prodded by your subconscious memories.

When you practice Ho'oponopono, you are actually working with Divinity, which is omniscient and omnipresent. This almighty divine power admits no defeat and has no limits. With the continuous application of this technique you will become more inspired and insightful; your entire life will become more meaningful and graceful.

3. Benefits of doing Ho'oponopono

It is important to highlight that the benefits which you can obtain from the use of this technique are closely correlated to its frequent application. You can never use this technique too much.

Some changes will take some time to appear; but sometimes you can benefit from this tool almost instantaneously. In all cases, you should always be very patient and committed to this technique. Some of the benefits you can gain from the use of Ho'oponopono are:

- *Elimination of your past subconscious programming*
- *Dissolution of physical and emotional pain*
- *Healing of any type of illness (emotional, mental or physical)*
- *Purification of your mind and body*
- *Boosting of your overall levels of energy*
- *Enhancement of your motivation*
- *Strengthening of your immune system*
- *Betterment of all other body systems (digestive, respiratory, reproductive, etc.)*
- *Rejuvenation of your cells*
- *Prolongation of your life*
- *Removal of any addiction*
- *Elimination of depression and feelings of loneliness*
- *More clarity and sharpness of mind*
- *More awareness of the present moment*
- *Increase in your creativity*
- *Frequent connection to the "zone" or state of flow*
- *Elimination of your worries and fear*
- *Ousting of your resentment, guilt and blame*
- *Improvement of your self-worth and self-confidence*
- *Achievement of better emotional awareness*
- *Solution of relational problems*
- *Development of better social skills*
- *Improvement in your career and job prospects*
- *Betterment of your financial situation*
- *Spiritual awakening and enlightenment*
- *Access to unlimited wisdom and Divine Guidance*
- *More peacefulness and happiness*

– *Experiences of forgiveness, thankfulness and pure love*
– *Access to a more meaningful life*
– *Significant contribution to your environment*

Chapter 2

Everything is Interconnected

1. Main aspects of Holism

The rich tapestry of life weaves its love in every atom and allows us to play in the vast field of infinite oneness.
– Harold Becker

Many masters say the Ho'oponopono is intimately related to the standpoint of Holism. The holistic perspective is applied by certain schools of thought in disciplines like Psychology, Theology, Anthropology, Philosophy, Sociology and Medicine. Holism states that every single thing or being that exists in the Universe is interconnected with all the rest.

Gutowski says that:

We are all connected by the very energy that forms us. This connectivity does not end with living beings; we are linked to the farthest star in the universe as well as every grain of sand in an earthbound desert.

A quite recent but very well-known discipline called Quantum Physics confirmed this principle too. Likewise, Metaphysics asserted this viewpoint for many centuries.

From the holistic perspective, you are united to everything. Ramesh Balsekar states that: *"all there is, is this wholeness and that wholeness is really and truly indivisible. In other words the human mind... divides what is naturally indivisible and therefore gets into trouble."*

It is important to know that the holistic standpoint is also related to the systemic perspective. In any system, all its factors are closely interrelated; they are continually affecting one another. Besides this, each system has a function and each of the components has particular functions which contribute to the overall function of the system. The behavior of any system is generally unpredictable. Statistical science knows this and takes into account error margins in the estimation of the systems' activities. The comportment of a system cannot be estimated with extreme precision because of the multiple relationships among its components.

From this perspective, the whole (or system) cannot be explained throughout any of its components (or parts). When you focus on only a part of the whole, the knowledge about that part will be partial. To thoroughly understand any factor of the system you have to take into account the wholeness this factor belongs to.

You can apply this systemic approach to your body and its organs. Societies can also be considered as systems. The same perspective can be applied to nature and its phenomena and elements. The market itself is a system where there exist producers, consumers, government and other agents.

Cultures are systems which have specific factors, such as verbal and non-verbal language, customs, food, dance, history and others, which are closely related to one another. Organizations are also systems which have internal structures (departments, sections or divisions) which vary according the organization analyzed. Organizations, in turn, belong to bigger systems like associations, confederations, sectors, etc.

The Universe can also be considered as a big system itself, with different (countless) components. Everything that exists can be considered as part of an overarching and complex system, the Universe. Besides, the Universe itself is a set of self-contained systems.

2. You are a system

We are, all of us, creatures of parts, used to beginnings, middles, and ends because our lives are divided that way, and our language... follows the same logic... But the spirit is one and undivided, without parts, not chained to beginnings or middles or ends, and thus not dependent upon sequential reasoning... its province, its everything, is wholeness.

– Ann and Barry Ulanov

You, as an individual, can also be considered as a system. You, as a human being, are a system which is made up of several subsystems. These subsystems are your organs which are made up of cells. These cells are composed of molecules; molecules are made up of atoms. You are a set of self-contained systems.

From the medical perspective, mind and body work in a coordinated manner, as part of an integral system. Medically speaking you can also recognize many systems in your body, such as the respiratory system, nervous system, endocrine system, circulatory system, digestive system, among others. Your mind can also be considered a system, composed of three subsystems: your super conscious mind, your conscious mind and your subconscious mind.

You as an individual belong to bigger systems, such as your family, your work team and your friends groups. Other systems you belong to are your local community, your country, the world and the Universe.

All the components of the systems you belong to are affecting you and vice versa. The same happens with all the subsystems within you. For this reason, you, as an individual, cannot be entirely analyzed without considering the environments (systems) where you operate and the subsystems you enclose.

3. You share the essence with all that exists

There is a thinking stuff from which all things are made, and which, in its original state, permeates, penetrates and fills the interspaces of the universe.
– Wallace Wattles

From the holistic viewpoint, you are linked to all that surrounds you and you also experience the state of sameness regarding all that exists. Regarding this, traditional Physics says that every single thing that exists is made up the same substance, which is energy.

Over many centuries many metaphysicians also state that all things are made up of vibrating living energy. Nonetheless what differentiates one thing from another is the particular information it encloses, as well as its particular vibratory rate.

In a different tone, some mystics say that the main essence of everything that exists in the Universe is love, which is the most pure energy. Likewise, DeNoyelles states that:

Love... is the foundation for all existence. Everything manifest is birthed upon the waves of this frequency, so it is this fabric of love that binds us together, individually as well as collectively.

This author also says that: *"Our relationship with our essence (love) has been compromised due to the emotional chaos and deep grief we have experienced as humans. We suffer under the illusion of isolation, of separateness from love, our source."* From the Ho'oponopono perspective you generally tend to feel as if you were separated from the source of love because of the memories held in your subconscious mind, which are also the cause of all the pain in your life.

4. Separation and the holistic perspective

As was said, the holistic paradigm recognizes that everything which exists in the Universe is interconnected. The metaphysical Law of Unity states the same: separation does not exist, it's just an illusion. Eisenstein says that: *"separation is not an ultimate reality, but a human projection, an ideology, a story."* The common thread that unites everything which exists can adopt different names (such as love, God, etc.) according to various perspectives.

Nonetheless most people cannot actually perceive that they are connected with all that exists. When you cannot perceive your interconnection with all that exists you tend to control your environment. When you are driven by a perception of separation, you tend to manipulate the world according to your needs, in many cases by any means possible.

When you feel disconnected to everything that exists, you avoid taking full responsibility; moreover, you tend to behave in a condemning manner, casting guilt on external factors for what is going on in your life. You also tend to dwell in states of fear or anxiety regarding your external circumstances. This also can bring about a tendency to judge and manipulate the "external factors." You also tend to think that scarcity is the common factor in this world, which means that for you to have more, others must get less.

5. Holism and wholeness

We are spokes of a wheel, radiating from the same center.
– Marianne Williamson

We are the Power and Presence of God. We are a consciousness of Oneness that is perfect harmony, joyful, all-knowing, infinitely abundant and all-powerful.
– Arnold Patent

Many spiritual masters state that everything has the seed of Divinity. Moreover you are the natural expression of the Divine. Nonetheless, your divine traits are generally obscured by countless subconscious memories, running in the fathoms of your mind.

Many ancient cultures support the idea that every single thing, even apparently inanimate objects (such as a chair, a house, a piece of land, etc.), have their inherent living spirit. Likewise, some philosophies say that every single thing has a soul or consciousness.

From this perspective, your spiritual part is connected to the spirit of everything that exists in the Universe. The core essence of every single thing is pervaded by the divine universal energy. This source can be called the Divine, God or Love, and it originated and animates everything that exists.

When you regularly say the four Ho'oponopono sentences ("*I am sorry*", "*Please forgive me*", "*I love you*" and "*Thank you*") you reconnect with the Divine, which is the source of pure limitless love. This tool transforms your life from a state of brokenness to a state of wholeness. This technique helps you remove your subconscious programs but it also fills you with pure divine love.

When you are fully connected to Divinity, which means you have removed all your subconscious memories, your life tends to flow effortlessly. In that state, called zero point, you are constantly supported by the Divine; you are naturally driven by divine wisdom. In accordance to this, Jirsch and Cafferky say that: "*the more separate we feel, the harder life is.*"

6. Other aspects of the holistic perspective

True spirituality also is to be aware that if we are interdependent with everything and everyone else, even our smallest, least significant thought, word, and action have real consequences throughout the universe.

– Sogyal Rinpoche

Ho'oponopono also supports that everything is interconnected. Every action that you perform or thought that you hold has an effect on you and others. When you see an inharmonious situation outside, there is a subconscious memory inside your mind which is not balanced and is manifesting that very situation in your environment. Your life circumstances are a reflection to past memories you hold on your subconscious level.

In Metaphysics there is a universal principle called the Law of Causality. This law states that every cause has an effect and vice versa. From the Ho'oponopono perspective, every circumstance you experience in your life is a mere consequence of past memories playing out in your subconscious mind.

As a consequence, when you delete these subconscious programs, by regularly doing Ho'oponopono, your life circumstances are completely transformed. Due to the holistic principle of interrelatedness, when you improve yourself you will positively impact on everything around you.

From this perspective, you also share subconscious programs with people around you. So when you delete your subconscious memories, not only will your situation improve, but this will also affect positively the lives of people in your environment.

7. Some examples of interconnectedness

Our lives are not compartmentalized; there is natural unity beneath apparent diversity and separation. You might sense that there is separation in everything that exists; that is just an illusion. From the Ho'oponopono perspective, this illusion is created by your mind, more specifically your subconscious memories. You can see below several examples of the symbiotic interdependence of everything that exists.

7.1. Maharishi Effect

The experiment named *Maharishi Effect* was conducted in several cities in the world. The researcher wanted to prove that when many people did meditation on a regular and coordinated basis, this practice could improve the life quality of the overall population in the cities where the practitioners lived. Some masters assert that continual practice of meditation connects you with everything that exists, creating positive effects in your environment.

After specific groups of people meditated for many days or weeks, the researcher observed that the quality levels of the people's cities improved substantially. This was due to the positive effects of meditation on their overall population, and not only on the practitioners. Some indicators of this were: decrease in psychiatric emergency calls, reduction of criminality rate, fewer accidents, among others. In relation to this McTaggart says that: *"the energy from a collective, intensely felt thought appears to be infectious."*

7.2. Hundred monkey experiment

There is a very interesting study known as the *hundredth monkey effect*. In a Japanese island there were a few monkeys learning how to wash sweet potatoes in order to eat them. After a while, this group was also imitated by all the other monkeys living in the same island.

When the amount of monkeys carrying out this task (washing the potatoes) reached a critical amount, this learned behavior spread beyond the original territory where these monkeys were located, for example, macaques located in other islands nearby. However, this phenomenon has been discredited by some skeptical people.

7.3. Other aspects

In the case of your health, you know that your physical aspects are interrelated to your mental and emotional ones; these aspects act like a system. The same analogy can be applied to your organs and cells. When one of your organs does not work well, this affects the overall state of your well-being.

In the case of the natural environment, you can see the intricacy of links among everything that exists. All species and natural elements are acting in state of complete interrelatedness. You can also observe that the global warming effects are just the consequence of the alteration of some of the critical components of the ecosystem.

In accordance to this, Rinpoche says that:

Modern science speaks to us of an extraordinary range of interrelations. Ecologists know that a tree burning in the Amazon rain forest alters in some way the air breathed by a citizen of Paris, and that the trembling of a butterfly's wing in the Yucatan affects the life of a fern in the Hebrides...

Lastly the prestigious scientist Dr. Hawkins says that there are different levels of consciousness and the most elevated types of energy are love, joy, peace and enlightenment. His research concluded that each person that experiences these powerful states (such as: love, joy, peace, etc.) counteracts the negative states (for example: anger, fear, guilt, etc.) of thousands of people in the world.

8. Solipsism

We may well go to the moon, but that's not very far, the greatest distance we have to cover still lies within us.
– Charles de Gaulle

Solipsism's distinctive philosophical perspective states that what is in your mind exists as *reality*. Every circumstance that you face up to in your life is a literal projection of your thoughts. Solipsistic supporters say that the outer world cannot be grasped directly, but only through your mind. Many sages have also stated that your outer world is just a reflection of your inner word; *reality* does not exist in an objective fashion, separate from you.

Ho'oponopono agrees with certain points exposed by Solipsism. For example, you are the one who creates, attracts or manifest your *reality* with the memories playing out on your subconscious level. The outer environment is just an accurate reflection of your inner world. These subconscious memories are the *lens* through which you perceive your outer world and act on it.

Metaphysics also says that you create your reality with the thoughts that you hold in your mind. Likewise Quantum Physics also states that you create things through your observation.

However, Ho'oponopono has a significant difference with the main essence of the solipsistic principle, which states that what is in your mind is your reality. In that effect, Ho'oponopono does not deny the reality of the consciousness of other people; instead solipsistic perspective does deny this. According to Perez, Ho'oponopono does accept the existence of the other human beings, which have free will by nature. Every time you are in contact with other people you have actually invited them to your world because of the subconscious memories you share with them.

9. Practical tips

You can find below some practical recommendations related to the topics explained over this chapter:

– You must always bear in mind that all things which exist are interconnected. Every single thing in the Universe is linked to one another. Interrelatedness is one of the main principles that rule the Universe. From a practical perspective, what you do always affects others, either directly or indirectly, and vice versa. Try to think about this idea as frequently as possible.

– You belong to different groups (family, friends, associations, etc.) that are systems. From a wider perspective, you are also inserted into even bigger systems, like cities, countries, etc. Try to analyze how the components of any of these systems you belong to affect one another.

– You are also a system on your own; you are a set of self-contained systems. For example, your body is a system made up of several organs which affect one another. And these organs are formed of cells, and so on. It is important for you to dwell on these topics frequently in order to have a more accurate perception of your own functioning, from a holistic perspective.

– There is another interesting exercise. Sit down in a comfortable place with your eyes closed. Breathe slowly for a while and relax your muscles. After this, visualize that every organ in your body is related to one another in a harmonious way. You can also imagine that all the cells of your body cooperate with one another to make your whole body work well.

– You can also repeat this sentence: *"I am connected to everything. I am part of all that exists. Every little thing is linked with the rest"* whenever possible. Then wait for some insights, take notes and read them carefully. Lastly, you should say the four Ho'oponopono sentences: *"I am sorry"*, *"Please forgive me"*, *"I love you"* and *"Thank you"* many times. This exercise removes all subconscious memories hindering your acceptance of the principle of interconnectedness.

– There is another well-known exercise. Sit in a quiet place, with your eyes closed, calm and relaxed. Slow down your breath and vividly imagine luminous threads connecting you to everything that exists. When you practice this, you will experience your connection with all that exits, in a more tangible way.

– There is second version of the exercise mentioned above.

When walking down the street or in any public place, imagine with your eyes open that you are linked by a radiant beam of light to everything that you encounter (people, buildings and any other thing) in the street.

– There is yet another version of this exercise. When you have a conversation with someone, you must imagine that you are linked to this person by an iridescent ray of light. After a while, the conversation will become more meaningful and the relationship with this person is strengthened.

– You can also apply the systemic approach to nature. You can do an easy exercise when you walk through a natural landscape. At that place, see that nature as components (such as grass, trees, birds and others) which are interrelated and in a complete state of balance and which have specific functions. Besides, sense that there is a common living force which makes that natural system work effortlessly. Lastly, you should try to feel the interconnectedness of every single thing in that natural landscape with you.

– There is a very interesting exercise you can do in your spare time. Any topic can be analyzed from different perspectives, which are all part of a system. For example, when you assess a national economy, it can be analyzed from different viewpoints: technological, cultural and financial, among others. These give you a more complete picture of the economy. These factors are relevant for a complete analysis, and affect one another. So, when you analyze any topic, try to use as many perspectives as possible and observe their inter-relation among the different factors involved.

– There is another well-known exercise: you must take into account one specific product you have at home, for example, tomatoes. From the system perspective, these tomatoes are a consequence of a complex series of activities performed by various factors, for example, people who worked in farms, the company who carried the packs with tomatoes and the grocery shop who sold them to you, among others. These factors are part of a coordinated system, from the holistic perspective. From the marketing viewpoint all these components or factors are called the value chain, because they all added value so that tomatoes reached your hands. You can do the same exercise using any other product or service.

– From the Ho'oponopono perspective, everything around you is a projection of your subconscious memories. So if you are affected by different problems, such as negative health conditions or financial difficulties, the most effective way to solve these problems is to remove your subconscious memories. You can remove these subconscious programs by repeatedly saying the sentences: *"I am sorry"*, *"Please forgive me"*, *"I love you"* and *"Thank you."* As previously explained, when you say these sentences, your life will improve and you will also positively affect other people around you.

Chapter 3

Your Memories are Playing Out Constantly

It's here in the beginning of a healing journey that we can recognize the stories we tell ourselves... Stories are mud. It is by attaching to the stories that we feel angry with a cause, justified or empowered beyond our norm.
– Lisa Marie Gutowski

The past lives in you as memories, but memories in themselves are not a problem. In fact, it is through memory that we learn from the past and from past mistakes. It's only when memories, that is to say, thoughts about the past, take you over completely that they turn into a burden, turn problematic, and become part of your sense of self.
– Eckhart Tolle

1. Your past is still in you

Each piece of information entering your brain – each feeling, remembrance, thought (including word, number, code, nutrient, perfume, line, color, image, pulse, note and texture) can be represented as a central sphere, from which radiates dozens, hundreds, thousands, millions of hooks. Each hook represents an association and each association has its own infinite number of connections. The number of associations you have already used can be regarded as your memory, database or library... in the mind lays a data managerial system that makes the analytical and storage capacities of the fastest supercomputer in the world... look tiny in comparison.
– Tony Buzan

From the metaphysical perspective, you have a natural state of perfection. You are the Divine in essence; you carry unconditional love and unlimited power and wisdom. However, you are constantly beset by umpteen subconscious programs clogging your mind. You have a thicket of countless memories of past situations, which include activities, people, places and things. All these programs obscure your connection with your divine essence.

These memories have different names, for example: beliefs, values, recollections, habits, paradigms and perspectives, among others. In all cases, this past data is embedded in your subconscious mind. In relation to this, you have two types of past programming. On one side, you have positive subconscious memories, which bring about beneficial situations in your life. On the other side, you also have negative subconscious memories, which manifest all painful circumstances in your life. From the Ho'oponopono perspective all your subconscious memories are limiting because they temporarily separate you from the Divine.

Every time you go through difficult experiences these situations are created by your subconscious memories. Your past does not actually exist because you cannot even grab it with your senses. The past only survives in you as programs you store in your subconscious mind.

However, most people feel the ominous presence of their past as if it were real. All people have the natural tendency to be attached to their own past experiences. Your subconscious memories are powerful relics of your past which are carried forward to the present moment and pervade all your life experiences, with no exception.

Your mind is full of past programs; you have thousands of them. Every single situation or experience that you went through over your life is indelibly etched on your subconscious level. This past programming dictates all your thoughts, actions, emotions and sensations. Moreover, these subconscious memories materialize every single circumstance in your life. You are continually held hostage to these past memories with no possibility to pay any ransom for your liberation.

Goddard says that:

> *Everything that has been is still in existence. The past still exists, and it gives – and still gives – its results… This going into the past and replaying a scene of the past in imagination as it ought to have been played the first time, I call revision… Changing your life means changing the past. The causes of any present evil are the unrevised scenes of the past. The past and the present form the whole structure of man; they are carrying all of its contents with it. Any alteration of content will result in an alteration in the present and future.*

You cannot change your negative life situations by fixing them, as many people try to do in a traditional manner. If you try this way, you can obtain some results, which will tend to be temporary because you did not deal with the roots (or causes) of the problems, only with their manifestations (or consequences).

From the Ho'oponopono perspective, your past memories are the opposite of your divine essence. Moreover, many of these programs carry energy which is opposite to love, that is the purest form of energy which exists. These negative memories are just manifestations of fearful states, such as sorrow, pain, regret, guilt, among others.

When you uproot the cause of your problems (which is the memories held in your subconscious mind) you solve all your difficult situations in a more lingering manner. This way you can improve all areas of your life (health, relationships, etc.) in an effective and lasting fashion. When you practice Ho'oponopono, you can effectively remove this past programming. The cleaning process of your subconscious memories progressively frees you from the tethers of the past, which allows you to thrive with no effort whatsoever.

2. Main aspects of these memories

a) Subconscious

These memories are not easily accessible because they are subconscious; they stray away from your awareness. Besides, it is difficult for you to remember most of these past experiences with clarity. You cannot access them with your rational mind, at least directly. In most cases, you don't even know when or why the memories went into your subconscious mind or what those memories are about.

These past programs have locked-in energy which keeps them alive and in place over time. Your positive memories have high vibratory energy, and your negative programs have low vibratory energy. In all cases these memories keep on playing out continually under the level of your awareness.

These programs are working behind the scenes, secretly. Some masters say your mind becomes the stage on which these memories play their specific roles, even when you are not aware of this. In accordance to this, Goddard says that:

> *man and his past are one continuous structure. This structure contains all of the facts which have been conserved and still operate below the threshold of his surface mind... The past still exists, and it gives – still gives – its results.*

These subconscious tapes gradually take over all the available room in your subconscious mind. As a consequence, these old tapes leave no spare space in your mind to receive divine inspiration, which is unlimited wisdom. Your subconscious programs tend to become completely unquestioned over time.

From the psychological viewpoint you develop attachments to

the memories held in your subconscious. Your mind becomes familiar with these subconscious memories, which makes it more difficult to challenge them. For this reason, the memories etched in your subconscious are difficult to remove using traditional tools, such as positive thinking, visualization or others because you tend to be attached to these programs.

These remnants of the past are evoked continually, in most cases without even you noticing this. At all times, you are unwittingly reliving these old tapes, and this sets you totally trapped in them.

One of the most toxic memories your subconscious can hold is that you are a helpless being who is separated from the Divine. This is just an illusion because you can never be completely severed from Divinity. Subconscious memories obliterate this essential connection with Divinity, but only temporarily. With the frequent application of Ho'oponopono technique, you gradually return to your essential home, which is the Divine.

b) Reality distorting

The past is over, don't relive it and waste today in its wake.
– Stephanie King

Reality making is reciprocal. You make it, while it makes you.
– Deepak Chopra and Rudolph Tanzi

In accordance with McRaney, there is a mental process called priming that occurs when you are affected by the past in a way that you act, think or perceive the stimuli of your environment. The process of priming is automatic and ongoing; it is performed below the level of your awareness.

Your past programs are related to the process of priming because they naturally interfere in your perception and interpretation of reality. By nature your subconscious memories are intrinsically selective. They always exclude some elements of "reality" and delineate your personal and distinct map of it.

Your subconscious memories make you concentrate your attention only on things or circumstances which are consistent with them. This makes your knowledge of your environment essentially limited and naturally biased.

These subconscious programs also help you assign meaning to things, people and circumstances in a very specific way. If your subconscious programs are adverse, they act like a negative point of reference regarding your reality. Instead, when your subconscious programs are positive, they help you perceive the beneficial aspects of your environment.

These subconscious programs take over every dimension of your life, constantly coloring your perception, actions and thoughts. Your past has a very significant impact on your current circumstances, shaping your present experiences accordingly. From a psychological viewpoint, the memories held in your subconscious also give you a sense of certainty and congruency because they constantly dictate how you should act, feel, sense and think at any time.

From the Ho'oponopono perspective, all your subconscious memories represent stagnant energy which not only pollutes all your life experiences, but also temporarily severs you from Divinity. From this particular viewpoint, these memories limit your potential. The frequent practice of Ho'oponopono actually works like an antidote which eliminates that venom regarding these past memories.

Some masters say that these programs are like a tape being played out constantly in a hi-fi system. You can liken this to a hi-fi system which is quiet, almost imperceptible but the tape (your subconscious memories) is still playing (affecting your whole life), even though you cannot hear it.

c) Limiting and disempowering

The power of thought is the highest power in the universe... It is this mental vibration that is at the center of our creative center, enabling us to be co-creator of the manifestations in our lives.
– Martha Davis, Elizabeth Robbins Eshelman and Matthew McKay

From the metaphysical viewpoint, all positive memories held in your mind are energy uplifting. However, all your negative subconscious memories exhaust your vital energy. Negative subconscious programs, which are originated by emotional wounds, faults and others, literally contaminate your current and future experiences.

Some Ho'oponopono masters suggest that there is no such thing as bad memories or good memories. All data held in your subconscious mind must be cleaned because it hinders your natural connection with Divinity. This programming is preventing you from becoming information-free, which is that state called zero point.

When you do the cleaning process you will be assisted by the Divine. Divinity always knows what memories you have in your mind, and how and which of them must be removed. So you don't even have to worry about this, but just do the cleaning process on a frequent basis.

Even though these subconscious programs can be considered detrimental because they temporarily sever you from Divinity, they give you the opportunity to reconnect with Divinity by removing them.

If we use a metaphor, it is possible to equate your subconscious memories to food. In this example, whenever you hold subconscious programs, your mind tends to become constipated. In this case, the regular use of the Ho'oponopono tool acts like a laxative, which makes you feel more comfortable and at ease.

Your subconscious scripts don't allow you to experience a

lingering state of pureness, stillness and comfort, which you are naturally entitled to. You are generally unaware of the fact that these subconscious memories take you away from your authentic divine essence.

This subconscious programming stands in the way of your personal evolution; they actually keep you from accessing your most prized inner resources, which are unpolluted and limitless. These negative subconscious memories don't allow you to achieve:

> – *The best state in all your relationships*
> – *Your personal mission, which is the most important purpose in your life*
> – *A prospering situation in all areas of your life*
> – *A comfortable and effortless lifestyle*
> – *Spiritual, mental, emotional and physical well-being*

All illnesses, financial shortages, lack of opportunities, relationship breakups or conflicts, accidents and any other negative situations you experience in your life are created by your subconscious programs. These memories act like a snare or trap: they take you in and they do not let you escape it.

It is important to understand that every time you classify, judge, categorize and even feel about things and circumstances, you always do so based on your subconscious programs. In most cases the subconscious memories dictating your thoughts, emotions or actions are not even relevant or related to the situation at hand; they might be totally counterproductive to your progress; they downgrade your life.

These memories represent the most important boundaries in your life. But the good news is that you can go beyond these boundaries by doing Ho'oponopono on a frequent basis. In relation to this, one of the main characters in the film *Cloud Atlas* says that *"... all becomes clear... all boundaries are conventions waiting to be transcended."*

According to the discipline called Psychoneuroimmunology your thoughts (and subconscious memories) actually affect all your bodily functions, for example the working of your circulatory system, digestive system and respiratory system, among others. These programs impact on your overall state of well-being.

In relation to this, Hanley and Deville say that: *"your body's biochemistry is heavily influenced by the way you think, feel and believe."* Moreover, there are some scientific studies which confirm that some of your subconscious memories can also have a damaging effect on your DNA. This means that your subconscious memories affect your overall health conditions. For this reason, when you do Ho'oponopono, your health tends to improve almost magically.

If you are like most people, without you even realizing you are constantly being driven by negative habits, which don't allow you to be creative and authentic. These habitual activities are also sustained by your subconscious memories. From Ho'oponopono's perspective, you can eliminate these automatic patterns when you remove the subconscious programs underpinning them.

All your habits, either good or bad, are intrinsically limiting, because you always tend to do things in a certain way. When you have a habit you are not free because you are driven by your subconscious mind. When you do Ho'oponopono on a frequent basis, you can access your natural state of freedom.

Many sages say that your subconscious memories set you on a survival mode, instead of allowing you to be on an evolutionary mode. From Ho'oponopono's perspective, your subconscious memories don't allow you to expand your life; they keep you in a rut not allowing you to harness your unlimited creativity.

These memories are very resistant to change. In that effect, Branch and Willson say that your memories resemble: *"well-trodden paths through an overgrown field. You can walk quickly and easily down these paths, as they've been worn down from years of use."*

The most effective way to remove this subconscious programming is by doing Ho'oponopono on a regular basis.

d) Chances to connect to the Divine

Many oriental philosophies state that you are a natural extension of Divinity. This means that you are always connected with the Higher Planes. Nevertheless, over time your mental kingdom becomes besieged by relentless and obnoxious intruders, which are your subconscious programs. With the regular use of Ho'oponopono you can dethrone these uninvited interlopers in order to regain total sovereignty over your life, and inhabit your natural divine essence.

Your subconscious memories transitorily hamper your connection with the Divine, but they can never thwart it completely. Dr. Len says that you must consider your own mind as if it were made of crystal clear glass through which the ray of Divinity goes through.

Following this analogy, your subconscious memories represent a black thick screen of dust covering up the glass of your mind, impeding the divine beam of light to go through. You can actually remove this black screen by continually doing Ho'oponopono. When you render the glass clear of dust, you arrive to that natural state of zero point, which allows the light of Divinity to go in.

In relation to this, Goddard says that: *"A cut flower soon wilts and dies because it has been taken away from the source of its life."* Something similar to this happens to you when you get temporarily disconnected from the Divine. When your life is taken over by your subconscious memories, you are in some way dead too.

Some oriental philosophies support the idea that no experience in your life is a waste; on the contrary, every single thing that occurs in your life is for a wise reason, in many cases unknown. Each experience in your life is just a preparation for the next obvious level on your path to your personal evolution. According to this viewpoint, all your subconscious memories are just prized opportunities to clean them up and transform your life significantly. So even though these programs seem detrimental at first, they allow you to strengthen your link with the Divine by removing them all.

Some sages say that you should never go against your enemies. From this standpoint, your subconscious memories can be perceived as your enemies. Moreover, some philosophies and religions state that you must love your enemies, embrace them lovingly. In accordance with this, you must acknowledge these memories, accept them and embrace them lovingly. You must pervade these programs with the love energy of the Divine, in order to remove them by practicing Ho'oponopono.

You can also consider these subconscious programs as your teachers. These negative programs are indicating that there is something in your subconscious mind that must be removed. They give you a valuable lesson you must be aware of, which is that you have to clean them all.

Other masters state that these subconscious memories are just useless distractions; they temporarily prevent you from receiving inspirational messages from Divinity. From this perspective, these tapes must be removed, as soon as possible, with no delay or hesitation.

e) Other aspects

When to the sessions of sweet silent thought
I summon up remembrance of things past,
I sigh the lack of many a thing I sought,
And with old woes new wail my dear times' waste
Then can I grieve at grievances foregone,
And heavily from woe to woe tell o'er
The sad account of fore-bemoaned moan,
Which I now pay as if not paid before
– William Shakespeare, Sonnet 30

It is important to highlight that your personality, your character, your talents and shortcomings, beliefs, values, habits, health conditions and phobias are also subconscious memories. These programs are also the basis for all your expectations and assumptions. All your strategies and decisions are motivated by your subconscious programming.

From the metaphysical perspective, your subconscious memories are just attachments, which entail specific and structured ways of perceiving, feeling, thinking and performing actions. These subconscious memories are actually your jailors; you show continuous allegiance to them, although on an unwitting level.

These memories buried in your mind are like a computer virus. In this analogy, the computer is your own mind and these subconscious memories act like viruses which *disrupt* the correct functioning of your mind and create all sorts of problems and difficulties in your life. So Ho'oponopono works like an antivirus program.

From the psychological perspective, you have different types of memories. They can be related to you (for example, a memory that says: *"I am a failure"*) or other people (for example, a subconscious program that states that: *"Every person that I meet wants to deceive me"*). These programs can also be related the world in general (*"This city is not a safe place"*). Nonetheless, all your subconscious memories are about you, either in a direct or indirect manner.

Some subconscious memories provide you with an explanation about how things work in reality. Nonetheless, all your subconscious programs are intrinsically limiting. You can only interpret reality in the specific ways dictated by your subconscious memories.

Some subconscious programs help you predict possible outcomes for your projects. These projections are also called expectations, which are akin to a fortunetelling skill which most people pretend to have.

As said before, from the Ho'oponopono point of view, you also share some of these subconscious memories with the people that appear in your life. For example, if a person treats you badly, there are some subconscious memories you share with this very person. By removing your subconscious programs not only will your situation change but also this person's.

You don't only have shared memories with people you are in direct contact with, like relatives, friends, acquaintances, colleagues and others. You also have shared subconscious programs with the rest of the people around you or in your awareness, even the ones who affect you in more indirect ways.

In the story told at the beginning of this book, Dr. Len was affected by the prisoners in the ward he was working at, even though he did not personally know them. They were in Dr. Len's awareness so he had shared subconscious memories with these people. When he removed these shared programs from himself, by doing Ho'oponopono, these inmates recovered almost magically.

There is another interesting topic to explore. Throughout his talks Dr. Len refers to the subconscious memories as *"the mortgage of the soul."* According to his viewpoint, until you delete these subconscious memories you are indebted, which means you are chained to your past programming.

Following this example of the mortgage, once you rid yourself from your subconscious programs (*"mortgage"*) you actually avoid any possibility of going into foreclosure. According to this analogy, when you pay the mortgage you become the full proprietor of your house. Likewise, as you delete your subconscious programming you become the full proprietor of your life. You can only be free from this "mortgage" when you repay it, which entails doing Ho'oponopono on a consistent basis.

Your negative subconscious memories were also examined from the Jungian perspective. Jung the renowned specialist said that every person has aspects which lay completely hidden from other people, sometimes even from themselves, called shadow aspects of consciousness.

From this perspective, these dark aspects tend to emerge frequently and are prone to sabotaging your best intentions. In some cases, you can also project those dark aspects onto other people, attributing these very qualities to them.

There is another relevant point to highlight. Each memory held on your subconscious level has a particular energetic signature or frequency, which brings into manifestation similar circumstances into your life. This perspective is consistent with the so-called Law of Attraction which states that your thoughts attract alike things.

In relation to this, Dr. Loyd suggests that negative cellular memories alongside with stress and negative energy are the fundamental causes of people's failure in life. From this perspective, this renowned specialist states that these negative memories can and must be cleared. In that effect, he says that: *"Success-related memories vibrate at healthy, positive frequencies, but failure-related memories vibrate at unhealthy, negative frequencies."*

3. Origins of the subconscious memories

We all have painful memories that have occurred in life, and no one gets by without lumps and bumps. Being born is in itself a traumatic event. The transition from womb to worry is automatic at the very end of the birth canal... No one escapes his or her own personal terror. So many bad things happen to so many kids, and the memories begin to pile up quickly. It is amazing that we can even escape childhood in one piece.
– Robert Ray

Your subconscious memories include general knowledge or specific experiences you have had all over your life. These programs are organized in modules or neural units and they are interconnected in an intricate network, which allows them to be fired in very swift manner. You accrue countless memories on your subconscious level, not only after you were born, but from your first spark of life.

In accordance to this, Gutowski says that:

from the instant we are conceived, we have been retaining information. Our father provided his data through the sperm, our mother gave not only her input through the egg, but continued downloading information to our atomic recording devices (our cells) for the entire pregnancy. Every thought, emotion and nutritional frequency that the mother came into contact with is in us along with the genetic energies from generations of ancestors.

This position is totally consistent with Ho'oponopono's perspective. Not all memories you hold in your subconscious mind are yours: you inherited some of these programs from your ancestors; these memories came to you through your DNA. They are related to your genetic lineage. These memories predispose you in specific fashions. According to Hanley and Deville, not only do you inherit the main traits from forebears but you also naturally learn their main fears and values, what these authors call *"psychogenes."*

All your past programs, even the ones genetically transmitted by your ancestors, can be deleted by doing Ho'oponopono on a frequent basis. There are some spiritual perspectives that assert that you also hold programs in your mind which were inherited from your previous reincarnations.

In the past there was a widespread scientific perspective that supported the idea that some of your characteristics were predetermined by your genetic patterns which have the tendency to remain unchanged over your life. According to recent scientific studies your genetic structure is actually malleable; it can really be changed through modification of your thoughts, which implies modifying your subconscious programming. And you can remove these subconscious programs by doing Ho'oponopono regularly.

From a psychological perspective, most of the other restraining programs you hold in your mind were imprinted at a very early age. Those years, all information received from your environment was absorbed by your subconscious mind in a totally unquestioned manner because you were highly impressionable.

Besides, you have been accruing subconscious memories during your entire lifetime, through your interactions with your parents, friends, acquaintances, colleagues, partners, lovers and also organizations (media, church, workplace, etc.), among others. Most of the people you were in contact with affected you in a direct or indirect manner.

Bavister and Vickers say that your subconscious memories have several origins; for example, all imprinted experiences in your childhood, influences of your cultural environment, messages from the media and your unconscious replication of the behavior of people around you. These authors also include among the main causes of your subconscious programs the feedback received from people related to you, the activities you repeated over time and your groups of influence and reference.

Over time your subconscious has been gradually filled with a collage of data from varying sources. The summation of all your different life circumstances and experiences were duly recorded as memories in your subconscious mind.

At any moment you are constantly bombarded by umpteen stimuli from your environment. Most of these bits of information badgering you actually enter your subconscious mind, even though you are not even aware of this fact most of the time.

Most of your subconscious memories are related to specific contexts. These programs tend to be specifically activated or retreated when you are in similar situations. There are memories called autobiographical, which are related to your own life. These programs tend to be organized by specific periods of your life, for example: childhood, adolescence, etc. In all cases, the memories stored on your subconscious level have specific emotional patterns. Some memories are related to emotional states not fully expressed.

Even though your subconscious memories are resistant to change, they naturally and spontaneously go through several transformations over your life. In relation to this, McRaney states that: *"Memories are constructed anew each time from whatever information is currently available, which makes them highly permeable to influences from the present."* Your subconscious memories are continually reformulated and shaped by themselves. This happens because of the incorporation of new information in your mind, which is mixed with the previous one residing there.

Your subconscious databank is made up of different types of judgments, classifications, expectations, and prejudices about yourself, people and specific life experiences. This information storehouse also includes various emotional states, such as hatred, resentment, envy, happiness, etc.

This database includes memories which create a state of disharmony, for example: illnesses, tension, lack of clarity, doubts, insecurity, etc. It also includes other memories which manifest states of harmony, such as peacefulness, glee, easiness, among others. As said before, from the Ho'oponopono perspective, all subconscious memories must be removed in order to arrive at your natural state of purity, which is the Divine.

It is not really your fault that you have these subconscious memories. These programs have been introduced in your mind on a constant basis, in most cases unwittingly. You are continually incorporating new programs into your subconscious mind, as easily as you can catch the flu. For this reason, you should never feel guilty for holding these programs.

All these memories are subconscious so you cannot access them, at least directly. In many cases, when the experiences originating these memories occurred you were not sufficiently aware of them. Other subconscious memories cannot be recovered effortlessly because they were imprinted in your mind in a preverbal stage of your life. When you were a neonate or in the early years of childhood you were not even able to talk and your brain was not fully developed. So you did not have any words to interpret the experiences you were going through.

As said before, countless stimuli from your environment continually imprint your subconscious, without you even noticing them. In this case, it is impossible for you to retrieve information you were not even aware of when it was introduced in your mind.

The accumulation of memories is a process that never ends; every new experience in your life generates more programs to be stored in your subconscious mind. The only thing you can do to declutter your mind is to do Ho'oponopono on a non-stop basis.

4. Mental mechanisms to hold memories

According to traditional psychology, there are several mental mechanisms all people frequently use in a subconscious manner. The main purpose of these mental defenses is to prevent your subconscious memories from surfacing into your awareness.

These defenses are generally triggered when the memories you hold on your subconscious level are unacceptable, threatening or antisocial. To put it more simply, these defense mechanisms are usually activated when you have disagreeable thoughts or feelings which you refuse to acknowledge properly.

The most well-known defense mechanisms are: repression, suppression, projection, regression, reaction, formation and sublimation.

a) Repression and suppression

Repression means that you keep negative, and generally intense, memories below the level of awareness; you are actually denying their existence in an unwitting manner. Nevertheless, in the case of suppression your memories are kept below the level of awareness as a consequence of your conscious control over them. As mentioned before, according to Jung, the negative aspects of ourselves we conceal from other people (and sometimes also from ourselves) are called *"the shadow."* According to Watson, this shadow is composed of a set of disgusting traits about your personality, which you don't want to admit or accept fully. Therefore these aspects tend to remain secluded in the back of your mind, albeit that they can also surface and show up in the most unexpected situations. In that effect, Jung encouraged people to fully own their dark part in order to achieve an overall state of well-being.

b) Projection

This well-known mental mechanism entails you acting as if your negative memories were not yours. Instead, you tend to project these negative programs onto other people. You assume that these memories (and qualities related to them) actually belong to others, and not to you.

Every time you project you tend to use your mind like a projector playing a movie. For example, you might tell other people they are untidy, when you are actually the one who is disorderly.

From a wider perspective, when you project you perceive people and circumstances through the lens of your past memories. In accordance to this, many masters say that your outside environment is just a literal projection of the movies being played in your mind.

c) Regression

When you regress you are incapable of behaving in a mature manner. You become stuck to subconscious memories related to previous periods of your life, not the current one. Past memories (more specifically, the ones related to the critical period of your life) keep you ensnared in the thoughts, emotions and actions of that past time. For example, if your adolescence was a traumatic period of your life you might become stuck to the behavior typical of that period, acting like a teenager.

d) Reaction formation

This mechanism is activated when the result of acting in a certain way (for example: being physically aggressive) is socially unacceptable. In this case, this mental defense converts the resulting unacceptable behavior into its opposite (in this example, you might tend to act in a peaceful fashion).

e) Intellectualization

This defense mechanism makes you concentrate on the intellectual aspects of your memories. Your attention is focused on the rational aspects of your subconscious programs, instead of their emotional traits. This mechanism tends to be activated when your subconscious memories are charged with intense negative emotions.

f) Sublimation

In the case of sublimation, you tend not to act based on your subconscious memories overtly and fully, because the behavior would be considered socially unacceptable. In this case the behavior triggered by the memories becomes more enticing to the social environment, but less authentic.

5. Your subconscious memories bring about your life experiences

Problems are repetition of our memories... Problems repeat themselves because when they appear, we react and hold on to them. We don't stop thinking about the problem, and so we get trapped.

We attract even more problems, when we could simply choose to let it go... Our reaction to problems is a repetition to our memories.
– *Mabel Katz*

Your world is formed in faithful replica of your thoughts... A negative thought, if not erased, will almost certainly result in negative conditions.
– *Jane Roberts*

You already know that there are countless memories continually playing out in your subconscious mind. The energy of these memories produces ripple effects on your environment. The vibrations emanated by your subconscious memories draw back to you only circumstances congruent with these programs. Some metaphysical masters use a very meaningful saying that goes: *"Like attracts alike."*

In relation to this, Allen says that: *"men do not attract that which they want, but that which they are."* There is also a saying in the Talmud which says that you never see your life circumstances as they really are, but as you are. From this perspective, you are essentially your subconscious memories.

Your subconscious memories and your life experiences are always a perfect match. In relation to this, Allen metaphorically says that: *"nothing can come from corn but corn; nothing can come from nettles but nettles."* To that effect, Jung also reflected that: *"when an inner situation is not made conscious it appears outside as fate."*

On a continuous basis you tread your path in life by making decisions which are entirely based on your past programming. In that effect, Elrod states that:

Our subconscious minds are equipped with a self-limiting rear-view mirror through which we continually relive and recreate our past... As a result we filter every choice we make... through the limitations of our past experiences.

Your subconscious level demands expression. Your negative subconscious memories tend to manifest negative situations, such as health problems, troublesome incidents, financial difficulties and relational conflicts, among others. To that effect, Bailes says that: *"destructive thoughts continue to work negatively beneath the surface, and in due time will yield up some outer experience that corresponds to them."*

The incessant stream of painful memories held in your subconscious mind is the only cause of all your negative emotional states, such as anger, guilt, envy, worry, despondency, loneliness, revenge and guilt, among others. Like most people, you might tend to attribute the changes in your mood to external circumstances.

Many masters say that when you experience problems, this is an evident sign you are affected by your subconscious memories. This is also a signal that you are away from your core essence, which is intrinsically pure and problem-free.

From the metaphysical perspective, when the memories held on your subconscious level are positive, they will materialize positive circumstances, cheerful events, happy relationships, healthy conditions and economic abundance. In relation to this Ray states that: *"what we perceive as ourselves in our world exists only in the Mind, and this is the direct result of the data, playing largely as memories that can be found therein."*

However, from Ho'oponopono's perspective, all your subconscious memories must be removed. In that effect, all your subconscious programs are limiting by nature, regardless of the quality of energy they hold (which can be positive or negative energy). This is because all your subconscious programs temporarily sever you from your pure essence, which is Divinity.

Every experience that you go through goads a series of mental associations in relation to your subconscious memories, which bring about certain emotional states in you. The real cause of your varying emotions is never outside you (for example, your life situations) but always inside you (subconscious memories). You are always enslaved to your subconscious programming; your subconscious memories substitute your straightforward contact with the world, and replace it with your past programming. In relation to this, Tolle says that: *"since the mind is conditioned by the past, you are conditioned to re-enact the past again and again."*

It is important to understand that the memories playing out on your subconscious level actually manifest each and every one of your life experiences. In total accordance with this, Murphy says: *"it is the world within, namely your thoughts, feelings and imagery that makes the world without."*

6. Your subconscious memories and your problems

... reality is not fixed, but fluid, or mutable, and hence possibly open to influence.
– Lynne McTaggart

Your subconscious programming is the origin of states of powerlessness and restlessness you might experience in your life. In these memories also originate all your financial difficulties, lack of love and illnesses you go through over your lifetime. Your subconscious memories are like thermostats which set (create) the conditions (your circumstances) in your outer environment.

It is a blatant lie that your problems are originated by your environment. Goddard states that: *"man's problems are mental in nature; they have no existence outside of themselves."*

If you are like most people, you might be continually obsessed with your problems. You are likely to dwell on difficulties on a continuous basis to work them out in an effective manner. If you act this way, you tend to consume lots of energy to solve troublesome situations. You might also have realized that when solving problems the results of your efforts in many cases were far from the ideal ones.

When you try to fix your troublesome circumstances, you are doing so by using the information stored in your subconscious memories, which is very limiting. From this perspective, you also deal with effects, which are the problems themselves, instead of tackling their causes, which are your subconscious memories originating them. On those occasions, you waste energy by overacting or by being ineffective because you do nothing to remove the actual origin of all your difficulties.

There is an ideal and long-lasting way to solve all your problems. You must just commit to cleaning up your subconscious memories on a regular basis. When you practice Ho'oponopono, you bring about more long-lasting results.

7. Memories versus Divinity

We can't solve the problems by applying the same kind of thinking we used when we created them.
– Albert Einstein

You have the divine loving essence within. You are naturally connected to the Divine. If you believe that you are imperfect, you have to know that this is not real. The only reason that you cannot perceive your natural seamlessness is because you have subconscious memories constantly playing in your mind which do not allow you to see that.

Nevertheless, when you delete your subconscious memories, by doing Ho'oponopono on a frequent basis, you can truly access the divine core in you. This state of truth, pureness and clarity is mentioned by the most widespread religions when they suggest that you are the exact image and likeness of Divinity or God.

It was explained that your subconscious mind is the natural warehouse of umpteen memories, keeping you transitorily disconnected from the Divine. Your subconscious tapes are, in fact, interfering with the natural divine flow in your life. At the same time, these innumerable memories create a natural state of resistance to receiving inspiration from Divinity.

You cannot receive divine guidance because your subconscious memories take up all the available space in your mind. Some masters say that your subconscious memories are one side of the coin; the other side is divine inspiration. In that effect, you cannot have both sides of the coin at the same time. You can be either driven by your subconscious memories or guided by divine inspiration.

Your subconscious memories are not authentic; they are not the real you. These programs can only bring bondage and deception. Nevertheless, as you clean your subconscious memories you realize that only your inspired actions are real; all the rest are absolutely unauthentic because they are driven by your subconscious memories.

The book *A Course in Miracles* states that: *"error is lack of love."* From this point of view, all your subconscious memories can also be considered mistakes because they keep you far from your loving pure essence.

When you do Ho'oponopono, one of the sentences you purposely use is *"I love you."* You use these words because love energy dissolves all your subconscious programs. This sentence not only removes your subconscious memories, but also makes you dwell in your natural home, which is Divinity.

The love force you harness when you do Ho'oponopono dispels all the loveless programs held on your subconscious level. Love is the easiest way to connect to Divinity, which is essentially pure unconditional love. It is important to remember that each time you practice Ho'oponopono Divinity helps you dissolve your subconscious programs with pure love energy.

Your natural right is to be pervaded by unlimited loving energy. The only obstacles to experiencing this pure and unbounded state are your subconscious memories. When you hold these subconscious programs you cannot restore your connection with the Divine forces. Furthermore, your subconscious information also prevents you from harnessing your unlimited power.

However, you must know that your connection with the Divine can never be completely eradicated, despite the interference of umpteen subconscious memories. This sacred connection is always there; it is hidden and untapped but it is present, underneath the myriad of subconscious memories. In accordance with this, Cabanillas says the only thing that severs you from God, the creator of all that exists, is your subconscious memories.

Using an analogy, you can imagine that you own a beautiful house, but you don't care for it at all. Instead you leave this naturally prized abode abandoned for ages. Over time, your residence will be gradually occupied by intruders. As these strangers move in, they will start to do whatever they want in that place, in a domineering and relentless manner.

In this example, these uninvited guests are your subconscious memories, which become owners in the house of your subconscious mind. Your subconscious memories are just vulgar copycats of the real proprietor of your mind, which is your natural divine essence. Ho'oponopono is the only way to evict interlopers from your subconscious house.

In relation to this, Lee recounted a very interesting mystic Hawaiian tale. According to this tale, in the ancient cultures, every child was born as a seamless bowl of light. However, every time the child became resentful, fretful or experienced other negative emotions, some stones were thrown into this bowl, gradually taking over the space of light.

When eventually the child accumulated too many stones inside the bowl he himself became a stone. At that moment there was no light left in the bowl. He was not able to grow any longer. As a consequence of this, in order for the child to become light again, he had to turn the bowl upside down for all the stones to fall and the bowl to be emptied. When he did so, the light pervaded the bowl again.

In relation to this story, your essential state is the Divine, which in the tale is described as the bowl of light. Over time, you tend to accumulate many stones (subconscious programs) which temporarily sever you from your divine state. All these stones are the main cause of all the suffering in your life. In that effect, Lee states: *"Negative, toxic thoughts over time turn anyone into a dense, dark stone."* When you use Ho'oponopono on a frequent basis, you can actually remove the stones taking up all the space of your bowl. In an alchemic manner Ho'oponopono converts the dull stones into precious divine light.

8. Some practical tips

– Remember that when you are affected by any negative condition, as most people are, you have to remove your subconscious memories because they are the causes of your difficulties. You should never try to force, control or manipulate external circumstances in order to fix them. You can eliminate your subconscious programming by practicing Ho'oponopono as frequently as possible. It is the most effective manner to turn around any negative situation in your life in a long-lasting way.

– You must also be aware that when you remove your past conditioning you can access divine guidance, also called inspiration. When your mind is crowded by subconscious memories you cannot receive the direction from the Divine, because there is no room in your mind for it.

– All people have mental defenses, such as repression, suppression, projection and rationalization, among others. Reread the description of each of the mental mechanisms and try to detect some of these defenses you might use in your daily life. For example, if you say that a person is ugly it is very likely that you are projecting your own ugliness on that individual. Go through each of the defense mechanisms in order to analyze their practical implications in your life. You can also take note of the insights. After this, say the four Ho'oponopono sentences (*"I am sorry"*, *"Please forgive me"*, *"I love you"* and *"Thank you"*) many times.

– It was explained that your subconscious programs are constantly affecting your perception. In relation to that, Dainow suggests a very interesting and well-known exercise. You must stand tall by an open window which has a glass in it. Firstly, you must keep the window open in order to see what is going on outside. Then you should close the window to see outside, but through its glass. Notice the differences in your perception of the environment outside. In some cases these differences might be very slight, but they could be more obvious if the window glass is cracked, dirty or it is not completely translucent. Lastly, see outside through the window wearing shades or eyeglasses. You will very likely notice the evident differences in your perception this time. Take note of any insights you receive.

– In relation to the previous exercise you can make an analogy of the window glass, shades and eyeglasses and your subconscious memories. In other words, your subconscious programs continually distort the view of the world, in the same way as the window glass, spectacles and shades. You must take note of further insights into this. Ask yourself the question: *"What is going on in me in relation to this?"* and write down further insights which might appear. After this, you must say the four Ho'oponopono sentences many times.

– Some psychological schools of thought suggest a very well-known and meaningful exercise. In order to do this exercise you must write a list of your main negative characteristics, for example, lazy, close-minded, etc. On this list, you can also include some of your negative actions, if possible the most noticeable ones, such as waking up late, swearing, among others. Lastly, you can include negative emotions such as being depressed, cross, grumpy, among others. All this information was actually elicited from your subconscious mind. That list is a reflection of your subconscious programs.

– In relation to the previous exercise you must read the list thoroughly and ask yourself *"What is going on in me that I am experiencing all this?"* After this, relax and stay at ease; try to see what comes up in your mind. Take note of any insights that might appear regarding this question. Then say the four Ho'oponopono sentences many times.

– Some psychologists suggest that you make a long list of characteristics that you don't like in people around you, for example: greedy, envious, and others. Every time you see something negative in others, there is something similar in you, in a bigger or smaller amount. Your relationships are a just reflection of you. When you don't like some features of other people, you tend to deny the same very traits in yourself. For this reason, what you see in other people, either positive or negative, has very valuable clues about yourself. After this, ask yourself: *"What is going on in me that I experience this?"* Stay calm and take note of insights and then repeat the four Ho'oponopono sentences.

Chapter 4

You Don't Know Anything

... our choices are not formed in a conscious, rational manner. Instead, they bubble up from our unconscious mind, and when they finally reach the surface of consciousness we take ownership of them.
– William Irvine

... only an "incredibly insignificant fraction" of our sensory experiences and memories can pass through our consciousness at any time... Most of what we can experience we cannot tell each other about.
– Tor Norretranders

1. Knowledge is unbounded

Knowledge is manufactured by scholars, by scientists and books. Wisdom is inherent.
– Khenpo Gurudas Sunyatananda

1.1. The world is complex

The only thing I know without doubt is that I don't know. Any kind of knowing in thought is not reliable. You think you know something one day, but then the next day you realize that it has all changed and you think you know something else.
– Unmani Liza Hyde

From the Ho'oponopono perspective, one of the most important principles to take into account is *"You don't know anything."* Your knowledge is very limited in relation to the variety of human experience.

Furthermore, from the Ho'oponopono viewpoint, your knowledge is intrinsically limited because it is always based on your subconscious memories, which are constraining by nature. All this might sound a bit disturbing for you; it is possible that you don't even admit that you don't know almost anything.

Many people certainly believe that they count on complete accurate information on several topics which are relevant for their lives. Nonetheless, Tony Buzan says that the scientists *"must still admit that total sum of the knowledge of our human mind is less than 1 percent of what is there to know."*

The world and the Universe themselves are overwhelmingly complex, which implies extreme degrees of unpredictability and variability. To that effect, your whole environment is affected by too many interrelated factors and dimensions which, in turn, can be analyzed and interpreted from countless perspectives.

All these elements, in turn, have intricate interdependencies which continually change over time. For all these reasons, it is almost impossible to have a complete and clear comprehension of what is actually going on, at least from our limited human perspective.

Despite this conspicuous fact, most people tend to display intense eagerness in order to make things as understandable as possible; they frequently look for clarity in many areas of their lives. In your daily life, you might have seen numberless proofs of this unstoppable quest for knowledge, for example:

– There are continuous technical, political and social analyses in the media, through umpteen programs, magazines and newspapers.
– In history, the main scientific disciplines have developed different paradigms to group and analyze their specific topics. These paradigms, which are particular ways to see the world, have been gradually replaced over time by new ones in all known disciplines.
– There are unstoppable scientific research activities on different areas (Medicine, Biology, Astronomy, Physics, etc.). This eagerness

for research brings about frequent and numerous discoveries. Some of these breakthroughs are actually revolutionary and ground-breaking.

– There is a steady multiplication of educational institutions on all levels all over the world. These organizations provide undergraduate and postgraduate courses, offline and online platforms and also informal and formal training.

– Most companies have an increasing budget on research and development (R+D) in order to know how to produce new goods, materials, packaging, etc.

– Many organizations devote lots of their resources to train and qualify people on how things should be done.

– There is a predominance of seminars, conferences, workshops and courses, which offer various techniques, tactics and strategies on countless topics.

– There is an upsurge of new disciplines which study specific fields of knowledge (Robotics, Psychoneuroimmunology, Genetics, etc.).

– The use of the Internet is widespread as a common source of knowledge (for example, Wikipedia, technical websites, forums, blogs, etc.).

– There are thousands of technical and self-help books and e-books being published every month.

– There is an increasing use of technological appliances (mobiles, iPads, computers, medical scanners, telescopes, etc.) to access specific different types of knowledge.

From the scientific perspective, there are many studies which have thoroughly demonstrated that most of the Universe cannot be perceived by human senses. The tangible aspects of the Universe you can actually sense are very small, between two and four percent of the total. We don't have direct access to most of the aspects of reality.

1.2. You always tend to control things

Many times we remain stuck and go around in circles in the same place for lack of faith or fear of the unknown. It is worth to learn from the seed, which despite its inability to imagine itself as an orchid has the courage to open, get broken, and give itself to the process entirely to sprout from the earth's surface and emerge to the light.

– Mabel Katz

Even though we know just an extremely tiny fraction as compared to what actually exists, there is a natural human urge to make things as comprehensible as possible. People naturally tend to have low tolerance to uncertainty; they try to dispel it as soon as possible. The majority of people are truly concerned by *"fear of the unknown."*

All unpredictable future situations look a bit gloomy, a least for most people. Most people are also very fearful of changeable contexts, especially the ones that can be modified according to undetermined patterns. For all these reasons, most people try to introduce certain levels of regularity and predictability into their lives.

Not knowing brings about insecurity, hesitation and in extreme cases even trepidation. In this complex and ever-changing world, people avoid not knowing in certain ways, for example consulting experts, pretending to know, avoiding tackling certain issues, feeling frustrated and defenseless, and experiencing a sense of embarrassment and incompetence. In other cases, we look for quick solutions, overanalyze or behave in a dramatic manner. People might also feel defeated, despondent, disoriented or with a lack of clarity.

In the market many industrial sectors usually make humongous profits on these basic human fears. Some examples are insurance activities, private security services, economic and financial predictions, among others. From the entrepreneurial viewpoint, companies try to reduce uncertainty about their future in different ways: setting of visions and missions, design of strategies and policies, research activities on the customer preferences, examination of trends and introduction of detailed terms and conditions in the contracts, among others. From a wider perspective, the public bodies of all countries try to reduce the levels of uncertainty regarding future scenarios through the design of budgets, issuing of legislation and implementation of bureaucratic procedures and policies, among others.

The unknown makes people feel uncomfortable and unsettled. Most people fear the unfathomable because they realize they do not have control over that. For this reason, people, by all means, try to avoid the unknown.

One strategic way to deal with uncertainty is to gather as much knowledge as possible to be ready for uncertain circumstances. Most people tend to control things, especially knowledge; they feel the urge to count on a minimum amount of knowledge in order to be in control of their lives to a certain extent. Most people are truly convinced that if they are minimally knowledgeable about certain topics they would not become defenseless in their social environment.

You can find below some examples regarding the need to control things through knowledge. In that way, you tend to control your environment when you want to know:

– *How to work problems out in the best way*
– *How to improve different areas of your life (finance, career, etc.)*
– *How to relate to others in a more harmonious fashion*
– *How things will unfold in the future*
– *How to select the most appropriate course of action in any situation*
– *How to know if your decisions are correct*
– *How to know what you are meant to do in life (which many call "your mission")*

In all these situations, people tend to count on their own knowledge (memories stored in their mind) and gather more if really needed. However, it is very uncommon for people to deal with their life situations from a perspective of no-knowledge, which means realizing that you actually don't know anything.

Paradoxically, when people really believe they have the basic knowledge necessary for their life circumstances, they tend to act in a very limited and uncreative manner. This happens because all their actions are dictated by their subconscious memories, which are constraining by nature.

However, when people realize they don't know anything they can face up to circumstances from a perspective of no-knowledge. When you realize that you do not know anything you are not constrained by your subconscious memories. From this standpoint, you don't have any preconceived ideas or prede-termined ways of doing things. You can be more exploratory, spontaneous and creative.

When you realize that you don't actually know anything, you are more likely to start removing your limiting subconscious memories. You also become more open to receiving guidance from Divinity also called inspiration. The boundless power and unlimited wisdom coming from the Divine makes your own limited knowledge look trivial.

2. Main hindrances to knowing everything

True wisdom lies in not knowing.
– Jacob Liberman and Erik Liberman

2.1. Your subconscious memories
If you are like most people, you surely have the illusion of being aware of everything that is going on in your life. However, your perspective of the world is, by nature, very limited and biased. Many scientific studies certify that your conscious mind is only

able to process up to 15 bits of information per second, which is a very unsubstantial amount. Nonetheless, your subconscious mind has the capability to process millions of bits per second.

Most of your actions are affected by information processed on a subconscious level. Moreover, many of your activities are performed in an automatic manner, like on autopilot. This simplifies your life because you don't have to think about every action you take. The downside of this is that this type of automatic behavior renders you powerless when you face up to new challenging situations.

In accordance with this, Dr. Bruce Lipton states that during the day only five percent of the time you are driven by your conscious mind; the rest of the time you are just taken over by your subconscious programming. This also means that you are not even aware of most of your actions. In relation to this, Irvine states that: *"we don't know our mind. It is entirely possible for us to make a decision without fully understanding why we made the decision we did."*

You must also realize most of your bodily functions are subconscious. There are trillions of cells in your body that change and communicate with one another below the level of your awareness. Each cell functions like a perfect tiny factory which carries out its own processes, and in turn is interconnected with other cells in a harmonious manner.

All these internal processes, which seem miraculous from our limited human perspective, are subconscious. This shows us that the conscious part of your mind has a very insignificant role in all your physiological functions.

Some psychologists suggest that there many mental processes (such as creativity, dreams, automatism, regulation of the bodily functions, etc.) that we do not control consciously and, for this reason, we do not have a clear overall understanding on them. Some other experiences like slips of tongue or altered states of consciousness also seem to be performed beyond your current level of understanding.

Your subconscious mind is unfathomable, like a sealed box; you cannot access the complete information held inside, at least in a direct manner. Nonetheless, you can deduce part of this information by using introspection. This tool will be explained in this chapter.

There are several scientific studies which confirm that you have thousands of thoughts per day, and you are not even aware of most of them. In this book it was also explained about the main traits of your programs you hold in your subconscious mind. In that effect, you are constantly creating and recreating your reality throughout these programs, which continually play out on a subconscious level.

Some of your memories appear to be deleted from your mind; nonetheless, these apparently lost programs are still running below the level of your awareness. You are not aware of these memories because they have been suppressed, repressed or affected by any other defense mechanisms. These mental defenses were thoroughly explained in the previous chapter.

To sum up, there is one relevant thing that you certainly know for sure now: all situations affecting you are materialized by your subconscious memories. However, what you really don't know is how your life situations will be manifested in the future by these very subconscious programs. You cannot know this in advance because you don't have any direct access to your subconscious memories.

There is another aspect which shows you that you don't really know anything. You don't even know which specific memories stored in your mind are the ones which cause the difficult circumstances that appear in your life. It is possible that, at first, this realization appears a bit disturbing for you.

However, you don't really have to know what memories are to manifest negative situations in your life. It is important to remember that whenever you practice Ho'oponopono and repeatedly say the sentences: *"I am sorry; Please forgive me; I love you; Thank you"* you are being assisted by the Divine. When you use the Ho'oponopono technique the selection of subconscious memories to be deleted is always the exclusive domain of Divinity.

2.2. Your desires

Every person has a very specific set of desires, which often conflict with one another. All your desires reside under your conscious level; they are, in fact, subconscious programs. In accordance to this, Irvine says that you do not have any control over your most significant desires.

You never form the desires consciously; they take shape deeply in the back of your mind, unwittingly, and pop out into your awareness. Some very well-known luminaries such as Freud, Schumpeter and Russell highlighted that all our desires belong to the domain of the subconscious mind.

Your desires are a consequence of multiple factors which boil in your subconscious cauldron, for example: your social programming (messages received from your family, friends, acquaintances, etc.); your genetic heritage from your ancestors; and the general influence of your environment (messages from the media, etc.). None of the factors originating your desires are actually under your control.

In some cases your desires are very deeply ingrained in your subconscious mind which makes it very difficult to deduce their real causes. You might rationalize and expose your own explanation on why you prefer certain things in your life rather than others. However, in all cases, the real causes of your desires remain a mystery, even to you.

From the Ho'oponopono perspective, your desires are just memories playing out in your subconscious mind. At the same time, your desires tend to change during your life and these transformations do not follow any specific and recognizable pattern. You cannot know (or predict) why or how your desires will change or how long they will last. Besides, you don't have any clue about why some of your desires conflict or interlock with others. You don't even really know why some of your intense past desires dithered over time.

Some specialists differentiate your desires into two definite categories, tangible things (such as a house, money, a new car, etc.) and intangible things (such as peacefulness, joy, love, comfort, status and enlightenment, among others). Nonetheless, if you analyze more deeply you will discover that each of your tangible desires has an underlying intangible desire supporting it.

For example, when you want a new car, you don't really want the car for itself, but because of your intangible things this car might be able to provide you with, for example: comfort, status, joy, etc. From Ho'oponopono's perspective, some important intangible desires you should always try to satisfy are peacefulness and love, among others.

In conclusion, your knowledge of your desires, which are fundamental factors in your life, is very limited. The only thing that you really know is that all desires are subconscious memories, which means you cannot have direct access to them.

2.3. Your perceptual system

You bring the outside inside through perception and you recreate it, interpret it.
– Michael George

Your perceptual system, naturally equipped by your five senses – taste, sight, touch, hearing and smell – is constantly scanning the information from your environment. Your senses are actually your most important interface with the world.

Your perceptual system never allows you to apprehend the wholeness of your environment. In order to deal with certain stimuli of your environment efficiently, you naturally dispose the rest on the way.

Many scientific studies confirm that your senses are flooded by millions of bits of information every single moment. Despite this, as it was previously explained, your conscious mind can only process a small, very limited, amount of bits of information every second because your attention is intrinsically selective.

Most psychologists state that with your attention you pick up only certain types of stimuli from the environment, and this selection is based on different criteria. For example, you might select certain stimuli because of their distinctive characteristics (such as frequency, color, size, etc.) or based on your own motivations (for example, your preferences, interests, etc.). It is interesting to know that some stimuli can also be misperceived because of distractions, blurred messages or lack of previous knowledge about the stimuli, among other reasons.

From Ho'oponopono's perspective, you can perceive only certain stimuli (and not others) because your subconscious memories guide your attention especially onto them. Your subconscious mind is primarily in charge of focusing your attention on specific things, and withdrawing it from others.

In accordance to this, Wilson states that:

we are equipped with a nonconscious filter that examines the information reaching our senses and decides what to admit to consciousness. We can consciously control the "settings" to some degree... The operation of the filter, however – the way in which information is classified, sorted and selected for further processing – occurs outside of awareness. The nonconscious filter does more than allow us to focus our conscious attention on one thing at a time. It also monitors what we are not paying attention to.

You always perceive reality through the lens of your limited past experiences, which is, by nature, a very limiting perspective.

Your perception of reality is always very incomplete and subjective. Many scientists such as Varela and Maturana state that what you perceive is not fundamentally the consequence of the messages received from your senses, but from internal processes of your brain that link the stimuli with patterns (or memories) held in your mind.

You might believe that you can grasp things clearly but your vision is always slanted. Your knowledge of your environment is partial and distorted. Norretranders states that your:

> *conscious will never be able to describe the world, neither within nor without itself. Both the person who is within and the world that is without are richer than consciousness can know about. They both constitute a depth that can be charted and described, but not exhaustively known.*

There are many stimuli you are not aware of which still imprint your subconscious mind. Norretranders states that: *"the senses... digest enormous quantities of information, most of which we never become conscious of... most of what goes in one person's mind is not conscious..."* There are some studies which confirm that during your dreams you can recall certain stimuli which imprinted your mind during your waking state but you were unaware of them.

Some psychological schools of thought state there are certain stimuli that are below your *"absolute threshold."* This technical term defines the point below which you cannot perceive a stimulus with your senses, for example, radiation. Another very well-known example is the case of subliminal messages. These messages can enter your subconscious mind without you even noticing them.

To sum up, the two main reasons why some stimuli are not registered by your senses are a) the intrinsic selective quality of your attention, which can focus only on a very tiny fragment of the endless stream of stimuli you are exposed to; and b) the absolute threshold below which a stimulus become imperceptible to your senses. In both cases, many stimuli still impact your subconscious mind imprinting it.

There is a third factor to add to this, which is repetition of the stimuli over time. The constant repetition of stimuli makes your mind familiar or accustomed to them, thus your mind is less likely to detect it. One example of this is the humming sound of the air conditioning, to which you get accustomed and which seems to disappear by becoming imperceptible background noise.

There is another topic which is important to pinpoint. It was mentioned before that your knowledge of reality is always limited. Some masters state that you don't get in direct contact with reality, but you always deal with representations of reality. These representations are very personal and they are far from being complete and accurate.

These representations of reality are produced and organized by your complex perceptual system. In that sense, Steiner states a representation *"is a concept that once was connected with a perception and retains the reference to this perception."* He also says that: *"our knowledge, to begin with, does not reach beyond our representations."*

The intrinsic characteristics of your sensory system impede you from having direct knowledge of the physical reality, except through your representations of it. Your representations of reality are always in accordance with your subconscious memories.

In accordance to this, Steiner continues: *"by contrast, the knowledge that goes beyond our representations – taking this expression here in the widest possible sense... is open to doubt."* He also adds that: *"except through thinking and perceiving, nothing is given to us directly."* Likewise Neuro Linguistic Programming (NLP) says that you have a map of reality, which is intrinsically incomplete and subjective.

Your own model of the world is composed of a set of factors, such as your beliefs and values, your personal history and experiences (in short, your subconscious memories). Your personal representations of reality are always significantly different from the reality itself because you subconsciously suppress, distort and generalize elements of reality in a very distinctive and personal manner.

There is another approach on perception which is solidly supported by Quantum Physics. This recently developed scientific discipline corroborates that everything is made of the same substance: energy albeit presented in different states. Every time you think and feel, you are affecting this universal field of energy and, in turn, manifesting things according to your feelings and thoughts.

From this scientific perspective, every time you observe things, you are actually prompting them to be. In the Universe every single element is present in the form of waves of energy. When you observe these waves they convert into specific particles, with specific time and place.

However, when you withdraw your attention from them, they return to wave form. In other words, all specific things in your life only exist because of your observation. These things cannot exist on their own, without your observation. This means that every time you observe, you participate in the creation of things and situations.

Every single thing you observe is driven by your subconscious memories. As it was explained before, every time you observe, you are creating your reality. For this reason your subconscious memories are what manifest your reality.

2.4. Your expectations

Many masters state that life unfolds in a mysterious manner, which means that in practice you never really know why things happen. You cannot really grasp the complexity and intricacies of the Universe and the wholeness of human nature with your limited intellect. You actually don't know anything.

If you are like most people, you might have expectations about different relevant topics in your life. Expectations are the result of complex processes of reflection, estimation, combination and synthesis of information. They are just another limited way to interpret your environment.

If we analyze the definition of the word *expectation* it refers to something you expect in a state of anticipation. You project possible outcomes regarding future situations in order to have more *certainty* about them. It is a peculiar way to access *knowledge* about future circumstances.

You can have positive expectations when you look forward to something in a positive manner. You can also hold negative expectations when you are fearful of something that might happen in the future. You tend to hold expectations on many things related to your life. You can hold expectations that things will work out, among others, regarding:

– *Your health (how you will be emotionally, mentally and physically)*
– *Your relationships (for example, how people should behave with you)*
– *Your projects (how different endeavors such as work issues, business, professional career and trips will unfold)*
– *Your wealth (how you will work out your financial difficulties, how prosperous you will be in the future)*

From the Ho'oponopono perspective, expectations are not useful because they are an unnecessary waste of energy. They are just based on guesswork; you try to predict the future. Your expectations are never based on any concrete evidence, so their accuracy is arguable. Your expectations are always based on your subconscious memories; moreover your expectations are programs engraved in your subconscious mind.

When you hold expectations on anything related to your life, you are deceiving yourself because they are essentially illusory.

They might give a sense of security, but it is totally baseless. You can never know how things will turn out in the future and how they will affect you physically, mentally and emotionally. Expectations are just superstitious and ineffective ways to dispel the uncertainty about your future. You are not clairvoyant so you cannot foresee the future.

This does not mean that you cannot be hopeful that your things will unfold well; in that sense, positive thinking is always better than a state of negativity. However, this positive attitude is different from predicting how things will unfold in a precise manner. Every time you have expectations you give all your power away to them.

All expectations pave the way to disappointment. If you thoroughly compare your past expectations with the real outcomes related to them, you will see they were never a perfect match. Things generally unfold in a different way, as compared with your expectations.

As a consequence, it is important not to have too many expectations. You must remember that all your expectations are just your subconscious memories, which are constraining by nature. When you have expectations you are trying to look at the future, using a rear-view mirror.

Every time you hold expectations in relation to any area of your life, you are trying to mentally force specific outcomes, which is another way of creating resistance. Expectations also imply some sort of concern about future scenarios. Every single time you have strong expectancy about how things should be, your mind is utterly structured and you are disconnected from the limitless divine flow.

So you might ask what the alternative to holding expectations is. When you don't rely on expectations you can embrace the intrinsic uncertainty of your life with all its potential gifts. With this attitude you are delighted with the uncertain future, instead of being fearful of it.

Every time you have expectations you are focused on an imaginary future, instead of being immersed in what is going on at present. Your expectations are subtle ways to escape the present moment, which is the only one that exists. So the best way to get rid of expectations is being fully focused on the present moment. When you fully surrender and connect to the current moment, the universal forces will always provide the best options in all dimensions of your life.

So your expectations are just another way of attachment because you get stuck to specific results you guess will occur. However, when you truly let go of all your expectations, you not only rid yourself from any attachments, but you also let the Divine operate in your life gracefully.

For example, when you face up to a difficult situation you are likely to have certain expectations. You guess in advance the possible outcome for this problematic situation. However, when you eliminate your expectations and trust the Divine, you harness far more power to transmute any difficult circumstance in your life.

Divinity can make things unfold in countless ways, most of which are beyond the boundaries of your imagination. The Divine will always find the best way to improve your life. The universal resources are unlimited and creative by nature, unlike your expectations. When you hold expectations you don't even harness a tiny part of this boundless power.

When you have no expectations you also you remove all the pain when things work out in a different manner, as they generally do. Besides, you can be completely open to the countless possibilities to be brought about by Divinity into your life. With this attitude you will feel utterly excited about the future instead of being concerned.

With an open attitude you will even look forward to receiving surprises, coming from the Divine through unexpected channels. When you have this attitude, even when things in your life don't appear to work out well, you will certainly know that, from the divine perspective, everything has a meaningful purpose, albeit sometimes hidden beneath apparent difficulties.

In this book it was explained that the only way to be connected to the divine source is by cleaning your subconscious memories, which include your expectations. You should hold no expectations but instead be at the mercy of Divinity, who cares for you in the best way possible. When you have this attitude you will soon notice that all troublesome situations tend to be resolved almost effortlessly.

On one side, some say that not having expectations is not necessarily at loggerheads with setting objectives in your life. From this perspective, it is actually good to set goals for your life. In that effect, every planning activity implies reducing uncertainty to a certain extent. Plans also specify ways to structure future scenarios according to the objectives you set. Nonetheless, because all future circumstances are always unpredictable, you should always try to be as open-minded and flexible as possible when you design and implement your plans. Every time you set goals you actually don't know all the variables affecting these objectives in the future. So you should always be open to the possibility that your objectives are not achieved or that they are attained in a different way. When this happens, it is very common that the Universe brings about something even better for you. Nonetheless, in order for this to happen you have to release any expectations on specific results; as a consequence, you can veritably connect to the limitless wisdom of the universal forces.

On the other side, a prestigious Ho'oponopono specialist like Dr. Len recommends that you should not plan anything, whenever possible. From this perspective, every time you plan you only use the limited information at hand contained in your subconscious memories. So planning is limiting by nature, no matter how thorough your plans are and how complete your research on future prospects is. None of these elements can anticipate how things will unfold in the future in a very precise manner.

For this reason, Dr. Len suggests that, instead of planning, you must always rely on Divinity. With no plans in your head, you become more open to receiving divine guidance. From this perspective, you do not need to plan anything; you are more willing to surf the waves of your life. You are more inclined to get into a state of flow. By knowing that you don't know anything and you don't need to do so, you will find that it is useless to plan. In that way, you can surrender to the Divine more easily.

When you let go of your plans, the Higher Planes will guide you on the right way to act, the best timing and the most appropriate resources to use. In that effect, every time you are stuck to plans you tend to forsake your most valuable inner resource, which is your connection to the Divine. You should be aware that the Universal Source always manages infinite possibilities.

To sum up, when you rid yourself of plans and expectations, you can feel comfortable with the idea that you don't know anything. When you have this attitude, you understand things will always work out in the best way possible, because you are continually assisted by Divinity. Metaphorically speaking, you don't have to know all the specific details of your life movie in order to enjoy it. You just excitedly watch this film as it gradually unfolds before your eyes.

2.5. Your cognitive distortions
Another important reason for your intrinsic lack of knowledge is your natural tendency to misapprehend situations. Every single thing that you are aware of is tainted by your subjective interpretation; you never capture raw information in a literal manner.

In other words, your interpretation of reality is always colored by the programs which lay hidden in your subconscious mind. Your misinterpretations of reality are caused by your numerous cognitive distortions. These distortions are also called cognitive errors, mental biases or mind fallacies. In that effect, Dobelli states that a cognitive error is *"a systematic deviation from logic – from optimal, rational, reasonable thought."*

These distortions consist of ingrained patterns of thought that lead you to an incorrect reasoning. You tend to twist the interpretation of facts in a certain way, censor some relevant information or highlight specific pieces of data. McRaney states that:

> *there is a growing body of work coming out of psychology and cognitive science that says you have no clue why you act the way you do, choose the things you choose, or think the thoughts you think.*

These distortive patterns of thought prevent you from accessing knowledge related to your environment in a useful and effective manner. Some scientific studies state that these biases are just a product of unreflective swift judgments of your environment and yourself. All these patterns of thinking are subconscious.

If you are like most people, you might not even notice these distortions in yourself or others or disbelieve their existence. You have to bear in mind that, from the Ho'oponopono perspective, all these cognitive distortive patterns are just memories playing under the level of your awareness.

These routine ways of thinking are more common than you think and they work on a very subtle level. Every time you interpret your environment you are being affected by these biased patterns. In that effect, there is no such thing as *"an objective interpretation of facts"*; instead every person has a distinct perspective on reality. Your cognitive distortions make your own perspective on things and circumstances unique and different from others'. Your cognitive distortions affect you in a distinct fashion; these mental distortions vary from person to person.

You are always assigning specific meanings to all things, people and situations around you. This particular set of meanings you use to interpret reality is based on your subconscious memories. For this reason, the origin of these particular patterns of thought is mostly, as any other subconscious memory, social conditioning (from family, friends, media, government, etc.) received all over your life and your genetic lineage.

In order to give specific examples of cognitive distortions, you will find below an indicative list including some of the most representative biases. For more detailed explanations on these mental fallacies, it is advisable to go through the specific bibliography mentioned at the end of this book. In that effect, according to numerous scientific studies, these are several examples of cognitive biases:

– *Focusing only on information confirming your own beliefs and leaving aside all data that does not validate them.*

– *Categorizing and labelling situations, people and things in a subjective manner; this includes stereotyping, which means assigning similar characteristics to all representatives of specific groups.*

– *Making everything personal or addressed to you, even things which are completely unrelated to you.*

– *Neglecting the positive aspects of any situation, focusing exclusively on its negative traits.*

– *Dismissing significant changes in your environment especially when you don't pay close attention to them, which is scientifically called inattentional blindness.*

– *"Reading" other minds, being completely sure what other people are thinking.*

– *Giving credibility to a fact just because it is believed or preferred by a majority.*

– *Believing that you control all things in your life, despite countless evidence of uncontrollable factors affecting you.*

– *Jumping into conclusions based on incomplete information.*

– *Using presumptions; this means interpreting facts in a certain*

manner without any valid evidence supporting it.
– Correlating factors without having solid evidence of the relationship between them.
– Minimizing or exaggerating the traits of current or future situations.
– Discarding relevant information necessary for the analysis of a situation.
– Remembering your past experiences in a distorted manner.
– Deciding based on your feelings rather than on your rationale; assessing potential risks and benefits of situations primarily based on your emotions.
– Acting based on your own or others' expectations.
– Being easily influenced by experts or people with authority, without challenging the validity of their opinions.
– "Predicting" the future; tendency to overestimate or underestimate future outcomes: this can include black or white thinking which implies narrowing down possible consequences to two opposite ones.
– Believing that every circumstance is brought about by one or a few causes, dismissing the multi-causality of all situations.
– Believing that the future is equal to the past and acting accordingly.
– Overvaluing scant resources, believing that scarce resources are actually abundant.
– Keeping the status quo of things, even when more positive choices exist.
– Believing that other people interpret situations in the same way as you do.
– Being affected by first impressions and becoming unable to substantially modify them over time.
– Magnifying your strengths and dismissing your weaknesses, tending to overestimate your own knowledge about a topic.
– Generalizing one-off situations, taking them into account to draw general conclusions.
– Assigning meaningful relevance to random events (this includes superstitious behavior, etc.).

– Accepting odd explanations for things or events you don't clearly understand.

– Believing that your recollection is made up of literal reflections of past circumstances, dismissing the fact that your memories are transformed and distorted over time.

– Analyzing facts based on the most available information in your memory, without considering its suitability.

– Being affected by contrast in your decisions (for example, as a buyer, you are more likely to accept a discount of £10 on a product costing £20, than a discount of £10 on a good costing £1000, even though the discount is the same in both cases).

– Not knowing if your actions are actually guided by divine inspiration or driven by your past subconscious memories.

In relation to your memory skills, you are naturally affected by some distortions regarding recollection. In that effect, the retrieval of information from your mind is mainly based on association of the pieces of information held in it. You tend to remember experiences in a selective manner, primarily based on mental associations. For example, you are more likely to recollect information which is directly or indirectly associated with data at hand.

You are more prone to retrieve memories which are full of sensory aids, such as images, touch and scents, etc. The same applies to these recollections charged with intense emotions. Besides, when you recollect information your mind tends to give priority to data which is clearly distinctive from the rest (for example, its size, color, shape, symbolism, ways of its display or movement, etc.). Your mind is also more likely to call back information which has been repeated over time.

Geley states that: *"The fact of the re-emergence of forgotten memories which the mind wrongly takes to be new and unpublished matter is… much more frequent than it is supposed."* This well-known memory bias is called cryptomnesia. To put it more simply, when you experience cryptomnesia you tend to think that you are original with some ideas which come up in your mind. However, your *creative* statements are based on memories, which you have completely forgotten.

It was mentioned before that all people are affected by these cognitive distortions in specific ways. The upside of these subconscious shortcuts is that they help you interpret the intrinsically complex aspects of reality in an easier and hastier way. Mental biases provide you with a quick sense of certainty before ambiguous situations.

However, the downside of this set of biases is that they distort your perspective facts and circumstances. These biases don't allow you to have an unpolluted perspective of reality. On many occasions, these biases don't allow you to evaluate situations thoroughly because, by their essence, they narrow your discernment skills. These fallacies might lead you to draw incorrect, unelaborated or just baseless conclusions.

2.6. Other aspects

There are a few more points related to this topic which must be necessarily highlighted, as follows:

a) Your ego distorts your perception

It is interesting to note that your ego also distorts your perception and interpretation of reality. The main aspects of ego will be thoroughly discussed later in this book. It is important to pinpoint that when you are identified with your ego, which is a false pretense replacing your true self, your perception tends to be naturally disfigured.

You have to understand that you identify with the main aspects of your ego most of the time. For example, you are constantly identifying with your race, nationality, position, gender, physical appearance, occupation, among others; you are fully attached to these specific traits which are related to your ego. This set of personal characteristics actually clouds the way you perceive reality. From the Ho'oponopono perspective, these traits are just subconscious memories which rule your life.

According to many oriental philosophies, most people tend to be entangled in the network of attachments related to their ego features. From this perspective, these attachments represent the major cause of most suffering in humanity.

b) Everything is neutral

Many masters state that things and events have no meaning at all, except the one that you personally give them from your unique and distinct perspective. In other words, the interpretation, explanation and description of reality are always subjective. The specific meaning you give to anything in your environment is unique and personal. It is very important to highlight that the specific meanings you assign to things, people and situations is always based on the information stored in your subconscious mind.

c) You tend to perceive parts not the whole

Some sages state that you only see fragments of what is going on in your life. In some cases, you can have a very inaccurate approximation to the overall situation when you analyze things retrospectively.

Even the most trivial situations are the consequence of umpteen causes and multiple relationships of several factors of which you are generally unaware. In many cases, you don't even know some of the factors affecting a situation. At the beginning of this book it was explained that all things which exist are connected to others in an intricate net of links. This complex maze of connections cannot easily be grasped by your limited intellect. This principle can apply to any circumstance in your life.

In other words, it is very difficult for your rational mind to see the complete picture of any situations or circumstances because, in general, they are affected by many other facts, some of which you have not even noticed. Even when you could notice all factors involved in a situation you would still be unable to understand the complex relationship among them all. You tend to have a partial and limited perspective on things which are opposite to the principle of wholeness and interconnectedness explained in the second chapter of this book.

3. What you really have to know

All the previous topics explained over this chapter confirm the principle that says: *"You don't know anything."* Your access to knowledge through your thinking, feeling, sensing, perceiving or emoting is always limited because in all cases you are driven by your subconscious memories. And these programs are always a reflection of your past, which is naturally constraining. You can never arrive at a state of clarity and certainty when you are continually snared by your own subconscious memories.

In that effect, limitless wisdom and complete knowledge can never come from your subconscious programs. The only way that you, and all people, can access pure and unbounded knowledge is through divine inspiration. The Divine is the most graceful, omniscient and almighty source of all wisdom that exists.

When you truly realize that you don't know anything you are showing humility and nobleness. This attitude also allows you to take responsibility for not knowing anything. When you don't deny this evident truth, you can truly start walking the path of wisdom. It is really important that you acknowledge this principle and embrace it as soon as possible.

Some masters say that when you truly accept that you don't know anything, you end up knowing something which is very significant: the fact that you don't know anything. This is one of the most important steps that you can take on the path of your personal evolution and life transformation.

From the Ho'oponopono perceptive, there is one thing which you can always be certain about: one of the most important purposes in your life is to clean all the memories playing out in your subconscious mind. This is actually one of the most significant pieces of knowledge you should always bear in mind.

It is also important to know that you can never be totally separated from the Divine, because it is your natural pure essence. All the memories you hold in your subconscious mind transitorily obscure your connection with Divinity, but they can never thwart it completely.

Another very important point to know is that you are naturally responsible for everything around you. You have to know this without any doubt. Every situation which appears in your life is the natural reflection of the memories playing out in your subconscious mind, and you are responsible for it.

You also have to know that by practicing Ho'oponopono on a frequent basis, you can remove your subconscious memories, and in turn dissolve all your problems effortlessly. Your subconscious memories cannot be deleted by themselves; but you can remove these programs by consciously repeating the four Ho'oponopono phrases regularly.

Another thing that you must know is that when you are committed to using this cleaning tool you also reconnect to the divine love energy. Whenever you repeat the four Ho'oponopono phrases you are naturally assisted by the Divine with the removal of your subconscious memories. Divinity can only help you when you grant it permission, and you do so by practicing Ho'oponopono regularly.

Lastly, there is another important thing for you to know. As you gradually remove your subconscious programs, you get nearer to the zero state, where there are no subconscious memories limiting you. In that state you are more prone to receiving divine inspiration.

4. Knowledge about yourself

4.1. General aspects of introspection

Self-awareness carries the power of transformation: it will always open your heart and mind to new levels of experience and will infuse you with fresh energy and understanding.
– Lynda Field

During the following points we will analyze the main aspects of self-knowledge (knowledge about your own inner world). There are some questions we will try to answer over the following points in the best way possible, such as:

– Can you really know yourself well?
– Can you truly access information related to your subconscious memories?
– If so, is that information trustworthy?
– If not, why can't you access that knowledge?

From the Ho'oponopono perspective, in order to know more about your subconscious memories you can use a very well-known tool called introspection. In relation to this, some psychologists like Fritz Perls make a clear distinction between introspection and awareness. On one side, introspection is the purposed process focused on finding out the meaning of what goes on inside you. In that effect, introspection is intrinsically intentional, interfering, and controlling.

On the other side, awareness is sensing what comes up in you, without you purposefully looking for it. Awareness is always spontaneous; you do not prompt any insights to emerge. However, from the purpose of this text, both terms will be used alternatively.

Introspection is a tool you use when you practice

Ho'oponopono on a frequent basis. To put it simply, introspection, also called self-observation or self-awareness, implies reflexivity, because you are purposed to examine your sensations, feelings and thoughts thoroughly. You try to make them as clear as possible so that you can gain new perspective on them. Some authors like Field say that introspection is intrinsically nurturing and contributes to your self-development.

Introspection implies intended reflection upon your inner world, more specifically your subconscious memories. It is about being fully aware of what you are experiencing in the present moment.

For introspection you have to pay undivided attention to whatever is occurring inside you. The term *introspection* is related to what Gardner defines as intrapersonal intelligence, which is the skill to concentrate inwardly. In the words of this author, intrapersonal intelligence: *"is the capacity to form an accurate, veridical model of oneself and to be able to use that model to operate effectively in life."*

Some psychological schools of thought relate introspection to the processes of meta-awareness (which means being aware that you are aware) and metacognition (knowledge about your own knowledge), which is also called metacognitive monitoring.

When you use introspection on a frequent basis you can deduce several aspects of the contents of your subconscious mind. We saw in this book that your reality is created by your subconscious memories; for this reason knowing about them is really crucial.

The final objective of introspection is to articulate or to put into words your internal states in relation to specific situations affecting you (for example, breakups in relationships, financial problems, or health conditions, etc.). When you introspect at the same time you place yourself in the experience but also outside it, in order to see what is going on inside you in relation to that very situation.

When you go through the introspection process, you have to ask some questions of yourself and then concentrate on your answers to them which can appear. Your answers can be expressed in different ways: physiological sensations (for example, tension, agitated breathing, etc.), emotional states (such as sadness, fear, etc.) and thoughts (spontaneous ideas, obsessive ruminations, etc.). All this information provides you with clues or insights into your subconscious memories.

Introspection implies stepping back from your current life circumstances in order to carefully observe how you brought them into reality through your subconscious memories. Introspection can be considered a useful tool for inner work. It can assist you in the process of removing your subconscious negative programming. At the end of the introspective process you have to repeat the four Ho'oponopono sentences (*"I am sorry"*, *"Please forgive me"*, *"I love you"* and *"Thank you"*) many times in order to delete your subconscious memories.

4.2. Types of questions used in introspection

Introspection is a self-awareness therapeutic tool which works like an interview. The only difference with an interview is that, when you go through the introspective process, you are both the interviewer and the interviewee. Once you asked the questions of yourself, you have to let the answers surface from your subconscious mind in a spontaneous manner.

When you ask questions during this process you must cast away any criticism, prejudice and even expectations about the possible results. When you introspect you must be truly inquisitive about yourself; you must also be a careful listener, you must deepen your listening in relation to what comes up to your mind. During the introspective process you must try to be as present as possible.

You should also be patient, humble and open-minded. In that effect, you should never use introspection to criticize yourself.

You should act like a little inquisitive and adventurous child who wants to know more about his or her environment.

Some suggest that you should not ask the questions in a formal or mechanical manner. Instead you always try to *live* the questions you ask, or even feel them organically. There are many different ways to pose the questions. You can find below an indicative list of examples of questions you can ask yourself.

> *– What is going on in my life that I am manifesting this?*
> *– Why did I manifest this situation in my life?*
> *– Why does this circumstance emerge in my life and what do I have to do with it?*
> *– What does this have to do with me?*

You can also try a more indirect approach with other questions such as:

> *– If it happens that I caused this problem how would I feel?*
> *– How do I feel about being responsible for this situation?*
> *– What is occurring now in my inner world?*
> *– What is this situation showing me?*
> *– What is the hidden meaning of this?*
> *– How is this for me?*
> *– Who am I?*

This last question is related to your own self-concept, which might change over time. You focus on your true core, your authentic essence. From the psychological viewpoint this question is also related to self-realization.

You can also ask additional questions to obtain more specific answers using some models known as Meta model or Milton model. These aspects are explained in detail in Appendix E at the end of this book.

All questions you use must be short, clear and simple. These types of questions engage your critical thinking more easily. You must use open questions, which can be answered in many different ways. With these types of questions you have the chance to be more explanatory; they help you obtain a great amount of information about your inner world.

As you probably know, open questions always begin with words starting with *"w"*, such as *"What...?"* and *"Where...?"*, among others. You should never use closed questions, which are restrictive by essence. An example of a closed question is the one which can only be answered with *"yes"* or *"no."*

All these questions are related to yourself, not to other people in your life. Questions focused only on yourself are the best when accessing your subconscious programs. The main purpose of these questions is to perform a voluntary deepening self-scrutiny, which implies an equidistant and non-judgmental observation of your inner world.

When you go through the introspection process, you try to analyze an outside situation from an internal perspective. This means that you focus primarily on your internal world to cast some light on it in relation to an external circumstance. You try to go beyond the conspicuous aspects related to situations affecting you; you go more deeply into your feelings, sensations and thoughts. Introspective questions represent pathways to access your inner wisdom.

Another point to highlight is that all questions must be focused on what is going on at present. In that effect, you should never ask questions like *"What was going on in me in the past"* or *"What will be going on in me in the future?"* The information of your past programming can only be explored in the now.

4.3. Your attitude regarding introspective insights

You must ask questions of yourself in order to prompt infor-mation regarding your subconscious programs to emerge. You should never shut yourself down to any answers you might receive; none of these answers are meaningless. They are your personal perception or reflection on what is occurring inside you. You have to always be open-minded and show authentic concern about what is going on within you at the present moment.

You have to hone your inner listening skills to access your inner knowingness more effectively. You should pay close attention to whatever you answer in an empathetic manner, as if you were a professional counsellor. It is really important to avoid any judgments in relation to the answers that come up.

You can also write the answers to those questions in detail on a piece of paper. You should never try to change their content, deny it, criticize it or modify it. It is important not to jump into any hasty conclusion about the insights as well. In other words, grasp the answers as they come and acknowledge them completely.

Many scientific studies confirm that the very act of writing details about your insights represents a very powerful tool to access your subconscious programming. Your insights are probable interpretations of your subconscious programs. This lack of accuracy does not invalidate the use of these insights at all.

In relation to this, every time you introspect you use the so-called *possibility thinking*. In relation to this, de Bono states that: *"possibility is not truth and should never pretend to be... (it) is a framework in the mind that makes it easier to move forward to what might be truth."*

When you are aware of what is going on inside you, you are contributing to the cleaning process of your subconscious memories. Once you take note of these insights, you must then say the four Ho'oponopono sentences many times.

4.4. Introspection and emotions
The process of self-observation called introspection includes not only thoughts but also emotions. Your emotional states tend to

complement your rational aspects providing you with very useful information about your internal world. Your emotions are complex and varying; they are energy in motion.

Your emotional states color all your experiences. Every time you are not truly aware of your emotions, you are more likely to be taken over by them. In relation to this, Goleman coined the term *"emotional awareness"* which is the capacity of recognizing your own feelings and their causes, as soon as they emerge. The capability of observing your own emotions is a skill this author calls *"Emotional Intelligence."* Many people tend to be over rational or completely disconnected from their emotions, which hinders their emotional awareness.

When you are emotionally introspective you can develop a thorough understanding of your own emotions at all times. When you use this tool, you truly understand the main causes of your feelings, which are always related to your subconscious memories.

When you use this tool you can differentiate and label your emotions. For example, you can assign specific names to your feelings, such as: sadness, fear, etc. For this reason, in order to be more emotionally aware, you should ask yourself questions like:

– *What am I feeling now?*
– *What is this feeling about? What is its specific name?*
– *What is going on in me that I experience this feeling?*
– *How does this feeling relate to my current life circumstances?*
– *What are the causes and meanings of these emotions?*
– *Why is the feeling of value for me?*

Throughout these questions, you not only acknowledge your feelings, but you also specifically relate them to your current circumstances. You don't try to stifle your emotions, by denying or suppressing them, but you fully own and express them. You might also discover that some feelings are recurring over time. It is also important to remember that your subconscious memories were originally imprinted on your mind accompanied by an emotional charge.

Your insights about your emotions can be expressed in a very indirect or subtle manner. For example, when you ask: *"What I am feeling now?"* you can receive some insights such as *"I am fed up of everything in my life."* In this case, you commented about your exhaustion, but you did not mention the emotions underpinning it. So your tiredness can be accompanied by various emotions such as anger, sadness and others.

In this case your specific emotions related to that issue were not shown explicitly. For this reason, you can explore your emotional states more deeply. You can ask another question like *"What specific emotions am I feeling now regarding this?"* This type of question provides you with a clearer picture of what is going on inside you from the emotional perspective. You can also use any of the questions of the Meta model or Milton Model, again which are thoroughly explained in Appendix E.

You should always be aware of not intellectualizing your emotions. You must describe your emotional states as organically as possible. It is also important that you don't judge your emotions as they emerge; you should never use emotional awareness to blame yourself or others.

Metaphorically speaking, your emotions are like the tip of an iceberg: the hidden parts of it are your subconscious memories. As mentioned before you can take note of any emotional insights you receive. You can reread these insights many times, and say the four Ho'oponopono sentences.

4.5. Introspection and sensations
When you are exploring your subconscious memories you can also receive introspective insights in the form of images, sounds or scents. You can even experience changes in your body temperature and other physiological sensations. All these wordless

indicators provide you with useful clues about the memories stored in your subconscious warehouse. Davis, Eshelman and McKay say that: *"internal awareness refers to any physical sensation, feeling, emotional discomfort, or comfort inside your body."* It is important to put all these signals into words whenever possible; you should assign meanings to these signs, as clearly as possible. In Psychology there is specific technical term for this called *desomatization.*

It was mentioned that sometimes you tend to retrieve information from your subconscious memories in a wordless manner, for example through the use of imagery. In relation to this, Robertson says that you can either be a verbalizer, when you prioritize the remembering of words or sounds, or a visualizer when you emphasize the remembering of non-verbal information. If you are visualizer you are more likely to experience physiological changes during the introspective process.

You can be more aware of your physical sensations if you take a thorough internal body inventory. When you scan every part of your body in detail, you can be more knowledgeable about what is going on inside you from the bodily perspective. You should identify different parts of your body with tension, discomfort or any other evident physical sensation. Once you discover any of these symptoms, you can ask yourself questions like:

– *What is going on in me that I experience these sensations?*
– *How does this symptom relate to any event going on in my life?*
– *What is the main cause of these sensations?*
– *What is the specific meaning of these sensations?*
– *What is my body telling me in relation to my problems?*
– *How is this sensation important for me?*
– *How is this sensation related to me?*
– *What are these sensations trying to tell me?*
– *Is there anything else I should know about these sensations?*

Once you have asked these questions, you should fully concentrate on your body to hear the answers coming from it. You put these physiological signals in words, as specifically as possible. You can also ask yourself questions about the emotional qualities of these physiological sensations.

When you know more about your sensations, you have more clues about your subconscious memories originating them. As said before, you can take note of the insights about your physical sensations you receive, reread these insights and say the four Ho'oponopono sentences.

4.6. Introspection and Ho'oponopono

All introspective questions help you examine what is going on under the level of your consciousness. It was previously explained that you cannot look directly into the internal functioning of your subconscious mind because of its intrinsic secluded nature. However, you can deduce some aspects of your subconscious memories in an indirect manner.

With the frequent use of the introspective tool you can also understand how your subconscious memories originate your life circumstances. Every question you ask during the introspective process pulls your memories from a subconscious mind into your conscious level.

From a wider perspective, the frequent use of introspective tools helps you change your life in a positive manner. You can become more knowledgeable regarding yourself so that it is easier to free yourself from the tyranny of negative subconscious programs. Holden says: *"the better you know yourself... the more effectively you will live... Self-knowledge is the jewel in the crown of success."* Besides, when you know the details of what is going on in you, you can live a more authentic and fulfilling life.

When you practice introspection on a frequent basis, you will gradually become more mindful with yourself. Over time it is also possible that you will reflect on your inner world in a more spontaneous manner. It is said that your life is fruitful only when it is lived in questions, instead of being lived in statements.

When you go through the introspective process, you ask yourself questions which also make your life more meaningful. There are scientific studies which confirm that people who ask themselves questions on a frequent basis tend to become more productive than the rest.

It is very important that during the introspection process after receiving insights you practice Ho'oponopono. You don't need to know all the specifics of your subconscious memories for the cleaning process to be effective. There are many cases in which you cannot articulate the contents of your subconscious memories. In other cases, you really do not know what these programs are about. And that is fine; you do not have to worry about this. In that effect, when you say the four Ho'oponopono phrases many times, your subconscious programs will be removed all the same, regardless of whether you know their contents or not.

4.7. Your personal stories on reality

In simple English, our lives are determined by what we tell ourselves to be true, even it is not. Each of us manufactures our view of the world; we impose meaning (e.g. our truth – with emphasis on "our") upon everything that happens.
– Gary Leboff

We spin our tales, but in doing so, our tales also spin us. They magic into existence the worlds of meaning we inhabit.
– Guy Claxton

It is said you cannot have an objective perspective on reality. You can never see things as they really are; your vision of the world is always based on your unique and distinctive perspective.

Neuro Linguistic Programming (NLP) states that your map of reality generally does not match up with the actual territory.

This topic relates to the introspective process. In relation to introspection there are two different psychological stances. The first perspective states that the introspective analysis works like a beam casting light on the dark fathoms of the subconscious level. You act like a curious explorer willing to unveil the most precious hidden gems of your past programming.

There is a second perspective which states that you can never access your subconscious level in a proper fashion. From this perspective, the whole introspective process seems useless. Any attempts to unveil the mysteries of your subconscious vault are totally unproductive. Your subconscious mind is unfathomable by nature. Every time you try to connect to your subconscious mind your access to it is naturally thwarted. In this book we support the first stance.

It is important to highlight another interesting point. Some spiritual philosophies assert that all things and experiences you encounter in your life have no intrinsic meaning. You are always assigning specific meanings to every single thing around.

You might say that there are things with very clear and unarguable meaning. Nonetheless, if you analyze this more deeply, even things that appear to have an undoubted meaning, that meaning was assigned by you, in many cases unwittingly. You are constantly assigning meanings to all things and experiences in your life, based on your subconscious memories.

Many specialists tend to play down the validity of introspection as a tool to access the truth of your internal states. They say through introspection you can never obtain trustworthy information about subconscious memories. Moreover, these psychologists assert that every time you use introspection, you are actually making a story which is only partially based on real elements of your subconscious programs.

From this perspective, every time you go through an introspective process you are not able to access the exact and complete information related to your subconscious memories because of their intrinsic intractable nature. Your introspective insights are just tales you make up; they are nothing more than a bunch of deductions mixed with fabrications.

You are always elaborating your stories with what is going on in your life, which tends to be naturally dubious and full of inconsistencies. In that effect, the introspective process is not the exception to this. You unknowingly tend to streamline the narrative of your real life episodes. Despite all this, you naturally tend to rely on the credibility of your own tales because they make sense to you; and this is the only important thing.

Your analysis and interpretation of experiences are constantly affected by these tales you tell yourself. Some of your stories might be pleasant; others actually prevent you from improving your life. These personal stories are very powerful.

Some of these personal scripts are very well known to you; others remain completely buried in your subconscious level, albeit they still influence your life. Many psychologists state that you tend to expect things to unfold in your life in accordance to these personal tales. These scripts can also help you calm down when you face uncertain situations.

In all these stories there is some connection to reality, which means that they are not completely fabricated. Nonetheless all your stories are tainted with your personal way of interpreting things. During the introspective process, you also make up personal stories called introspective insights.

These short tales are always connected to a more relevant story of yours. From the psychological perspective, this big story is called your life story or life plot. This major story includes the most relevant experiences you have been going through all through your life. This story has continually been written since you were a little child.

This life story has an ongoing plot, a leading theme and

countless related sub-stories. It also has a set of conflicts and plenteous characters (main and secondary ones) among other elements.

4.8. Your introspective insights as personal stories

When you use the introspective tool you always face up to a big challenge because all the pieces of information you try to deduce are not accessible, at least directly. All that data is buried in your subconscious mind.

As a consequence, when you introspect, you naturally try to deduce things that occur inside you in relation to your different life circumstances. In order to do so, you tend to naturally mix real elements with others, which seem truthful but are just plain inventions. The main goal of these introspective tales, called insights, is to make some minimum sense of what is going on in your life and your specific participation in it. Meaningfulness is the only objective of these introspective stories, not accuracy.

Some people believe that these stories are an absolute and literal reflection of the truth. This assertion is totally fallacious and daring. These stories are never absolutely respectful of the truth because most of the information in your subconscious mind is difficult to access in a proper manner, even with the use of introspective tools.

There is another important factor which impedes your access to the original meaning of your memories. Many of your subconscious memories were introduced to your mind a long time ago and they have been transformed over time once and again. As a consequence, these memories lost part of their original meaning.

Each time that you use introspection you are using guesswork. In that effect, introspection is intrinsically speculative and hypothetical. Each of your deductions is based on incomplete and provisional information. When you introspect, you unwittingly tend to make up the missing pieces of data related to your subconscious programs.

Your introspective insights are consistent and credible stories regarding your subconscious memories you make up; they are far from being veritable ones. Every time you have introspective insights you embellish and disfigure different aspects of these personal little stories and fabricate others. Some of these distortions are due to the use of your mental defensive mechanisms (repression, suppression, etc.), which were explained in this book in Chapter 3.

Each time you use introspection your mind generates insights acting as an excellent novelist which produces a rich and unique narrative. These tales are related to your peculiar perspective or reality and thus they become rationally self-justified. These stories include short descriptions, comments about your personal values and ethic assessments, among other elements. These introspective stories act like maps that tentatively guide you through the uncharted territory of your subconscious mind.

Some authors like Sogyal Rinpoche assert that you cannot even know anything about the essence of what is going on in your mind because your mind is always present in you. In other words, your mind is too near to you to be grasped in its wholeness. Some specialists suggest that other people can actually have better knowledge about you than yourself. Other people receive and interpret not only your words but also body language messages, which you cannot see. These non-verbal cues tend to communicate prized meaningful things, most of which you are not even aware.

4.9. You should really know who you are in essence
When you are using the introspection tool you can also ask yourself more transcendental questions. Dr. Len also suggests that you should ask a paramount question of yourself like *"Who am I?"* which is related to your own essence.

Many people feel that this type of question is actually frightening or overwhelming. Most people only grasp a very superficial part of their authentic inner core. Their deep true essence remains absolutely concealed most of the time.

From the Ho'oponopono perspective, you are just pure divine energy, an exact duplicate of the Divine. However, you might temporarily be deceived that you are less than Divinity, especially when you are driven by your subconscious memories.

When you truly know who you are, you understand you are not your thoughts, emotions, senses or background because all these are just subconscious memories. In essence, you are not your name, nationality, age, occupation, health condition, financial situation or any other of your traits. All these are just subconscious programs, which disguise the divine essence you truly are.

When you gradually strip yourself from your subconscious memories, by regularly doing Ho'oponopono, you can reconnect to the divine almighty source and realize that you are the Divine, in essence. You understand that you are naturally pure, unlimited and impregnable.

You can find below some hints of how you truly are, your divine nature. You will progressively discover this truth on your own, as you gradually remove your subconscious memories:

In essence, you truly are:

– *A memory-free being*
– *The exact image of the Creator*
– *Pure seamlessness and perfection*
– *Unbounded beautifulness*
– *Total freedom from the burden of the past*
– *Boundless freedom to do whatever you dream about*
– *The source of all good*
– *Limitless enjoyment of your present moment*
– *Liberation from all expectations*
– *Unconditional love toward all that exists*
– *Indwelling peacefulness and easiness*
– *Omniscient being with perfect wisdom*

- *Unwavering clarity and certainty*
- *Natural spontaneity and grace*
- *Unstoppable bliss*
- *Unfaltering well-being*
- *Loving interconnection with all which exists*
- *Continual abundance and prosperity*
- *Lively fearlessness and enthusiasm*
- *Inexhaustible fountain of resources*
- *Continual awakening and development*
- *Constant expansiveness and development*
- *Embodiment of your personal life mission*
- *An incredible state of limitlessness*
- *The divine light that illuminates everything*

5. Practical tips

– As previously seen, one of the principles in Ho'oponopono is *"you don't know anything"*; your knowledge of your environment is very limited. There is a very interesting exercise regarding this point. You should sit down in a comfortable place and write down a personal list of activities you performed to gather more knowledge about your environment. These activities can be simple (checking the price of a product on the Internet before buying it) or complex (attending a course researching a topic for coursework or for a thesis, etc.). Once you finished that list, you should ask yourself these questions: *"Were these activities enough to gather all necessary knowledge?"*, *"If so, why?"* and *"If not, how do I know?"* You should take note of the insights you obtain from these questions.

– In relation to the previous exercise, in case you were not pleased with the knowledge obtained from these tools you can ask yourself another question like: *"What other activities could have improved the quality of knowledge available?"* Then write down the answer and read it carefully. You will see the knowledge you obtained from different sources was never enough. You could always have improved the quality of the knowledge you gather every time. This process can go on forever; it never ends. There will always be additional sources of information you missed out. Using an analogy, knowledge is like a bottomless pit; you will never reach the ground. After doing this exercise you repeat the four Ho'oponopono sentences.

– There is another interesting but well-known exercise. Imagine that every experience, person and thing you encounter has no previous meaning for you, as if it is the first time you see them. Approach each of your circumstances from a fresh viewpoint, which means not being tied to any past classifications in relation to these situations. Avoid using any adjectives or nouns to identify things, persons or situations. You should also take note of any insights you obtain during this exercise. After this, you can say the four Ho'oponopono phrases many times.

– You should also try to start things without having an end result in mind. Perform the activity; try to feel comfortable with the unknowable upcoming circumstances. You should perceive every new situation you face as a space of evolution and learning. You should face every situation from a fresh, exciting, explorative and mysterious perspective. Adopt a naïve, open-minded and tentative mindset and avoid analyzing or categorizing things with the mental screen of your memories. You must also avoid any expectations, assumptions or preconceived ideas. Some oriental philoso-phies call this state the *"beginner's mind."*

– In relation to the previous exercise, and in order to approach things in the purest way possible, you can imagine that you were a little infant who is gradually discovering the world stepwise, little by little. Your attitude must be extremely curious, non-judgmental, playful and adventurous. You should try to feel surprised by any experience you go through. You should hold no presumptions or previous guessing on your environment. Some psychologists like Dainow suggest that you could also imagine that you perceive the world as if you are an extraterrestrial being. After doing this exercise, take note of insights and then say the four Ho'oponopono sentences many times.

– D'Souza and Renner suggest another exercise you can do every day. You can ask questions such as: *"What is my relationship with knowledge?"*, *"How does my knowing hamper my experiences?"*, *"How do I feel with knowledge?"* and *"How do I feel before the unknowable?"*, *"How do I feel when I say 'I do not know...'?"* After this, you can say the four Ho'oponopono sentences many times.

– You can also do another exercise which will help you gain more awareness of your natural cluelessness. Your knowledge on any topic is always limited even when you are somehow knowledgeable. You can explore any topic you might think that you know a bit about. After selecting the topic and thinking about it, ask yourself: *"What is going on in me that I truly believe that I know something about this topic?"*; wait for any insights and write them down. After this, you should say the four Ho'oponopono sentences.

– There is an interesting exercise you can do on your own. Make an extensive list of things you regularly do in order to control your future circumstances to bring more certainty into your life; for example, designing plans or budgets, taking insurance and researching, among others. Read the list and ask yourself these questions: *"Are these activities enough to completely eliminate uncertainty about my future?"*, *"Will these activities guarantee complete control over my future circum-stances?"*, *"If so, why?"* and *"If not, what other activities can I perform to eliminate uncertainty to the unknown?"* Take note of your insights and say the four Ho'oponopono sentences many times.

– You probably noticed that none of the activities you perform on a frequent basis are enough to predict or guarantee the future. There will always be other activities you can perform to bring more certainty about your future circumstances. You can never control future circumstances with complete accuracy. After this exercise, ask yourself: *"What is going on in me in relation to this?"* Then write your insights and say the four Ho'oponopono sentences many times.

– There is another exercise you can do; you must analyze what happened in the past on occasions when you tried to control your future circumstances. For example, you can examine what occurred when you planned to go on a trip. You will see that any instrument (plan, budget, etc.) which you used to control your future situations was far from being completely accurate and effective. Any tool used could have never predicted all situations which later on unfolded in practice. The future is always an incommensurable mystery; you can never grasp it in advance in a precise manner.

– When you do the previous exercise, you will probably discover that every time you used tools to control your future circumstances there were many things that unfolded differently. In hindsight, you realize you could always have acted more effectively and performed more activities to have more certainty about those circumstances. Nonetheless, on those past occasions your perspective was limited because you did not really know how things would unfold; you did not have the knowledge you have now in hindsight. This is another example of how limited knowledge always is, even when using plans or strategies to reduce uncertainty about the future. After doing this exercise repeat the four Ho'oponopono sentences.

– You can also think about past situations when you did not try to control things, for example an occasion when you did not plan so much or when you just engaged with the flow of things. In those cases, you are likely to discover that a sense of inner knowing has taken you through those situations in the best way possible for them. After doing this exercise, take notes of any insights and repeat the four Ho'oponopono sentences.

– There is another interesting exercise. You must be oriented to the future; you should start doing something, for example writing a letter to someone, without any definite plan. Try to be engaged in the present moment, without any expectations or assumptions. Eliminate any ideas about the end results of this process. After this, you should evaluate how you felt during the process. Take note of insights and say the four Ho'oponopono sentences many times.

– If you tried the previous exercise you will notice that when you have no plans or expectations you tend to feel less constrained and more spontaneous. Moreover you are also likely to feel more alive and creative. You can apply this approach of not having any plans or expectations to more significant situations, for example going on a short trip on your own. This exercise is not meant to encourage you to take unnecessary risk; its actual purpose is to make you feel more comfortable with uncertainty, without trying to strictly rely on any strategy to control things. When you practice this exercise regularly you will realize that you have a natural capacity to deal with uncertainty.

– You perform a range of activities automatically every day (waking, breathing, brushing your teeth, etc.). The main purpose of this exercise is to do any of these automatic activities as mindfully as possible. For example, whenever you brush your teeth you must be fully aware of the temperature of the water, the texture of the toothbrush, the taste of the toothpaste, among other stimuli. You should be fully concentrated on the now while you perform the activity. When you are mindful, your activities become more alive and less automatic. You can perceive more of their details and enjoy them more. After doing this exercise, take note of your insights and repeat the four Ho'oponopono phrases.

– As previously explained your desires are based on your subconscious memories. There is an interesting exercise you can do. Sit down in a comfortable place with a piece of paper and a pen at hand. Choose an activity you like (for example, drawing) which you think you truly know why you like it. Then ask yourself this question: *"What is the actual reason I like this?"* Wait for any insights to come up in your mind; cast aside any preconceived explanation about the origin of your preferences. After this, you should say the four Ho'oponopono sentences many times.

– As explained in this chapter, there are two definite categories of desires: tangible (such as a house, money, a new car, etc.) and intangible ones (such as peacefulness, joy, love, etc.). However, all your tangible desires are related to intangible ones. You can do a very useful exercise; make a list of your tangible desires and ask yourself: *"Which is the intangible desire underpinning this tangible desire?"* Be open to any insights and then say the four Ho'oponopono phrases repeatedly.

– You must remember that you always have a very limited perception of reality. There is a very interesting exercise you can do; you must perform any activity twice, for example you must read a book twice. When you reread the book ask yourself: *"What are the main differences in my perception regarding this book?"* Then remain still and wait for insights. You will discover significant details not perceived the first time you performed that activity. The knowledge you had the first time is likely to be significantly smaller than the second time. This helps you realize you can always increase your knowledge over time, and this process never stops. After doing this exercise, repeat the four Ho'oponopono sentences.

– As explained all things around you are neutral; you always assign personal meanings to everything in your environment. The same thing can have different meanings for various people. For example, a wood for a furniture producer can be perceived as a supply of raw material. However, the same wood for an ecologist can be perceived as a natural landscape to preserve. Reflect on this and wait for insights.

– There is a good exercise you can do which will help you widen your perspective on things. Select a topic and then try to consider as many viewpoints on it as possible. Let's suppose that you analyze the topic: *"How to improve your financial situation."* In this example, you can ask yourself: *"How will a millionaire perceive this issue?"* Then you can also ask yourself: *"How will a beggar perceive this?"* You can also pose questions like *"How will a monk perceive this?"* Imagine many different viewpoints on the topic you selected. Take note of any insight and say the four Ho'oponopono sentences many times.

– As explained, expectations are just projections about future situations based on your subconscious memories. Here is a very simple exercise; write down a list of your main expectations in different areas of your life, for example: health, romance and other relationships, career, finances, etc. Then ask yourself: *"What is going on inside me in relation to these expectations?"* to elicit information from your subconscious related to the expectations. Write down your insights and ask: *"What is the meaning of all this?"* Then say the four Ho'oponopono sentences many times.

– As explained, cognitive distortions color everything that we perceive, analyze, interpret and feel; they are distinct for each person. There is a very interesting exercise you can do on your own; sit down in a comfortable and quiet place and read the list of cognitive distortions that appear in this chapter many times. Then take note of the cognitive distortions that you see in yourself; try to be honest with this. Read that list many times aloud. Then ask yourself: *"What is going on in me in relation to this?"* You will surely receive very useful insights into this. After this, you must say the four Ho'oponopono phrases many times.

– There is a second version of the previous exercise. You must write a second list about cognitive distortions related to a person that you know well. You can use as a reference any person you are connected with, for example a relative or a friend. Then you must ask yourself *"What is going on in me in relation to this?"* and wait for any insights. After this, say the four Ho'oponopono sentences as many times as possible.

– As explained, there are a few things you must really know: you are a pure being in essence whose divine core is temporarily obscured by subconscious programming. You must also know that you can delete these programs by doing Ho'oponopono. Another important thing is that when you use this cleaning tool you are assisted by the Divine. Moreover, as you clean these memories you gradually reconnect to your own divine nature and you are more likely to receive divine inspiration. You must dwell on these ideas and ask yourself: *"What do these ideas mean to me?"* or *"What is going on in me in relation to these ideas?"* Wait for any insights and repeat the four Ho'oponopono sentences.

– Introspection is a tool you use to access information related to your subconscious memories. For example, when you face any problem in your life, you can ask yourself: *"What is going on in me that I am experiencing this now?"* or any other introspective question. Avoid judging the ideas that emerge in your mind; take note of them as they come. Then say the four Ho'oponopono sentences many times.

– In some cases, when you ask yourself: *"What is going on in me that I am experiencing this now?"* the insight is not clear. So you can ask for further details with questions like: *"What is the meaning of this?"*, *"What is this related to?"*, *"What are the specific aspects of this?"* or *"What is else is going on in me in relation to this?"* You can also use the meta-model questions or Milton model questions, which are explained in Appendix E at the back of this book. In all cases, after receiving the answers, say the four Ho'oponopono sentences many times.

– By using the introspective tool the insights you receive are scripts you make up based on information from your subconscious mind, which are never completely accurate but meaningful. As a practical exercise, you can act as if these stories were cinema movies or novels. The titles you choose for these stories must briefly summarize their main aspects. Enumerate the main elements of each story (for example, main characters, theme, type of story, etc.). Once you do this, wait for more insights and take detailed notes of them. After this, say the four Ho'oponopono sentences many times.

– In relation to insights or stories that come from introspection you can also use a metaphor to name the story. A metaphor is a sentence which relates one idea to a second one in a figurative or symbolic manner, for example: *"My present is a boxing match."* The two ideas used in the metaphor must have a certain level of similitude. Many psychologists say that metaphors allow you to access your subconscious mind bypassing your rational mind. Metaphors naturally mobilize your innermost emotions and bring about new meaningful insights about your subconscious memories. Once you have the metaphor, ask yourself: *"What is the specific meaning of this metaphor?"* and then repeat the four Ho'oponopono sentences.

– As explained, introspection entails having access to your emotions and sensations, not only your thoughts. In order to discover your feelings in relation to a situation, you can ask: *"What am I feeling now?"* Then wait for insights; take note of them. If the answers you receive are indirect, for example: *"I am fed up of everything in my life"* you can explore the underlying feelings you are experiencing. In order to do so, ask an additional question like *"What specific emotions am I feeling now regarding this?"* In the case of sensations, you can ask yourself: *"What physical sensations do I have now?"* Then wait for new insights and say the four Ho'oponopono sentences many times.

– You should use introspection at different places, for example in the park, at home, at work, among others. You will notice that your answers are likely to be influenced by the specific environment you are in at that moment. Discover the differences in the quality of the answers (insights) you receive in different places and detect the places which provide you with more interesting answers. If you have a busy life, you should use introspection primarily in the place that you get more elaborated answers. Nonetheless, use this technique in any place, as frequently as possible. In all cases, after practicing introspection say the four Ho'oponopono sentences many times.

– You can also try to be introspective at different times; for example, as soon as you wake, during mid-morning, at midday, in the afternoon, in the evening and before going to bed. The quality of the answers differs from one moment to another. Pay attention to the time of the day that you have more elaborative answers. If you don't have much time to use the introspective technique, select the time of the day when you get richer answers. As mentioned before, introspect as frequently as possible. Some coaches recommend to time block some minutes every day, at least, for introspection. In all cases, after doing introspection, repeat the four Ho'oponopono sentences.

– There is another interesting exercise suggested by Fontana, which consists of drawing several geometrical figures. In that instance, you must draw a circle on a piece of paper and ask: *"What is going on in me regarding this?"* Take note of any mental association regarding that figure and repeat the four

Ho'oponopono sentences. According to this author, the circle represents unity, wholeness and completeness. From this perspective, you can also draw a cross, which symbolizes expansion and life. You can also draw a square which from this standpoint represents stability and power. Lastly, you can also draw a triangle which represents the Trinity, or fusion of the masculine and feminine energy. You can also draw different combinations with these four figures. In all cases write down the insights about these figures and repeat the four Ho'oponopono phrases.

– Lastly we saw that you are Divinity in essence. The last point of this chapter mentioned several characteristics of your divine core, such as unconditional love, continual seamlessness, continual glee, divine wisdom and peacefulness, among others. As you gradually remove your programs you become more in contact with these divine traits of yours. You should carefully read the list of your divine traits many times and then ask yourself: *"What is going on in me in relation to these features?"* Wait for any insights and say the four Ho'oponopono sentences many times.

Chapter 5

You are Responsible for Everything That Happens in Your Life

Self-responsibility is claiming our ability to live fully. It is a swift path to embodying our sovereignty. Self-responsibility is the practice of acknowledging our role as the caretaker of our emotional, mental, physical and spiritual well-being, knowing that we are the creators of our life, in every moment.
– Alaya DeNoyelles

1. You are the creator of all your circumstances

1.1. Main aspects of total responsibility

Anything that enters my awareness becomes my responsibility, anything that was my responsibility I will be present with...
– Jacob Liberman and Erik Liberman

By reviewing several dictionaries there are certain commonalities in the definitions of the word *responsible*. Some of the definitions highlight that when you are responsible, you admit that you are the cause or origin of something. Other definitions state that when you are responsible you are using your rationale properly. In that sense, taking responsibility entails analyzing things soundly in order to act accordingly. Some other meanings of the word *responsible* are being able to respond, and being accountable for your acts.

When you feel responsible you are compelled to act in an appropriate manner. Responsibility also implies the idea of maturity, autonomy and self-trust. You can fully rely on your internal resources, which can help you succeed in any circumstance.

Some synonyms of the word *responsible* are *accountable,* *amenable* or *answerable,* among others. These words present subtle differences in their application, which will not be considered in this text.

Max Weber highlighted that people must not only be responsible for their intentions but also fully comprehend the possible effects of their own actions on the environment. Your responsibility covers the overall performance of your actions, not only your original intentions. You must acknowledge the relationship between your actions and their consequences, avoiding passing your responsibility onto others.

From the Ho'oponopono perspective, you must take full responsibility, which means accepting your responsibility for every single situation around you, which includes everything in your awareness. The concept of one hundred percent responsibility is very empowering and revolutionary. This particular perspective represents a big difference in relation to the traditional approach of responsibility, which states that you are only responsible for your own actions and nothing else.

When you take full responsibility you recognize that you are the only source of all your problems, and also accept your participation in the problems experienced by people around you. Everything that you perceive with your senses or which shows up in your life (and this includes your own problems and other people's problems) is just a natural result of your creation and you are responsible for every bit of it.

You cannot easily get unhooked from your responsibility. All situations you go through are experienced in your mind, even the ones affecting you in an indirect manner.

For this reason, if you want to change what you observe in your environment, the only way to do so is you to transform your inner world, which implies removing the past programs manifesting these very situations. Some masters say that there is no such thing as *"out there"*; everything outside is just a reflection of what is inside you. This implies a high level of awareness.

You take total responsibility for everything that appears in our lives, either unpleasant or delightful. Your subconscious memories are acting like a cinema projector which plays movies onto you and your environment.

According to the metaphysical principle of Mentalism, all that you see in your life is a manifestation of your thoughts. The Law of Correspondence also states that everything which happens outside always corresponds to what is going on inside. Each circumstance in your life (outside) is a literal manifestation of your subconscious programming (inside). In other words, Wilde states: *"There are no accidents or victims. Each one is responsible for his or her own evolution. Each pulls to him or herself the circumstances experienced in life."*

You should always take ownership of your life's negative situations, because you are responsible for them. Most people try to avoid difficulties, deny or fight them, which are all ways of resistance. You are the author of all stories directly or indirectly related to your life. These tales are only kept in your mind but have effectively materialized in your environment, concrete situations and circumstances that are in your awareness.

You are an intrinsic and fundamental part of everything that is going on in your life. In relation to this, Dr. Len says that you must realize that every time there is a problem, you are always there.

There is another important point to analyze. Some scientific studies demonstrate that a person has between 50,000 to 60,000 thoughts each day. Nevertheless, most of these thoughts are not new; they are just a repetition of past thoughts. They are just old memories playing out on your subconscious level.

As was explained before, these thoughts are the source of everything in your life. Bristol says that:

Thought is the original source of all wealth, all success, all material gain, all great discoveries and inventions, and of all achievement... Your thoughts – those that predominate – determine your character, your career, indeed, your everyday life.

So the only way to improve your life situations is by changing yourself, which means removing these subconscious memories. From this inside-out perspective, you must regularly practice Ho'oponopono.

1.2. Other aspects of total responsibility
When you are totally responsible you can allow change to happen in your life. If you don't take complete responsibility you actually disbelieve that you are the creator of whatever happens in your life and you tend to be more stuck to your current circumstances.

When you take full responsibility you don't forfeit your power through guilt, victimhood or blame. Instead you open your life to other possibilities, more thriving ones; you really own your life.

Total responsibility might be a great challenge for you. You might be accustomed to blaming others or criticizing them for whatever is affecting you in your life. When you have been avoiding your responsibility for a long time, you tend to be more attached to the status quo, which seems familiar and safe albeit counterproductive.

On your conscious level is where you really have a choice. When you are fully aware not only do you accept your responsibility for having accumulated countless programs in your subconscious mind but you also make the decision of getting rid of them, through the regular application of Ho'oponopono. You are committed to solving your problematic situations by using this cleaning technique.

When you are totally responsible for your life circumstances you avoid guilt, resentment, hatred or blame. These emotional states only make you extremely vulnerable and disempowered. When you recognize your total responsibility, your position is always one of strength; you go from being reactive towards a proactive attitude. You strip yourself from the veils of apparent external causes, by knowing that everything has its origin in you.

As was explained, every time you meet or interact with a person you have shared memories with this individual. The same principle applies to other people you are aware of, even when their issues don't affect you. As a consequence when you use Ho'oponopono you can eradicate these shared subconscious programs from your mind and also from theirs. So taking full responsibility also implies being responsible for the difficulties affecting other people; their problems are actually your problems. All problems, yours or others', are perceived and experienced in your own mind, in your awareness.

When you judge your current negative circumstances you are not accepting full responsibility regarding them; you keep your life situation stuck in the same place. Accepting your responsibility always represents a non-judgmental perspective; you accept your participation on all circumstances around you, which is the only way to transform your life for good.

Whenever you use impersonal statements such as: *"Things happen"* you are not taking full responsibility. If you use sentences like: *"She is the cause of all my problems"*; *"This person drives me crazy"* or other similar ones you are not accepting your responsibility either. With these sentences, very common in practice, you implicitly want to be exonerated from your responsibility regarding events in your life.

Rosenberg says that when you use vague or impersonal statements (for example, *"It's a terrible situation"*) you are not addressing your responsibility. From this perspective, you also elude your responsibility when your actions are exclusively driven by blind acceptance of social or legal rules. This author says that you also avoid your responsibility when you act based on irrational respect of authority figures or when you abide by group consensus without even questioning their ideas.

If you find that accepting your total responsibility is very difficult, you can ask yourself some questions like: *"What is the hardest part of accepting total responsibility?"* or *"What are the benefits and opportunities of accepting total responsibility?"* After this, you should say repeatedly: *"I am sorry for not accepting my total responsibility. Please forgive me for not taking full responsibility on all things going on in my life. I love you. Thank you."* In an assertive manner, you can also say: *"I am responsible for everything that is going on in my life."* You have to say these sentences as many times as possible.

2. Signs of being totally responsible

You must take full responsibility. Otherwise, you have no chance of ever getting out of the mess. If you attribute the cause to something other than you, not being true, you can never get out of the mess... Nothing happens to us that isn't caused by us... Everything that bothers you is not outside you. The bother is within you.
– Lester Levenson

There are different signals indicating that you are on the right course, which means being fully responsible. You are taking full responsibility when:

– You are being honest with yourself. You don't lie to yourself any longer.
– You take charge of your life. You accept your accountability for everything around you.
– You don't run away or escape your current circumstances. Instead, you recognize your life situation as it actually is.
– You don't attack yourself or others, in the form of guilt, blame or

resentment. You don't get immobilized before your life circum-stances either. You always tend to take action.

– You realize that all outer circumstances are a mirror of your inner world; you are the origin of all your experiences.

– You understand that you reap the fruits (your life circumstances) according to the seeds you sowed (your subconscious memories). You realize these memories are not alien intruders any longer; they are useless programs to be removed.

– You recognize that you have been deceived by your subconscious memories for a long time. These programs took control of your thoughts, emotions and actions in a tyrannical manner.

– You are not in a state of conformity to your subconscious memories any longer. You have now decided to challenge them, by removing them from your mind.

– You focus on yourself; you are interested in yourself. You recognize that changing yourself is the only way to transform others. You know that in every single moment exists the opportunity for your overall transformation.

– You are not in denial any longer. You don't dismiss your partici-pation in the creation of all your life circumstances. You humbly accept that you, more specifically your subconscious memories, create every single situation around you.

– You are being proactive and self-reliant. You understand that all motivation to transform your life is within yourself. You realize that you are stronger than you thought because you can actually delete your subconscious programming.

– You realize that your life is a journey on which you get the most valuable lessons. You understand that your subconscious memories are your best teachers; you benefit from the prized lessons.

– You cast faraway any state of enmity toward yourself; you can embrace yourself with unconditional love. You also befriend your subconscious memories to remove them all.

– You understand that the only way to be truly free is by removing your subconscious programs. You know that when you empty your

mind from these memories, you are more prone to receive divine inspiration.

– You are actually being assertive instead of behaving like a victim. You don't try to blame yourself, others or even God for your current life conditions. You don't project your own responsibility onto others.

– You set a new goal in your life, which is freeing yourself completely from the burden of your past programming. You want to become a memory-free being. You understand that your current negative circumstances are actually a call for cleaning your subconscious programs.

– You try to restore the natural state of peacefulness in your life. You realize that by deleting your subconscious programs you eliminate the emotional and mental turmoil caused by them.

– You are not doubtful or fearful anymore. You understand that any state of hesitation or dread does not allow you to connect to the Divine source.

– You are willing to go from a state of being driven by past memories to a state in which you are being guided by Divinity.

3. Main principles of total responsibility

3.1. You understand how things are

We are sending out thoughts of greater or lesser intensity all the time, and we are reaping the results of such thoughts. Not only do our thoughts influence ourselves and others, but they have a drawing power – they attract to us the thoughts of others, things, circumstances, people, "luck", in accord with the character of the thoughts uppermost in our minds.
– William Walker Atkinson

Joe Vitale says that taking full responsibility can be considered as an awareness tool. You truly understand that your subconscious memories affect your life in all dimensions. When you have this prized knowledge, your personal transformation seems more workable. Your clear understanding on this is like a potent beam of light dispelling darkness.

Once you are truly aware of the effects of your subconscious programs on your life, you are ready for cleaning them. You can also clear any state of confusion from your mind. No external factor can actually affect you because you are the only origin of all your life circumstances. There are no more mysterious factors affecting your life.

When you are totally responsible, that implies you also are self-understanding; you comprehend yourself in more appropriate way. Until you accept your full responsibility you will continue to be clueless. Total responsibility is also the key to your liberation from your limiting subconscious programs.

3.2. You are responsible for everything around you

Real self-responsibility means that you are 100 percent responsible for the quality of your life. You're in charge of your thoughts and emotions and the outcomes that you create.
– Sandra Anne Taylor

You must assume complete responsibility for every single situation around you; this means that you must not see yourself as partially responsible. You have created every single circumstance which is in your awareness, with no exception.

As was explained before, you are not only responsible for the situations affecting you, but also for everything else going on in your environment. For example, if you see people, known or unknown, who are affected by problems you are also responsible for their experiences at that moment. So when you practice Ho'oponopono to eliminate your subconscious memories, not only will you improve your own situations but also those people's experiences with whom you have shared memories.

When you see people around with problems, you don't have to mend their difficulties directly but should fix yourself by removing your memories. It is important to remember that all circumstances which affect you or other people are just projections of your inner world. Atkinson says that: *"each gets what he calls for over the wireless telegraphy of the Mind... a man really makes his own surroundings, although he blames others for it."*

You are always present in all your life situations. For this reason, all significant changes in your life begin within you; it cannot be otherwise. Once your subconscious memories are deleted, your entire environment is affected positively, including people around you.

Lastly, there is a very easy way to assert that you have accepted your responsibility. The frequent use of sentences such as *"This situation is part of me"*, *"I have created this situation"*, *"This has to do with me"* indicates that you have taken full responsibility.

3.3. You don't ignore problems affecting you

When you take full responsibility you do not pretend that there are no difficulties in your life or act apathetically before them. Taking responsibility is always a sign of maturity; it is unconditional acceptance that every single thing which exists in your life is originated by your subconscious memories; you accept your participation in all circumstances in your life.

This attitude helps you transmute any problematic situations in your life into positive ones. You cannot be fully responsible if you are in denial, which means ignoring the direct connection between your subconscious programs and your troublesome situations.

For most people, problems represent a very significant part of their lives. They struggle to solve their troublesome issues using their conscious mind. Nevertheless, when people use this strategy it is condemned to failure. In numerous cases, people end up being even more attached to their own problems.

A different approach should be used when you tackle any problem in your life. You always experience your problems within you, in your mind. So the most effective way to solve your problems is by changing your mind, more specifically your subconscious memories. As a consequence, when you have an attitude of total responsibility you never have to delay or second-guess getting rid of your subconscious memories.

3.4. You don't react

All people tend to perform certain activities in a reactive manner, without any previous analysis. In those cases, you are not using your rationale; you are responding automatically, completely taken over by the subconscious memories. When you react, you are not truly present; instead you are prompted by your past.

If we analyze the etymology (origin) of the word "responsible", this term can be traced back to the Latin word *responsus*, which literally means *respond*. To put it simply, the word *"responsibility"* means *"ability to respond."*

However, you can never respond effectively when you are driven by your subconscious programs. There is no prior analysis of the situation at hand, and your reactions resemble knee-jerk responses. For this reason, every time you react you are not being responsible.

Every time you react you behave as if you were the effect and not the cause of your life circumstances. By reacting, you are overly dependent on what *happens* in your environment instead of being responsible and acknowledging that you are the cause of everything around you.

When you are reactive, you are not free, you are totally ensnared by your subconscious programs. It is your subconscious memories which make you react to the outside circumstances without even you noticing this. The external facts take control over you; they trigger your subconscious memories, to make you act in an automatic manner.

When you react you also tend to experience intense dissatis-faction because you feel that things should be different; that you deserve a better reality. On those occasions, you truly believe that your external circumstances happen to you; you are convinced that life is against you. So your reactions become the easiest way to respond to situations.

Each time you react you might also feel a little sense of grati-fication because you temporarily satisfy these intense impulses driven by your subconscious memories. Your reactions act like powerful habits difficult to be removed; they resemble lingering addictions.

Whenever you react you actually give your power away to your external environment. You might feel that your environment should be treating you more fairly; it might look as if the world owes you something. In these situations, you are trapped in a state of powerlessness, with no possibility to make things right. Your awareness is temporarily clouded.

Taking responsibility is the capability to respond in an effective manner, which always implies a certain degree of freedom. When you react you are enslaved to automatic responses prompted by your subconscious memories.

When you take responsibility you become proactive, you can choose and you can harness your inner power. Conversely whenever you react you actually forsake your essential freedom; you can only *perceive* all circumstances from the narrow perspective of your subconscious programs, which are limiting by nature. You also tend to act in a defensive manner.

Whenever you react you are unlikely be tolerant and compas-sionate with yourself or others. Your reactions never allow you to connect to your core essence, which is pure love. Your reactions hamper your access to your unbounded resources.

Berg suggests that in order to not react, you can restrict your impulses; you must stop your urge to act reactively to be more aware of what is going on in your life. You can also ask yourself: *"What is going on in me in relation to this?"* Then you must wait for any insight and also say the four Ho'oponopono sentences.

You can also be less reactive by being fully present in the now. In a detached manner you must try to observe your impulses trying to take you over and let them pass by, which means not reacting.

3.5. You don't blame anyone, not even yourself

When we explain to ourselves and others why things have gone well or badly, we prefer explanations that cast the best possible light. Thus we are quick to assume that our successes are due to our sterling qualities, while responsibility for failures can often be conveniently laid at the door of bad luck or damn fool others.
– Cordelia Fine

It was previously commented that when you take responsibility you are capable of responding effectively. However, when you do not accept your full responsibility you tend to place that responsibility on your environment. You tend to place blame on people (family, friends, employers, employees, competitors or government), things or situations (financial crises, lack of luck, weather conditions, traffic congestions, car accidents), or even yourself. Taking full responsibility means accepting that you are the only person responsible to whatever is going on in your life, with no blame or guilt.

When you embrace your responsibility fully, you don't place any resistance on your current circumstances. Taking full responsibility implies not having a victim attitude, which implies feeling that you are not in control.

When you are a victim, everything and everyone seem to be against you; things are not fair for you. However, by being a victim you might enjoy that people feel sorry for you. You might feel powerless and defeated, looking for anything or anyone around you to be blamed for your misfortune. You might look for any excuse to justify the negative situations affecting you. You feel swayed by life circumstances which are beyond your control.

From the psychological viewpoint, the victim mindset works as a self-protective mental defense; it is supposed to protect your ego every time you face situations of failure. In relation to this Fine says that: *"Failure is perhaps the greatest enemy of the ego."*

Ferrini states that:

guilt and responsibility are mutually exclusive. Guilt holds on the wound and so it prevents it from healing. Responsibility is the first step in the healing process.

Guilt is one of the main hindrances in the way of your personal transformation. From the Ho'oponopono perspective, when you feel guilty this is a signal that you have some memories you have to remove.

You do not need to feel guilty about anything, not even your thoughts, emotions or actions; you must avoid any judgment to yourself or others. In relation to this, Robert Anthony states that: *"there are not victims only volunteers."*

It is not worth feeling guilty any longer if you realize that your subconscious memories create every circumstance in your life. When you grasp this there is no need to blame anyone, not even you; you avoid finding scapegoats for your maladies. When you take full responsibility you naturally become more compassionate and less judgmental.

Canfield says:

Lots of people overcame… limiting factors, so it can be the limiting factors that limit you. It is not the external circumstances that stop you – it's you! We stop ourselves. We engage in self-limiting thoughts and engage in self-defeating behaviors.

These constraining thoughts and comportments are just the results of your subconscious memories.

Judgment or condemnation to others or yourself not only fails to contribute to solve your problems, but also attracts more troublesome situations into your life. These negative emotional states render you powerless, hopeless, and defenseless. You cannot access your innermost resources to change your circumstances.

When you act like a victim you tend to feel the center of the attention because of negative situations affecting you. When you have an attitude of self-victimization you might use statements like *"It's not my fault"*, *"The world is against me"* or *"I have bad luck"*, among others.

On these occasions, feeling guilty appears to be the valuable *reward* you obtain for being stuck. You might even indulge in resentment or any other negative emotional state. This type of attitude is detrimental to your personal evolution and keeps you stuck in the same place.

When you truly accept one hundred percent responsibility, you actually regain control over your life; you can proceed to delete your subconscious memories. You can move away from any immobilizing circumstances, because you are open to transformation.

3.6. You realize you can choose

I am tired of people that drain society by manipulating in an unhealthy way, like... the criminal, the scam artist, and many other unsavory types. It all begins and completes within me; not by trying to force change on the outside. I have to change inside, so they can follow suit and change outside of me.
– Robert Ray

Viktor Frankl is a famous therapist and author who personally went through a horrific predicament for several years. During the

Second World War he was imprisoned in a concentration camp. From this terrible experience he learned that you are free to choose your attitude before all circumstances in your life, even the toughest ones.

Even in the most hurting and grieving situations, there is a chance to find a positive meaning of things. You are always free to choose how you stand before your life circumstances. In that effect you can either:

- *Do nothing, ignore reality, blame yourself or others and, thus, continue to be trapped by these subconscious programs; or*
- *Accept your responsibility for everything around you and proceed to delete your past memories.*

When you take responsibility, you recognize what is going on in your life and fully understand why this happens. As was explained you realize that all your life circumstances are created by your subconscious memories so you make the decision to remove them with Ho'oponopono.

Most people have serious problems with making the decision of taking full responsibility; they tend to feel uncomfortable with that idea. From mankind's perspective, many maladies are just consequences of people not having taken full responsibility. Some examples are: depletion of certain species, erosion of cultivable field, enlargement of the gap in the ozone layer and an increase in normal and nuclear waste, among others.

When you choose to take responsibility you implicitly recognize that you are naturally entitled to change your life; you are endowed with an unlimited power to do that. You also realize that you have been temporarily cut off from that power because you have entertained limiting programs in your subconscious mind. You also understand that you can be free from past programs by doing Ho'oponopono.

3.7. You understand that the outer world mirrors you

No man has a chance to enjoy permanent success until he begins to look in the mirror for the real cause of all his mistakes.
– Napoleon Hill

Some sages say that all your life circumstances are mere reflections of you; these situations are your outer mirror. You don't even have to thoroughly understand how your subconscious memories create these situations to take full responsibility. The only thing you have to know is that they manifest your life experiences.

Bailes says that: *"Our Dominant Inner Pattern of Thought becomes our Outer Dominant Pattern of Experience"* and *"Our outer world is our inner world objectified."* This means that all things that occur in your life, good ones and bad ones, are originated by your internal world. Your circumstances are never the result of other people, luck or any other external factors. You are the only one responsible for all that you see in your life.

Jampolsky and Cirincione say: *"our thoughts, and not the outside world, cause what we see and experience, and the world that we experience is the effect of our own thoughts."* When you take full responsibility you realize that your subconscious programs actually mold your life experiences.

Once you accept that you are responsible for whatever is going on in your life, you are positioned in a place of non-resistance. With this attitude, you can effectively delete your subconscious programming and, in turn, allow things to change effortlessly.

3.8. You feel empowered and proactive

People on the success curve live a life of responsibility. They take full responsibility for who they are, where they are, and everything that happens to them.
– Jeff Olson

Many sages say that you can only be free when you accept your full responsibility. When you realize that you are totally responsible, you take the first step to release the burden of the past.

It is important to understand that, even when you do not take full responsibility, you are still totally responsible for generating your life circumstances. In other words, your subconscious memories are constantly creating your life situations, regardless of whether you accept your responsibility for this or not.

Your personal transformation always implies that you address all circumstances affecting you, even the most troublesome ones, in an effective manner. And you do so by acknowledging that all your situations are created by your subconscious memories.

Jeffers says that when you are totally responsible you move from a position of pain and powerlessness toward a position of expansion and powerfulness. You can be either responsible for your life circumstances or a victim of them; you cannot be both at the same time.

Taking full responsibility is realizing that the point of power is within you. When you are fully responsible you don't ask anything or anyone to change; your personal transformation always begins within you. This is a very powerful perspective, which puts you in the driver's seat of your life.

When you accept your full responsibility for all your life circumstances, you don't succumb to any problems affecting you, but instead you rise above them. Every time you take responsibility, you daringly face any dire situations which come to your life, instead of eschewing them. As was explained, you know that by removing your subconscious memories all your dismal situations get solved effortlessly.

There will be times when you actually feel disempowered especially when you are affected by many challenging life circumstances. In those cases, it might even seem impossible to take full responsibility; you might be prone to blame, quit or resist the negative situations. If you are in this situation, you must bear in mind that you always have the power to change; remember that your problems originate from your subconscious programs.

If you feel discouraged to feel totally responsible, you must act as if you were totally responsible. Imagine how you would feel, think and act if you took total responsibility and proceeded accordingly.

As seen before, when you are responsible you are willing to deliver some responses in relation to facts or circumstances in your life. From this perspective, the term means not remaining passive.

So when you are totally responsible, you move yourself from a passive position (also called victim mentality) to a proactive stance. When you are proactive, you can act more effectively; for example, you can delete your subconscious memories by doing Ho'oponopono.

3.9. You realize that negative situations help you evolve

The purpose of life is to be restored back to Love, moment to moment. To fulfil this purpose, the individual must acknowledge that he is 100 percent responsible for creating his life the way it is. He must come to see that it is his thoughts that create his life the way it is moment to moment. The problems are not people, places, and situations but rather the thoughts of them. He must come to appreciate that there is no such thing as "out there."
– Dr. Ihaleakala Hew Len

When you assume total responsibility you admit that you have had enough of your subconscious programs manifesting negative conditions in your life. As a consequence of this, you are willing to transform your life circumstances by deleting these very memories by doing Ho'oponopono.

An attitude of total responsibility is always life-changing. Some ancient schools of thought pinpoint the importance of perceiving all obstacles you encounter in your life as opportunities to evolve. This stance is in total accordance with the perspective of Ho'oponopono because every negative circumstance you face gives you the chance to delete your subconscious memories and, in turn, reconnect to Divinity.

In other words, all negative situations that affect you conceal a valuable opportunity for you to become more enlightened. You are constantly learning valuable life lessons, even during your bad circumstances. Every situation has a relevant meaning, sometimes covert or hidden, for your personal evolution.

From a wider perspective, you have to understand all things in your life occur the way they should do. All your life circumstances make sense, even when you don't realize this. Your troublesome circumstances generally act like a springboard which elevates you to a higher position than before in your life path.

In conclusion, every time you face up to a negative circumstance there is a prized opportunity to do Ho'oponopono; that situation is a reminder that there are programs which must be removed. Lester Levenson states that: *"adversity is a prod to growth."*

4. The dilemma of full responsibility

Before you make the decision to take full responsibility, you acknowledge two opposite alternatives. You always have this choice; you can choose between these alternative courses of action:

– *You can either be conscious by wittingly deleting your past programs or be totally unconscious and trapped by your memories.*
– *You can either accept your responsibility for everything going on in your life (which implies a powerful attitude), or instead victimize*

yourself or others for your life circumstances (which entails a powerless attitude).

– You can either look for freedom (by removing your subconscious memories) or be comfortable with your state of bondage (which implies being enslaved to your subconscious programs).

– You can either choose to strengthen your connection to Divinity (as you clean your past programs) or be temporarily separated from the Divine (when you are taken over by your subconscious tapes).

– You can either opt for wholeness (when you are fully imbibed by the Divine force) or brokenness (when you are hopelessly trapped in your subconscious programming).

– You can either choose a proactive attitude (by taking action and removing your subconscious programming) or a state of victimization (by being stuck in your subconscious programs and blaming yourself and others).

– You can either let yourself be guided by the Divine (which is the source of limitless wisdom) or believe that you know everything (based on the limited information contained in your subconscious programs).

– You can either live in faith and love (which means connected to Divinity) or dwell in fear and pain (which means based on your subconscious programming).

– You can either concentrate on your natural equilibrium (which is brought about by cleaning your subconscious programs) or focus on imbalance (for example, diseases and any other maladies created by your subconscious memories).

– You can either be grateful and loving (when you eradicate your subconscious programming and are purposely engaged with the Divine) or be reproaching and judgmental (when you are enmeshed in your subconscious memories).

– You can either fill your heart with forgiveness and love or inundate it with hatred and condemnation.

– You can either tread the trail of your personal transformation and evolution (which entails cleaning your subconscious memories) or

trudge the path of stagnancy and resistance (in which you are controlled by your subconscious programming).

5. You do not have free will

5.1. General aspects

In this point we will analyze the topic of free will. In relation to the concept of *free will*, it is important to ask yourself these questions: *"Do I actually know if I am acting freely?"*, *"If so, how do I know this specifically?"*, *"Am I acting according to free will or being driven by my subconscious memories?"*, *"Do I know the real reasons for my actions?"* and *"Is my free will an illusion or it is real?"* By asking these questions you can obtain very meaningful insights into the topic of free will.

You can also ask yourself these questions: *"Can I always be responsible for everything around me?"*, *"Does the concept of freedom of action have anything to do with the principle of full responsibility?"* and *"Can I ignore the reasons of my own actions and still take full responsibility?"* When you regularly ask yourself these questions you can obtain very useful insights into this topic.

As was seen before, from the Ho'oponopono perspective, you are constantly being driven by umpteen subconscious memories. As a consequence, you actually have no free will at all. All your actions, even the ones you believe you freely choose and perform, are dictated by your programming.

From this standpoint, you still have one relevant choice to make; you can choose either to be stuck to your subconscious programs or to be completely free from them. If you make the decision to be really free from your subconscious memories, you must do Ho'oponopono on a frequent basis.

Over the previous chapters it was also explained that, like all people, you are generally clueless; you are always totally blind to the reasons that motivate your actions. This happens because you cannot have direct access to your subconscious memories.

Only when you use introspective tools can you actually obtain ephemeral insights on the innermost motives which prompt you to act in certain ways.

5.2. Some scientific evidence of your ignorance

Many scientific studies confirmed that people are not capable of discovering with extreme accuracy the relationship between their actions, thoughts and feelings and their real causes. As it was clearly expounded in this book, people naturally use conjectures about the reasons for their own actions, without knowing their actual causes.

You have millions of bits of information running inside your subconscious mind but you can consciously process only a few bits of data at each time. As a consequence, your motivations, goals and emotions are always driven by information which is below the level of your awareness. For different reasons previously exposed in this book, the memories that you try to recollect are far from accurate.

Many scientific studies confirm that you are subconsciously told what to do on any occasion, before you are even aware of this. These studies suggest all your decisions are originally prompted by the subconscious part of your mind. This means that all your intentions are subconscious; only the specific performance of the actions is actually conscious.

In that effect Norretranders says that: *"the desire to carry out an action becomes a conscious sensation long after the brain started initiating it. But consciousness does occur before the action is performed."* The Ho'oponopono perspective is in total accordance with this; all your actions are initiated by the memories embedded in your subconscious mind.

Some scientists will state that, once you received the message from your subconscious, you consciously opt to act on it or not, and this is called free will. This option is made in a very short period of time (milliseconds) by your conscious mind.

According to Assagioli your will means the ability of regulating the way that biological and psychological (subconscious) energies are expressed. The control of these urges does not imply the renunciation of your desires, but their expression in a more appropriate way (for example, in a more graceful, aesthetic, or enjoyable manner).

So according to these discoveries, your consciousness only decides if you should proceed or abort the actions initiated unconsciously. This is the real power of your free will. Each of your actions is always generated subconsciously, with no exception.

You might have believed that you always make your decisions on a conscious level right from the start. Nonetheless, vast scientific evidence contradicts this apparent truth. You tend to become more aware of your subconscious mind when it is at loggerheads with your conscious mind. This happens, for example, when you don't consciously want to perform an action which was prompted on a subconscious level.

Some authors such as Schwartz and Begley coined the term *"free won't"* which seems to be more useful than *"free will."* They say that: *"free won't refers to the mind veto power over brain-generated urges."* Your conscious mind acts like a censoring screen or gatekeeper in relation to all your actions, which are always originated by your subconscious mind.

There is another relevant point to highlight. When you perform any activity, it looks as if you were experiencing the action just in real time. Nonetheless, Libet clearly says that:

> *the brain needs a relatively long period of appropriate activations, up to half a second, to elicit awareness of the event... our awareness of our sensory world is substantially delayed for its actual occurrence. What we become aware of has already happened about 0.5 seconds earlier.*

Likewise, Norretranders states that: *"consciousness lags behind what we call reality"* and also states that: *"it takes a little time before we experience the outside world, but we just relocate the experience backward in time, so we experience that we experience the world at the right moment."* In other words, any action you experience to be performed just in time was actually carried out a very short time ago.

5.3. Your natural state of freedom and Ho'oponopono

Ho'oponopono states that you are never free, because you are always trapped by your subconscious memories. However these programs can never eliminate your natural state of liberty. You can always take an important step to achieve your natural state of freedom when you truly make the decision to using Ho'oponopono regularly. This cleaning technique is like the payment of a ransom which liberates you from your kidnappers, your past programs.

As you remove your subconscious programs, you get nearer the zero point. As you get nearer to this state you tend to feel differently as follows:

- *You feel freer in your actions, thoughts, emotions and perceptions*
- *You feel clearer about everything in life*
- *You feel more spontaneous regarding your behavior*
- *You feel more sympathetic and understanding*
- *You feel more present in the current moment*
- *You feel more integrated and connected to everything that exists*
- *You feel more grateful, loving and forgiving*
- *You feel wiser and more authentic*
- *You feel more graceful and flowing*
- *You feel more adventurous, explorative and daring*
- *You feel more creative and innovative*
- *You feel less automatic and constrained*

As a consequence, all your activities tend to become more meaningful and expansive. You truly feel, in the depth of your heart, that each of your actions makes complete sense. You progressively relinquish your lingering state of cluelessness.

6. Practical tips

– In order to take full responsibility you must be aware of not casting blame on others. As an exercise, take note of the times you use sentences like: *"It is your fault"* or *"You ruin every-thing."* You might also use vague or indefinite ways of casting blame, for example, when you say: *"Things happen"*, *"It is life"* or *"If only this happens."* Some excuses to avoid responsibility might be very subtle, for example when you say: *"I wish I could do this but..."* Read the list including the sentences you use, and repeat the four Ho'oponopono sentences.

– When people experience intense emotions they tend to believe that these emotional states are produced by external factors, which is a way to avoid their responsibility. The real fact is that your emotions are just reactions to external factors, but not produced by them. For example when you use sentences like *"You make me feel bad because of your character"* you are making another person responsible for what you feel at the moment. This is a subtle way to avoid your responsi-bility for what you are feeling at the moment. Take note of the times you use this type of sentence. Read the list including the sentences you use and repeat the four Ho'oponopono sentences.

– As a practical exercise, you can use the so-called Responsibility Language, which is very useful when you want to express your own emotions. You must word your sentences in a way that you take full responsibility for what is going on in you. Taking into account the previous example (*"You make me feel bad because of your character"*) this sentence can be reworded this way: *"I make myself feel bad about your character."* All your sentences should start with the word *"I..."* in order to own your thoughts and feelings in relation to specific situations, and to avoid blaming others.

– Dainow says that you don't assume responsibility when you use dissociations. Some examples of dissociations are *"My body"*, *"My mind"*, *"My emotions"*, *"My thoughts"*, *"My luck"* and *"My life."* When you say: *"My thoughts always make me feel confused"* you do not acknowledge your responsibility; you cast it aside to a *"stranger"*, which is *"your thoughts."* A good way to reformulate this sentence is *"I think and I feel confused."* As a practical exercise, try to reword the sentences you use in your daily interactions accordingly.

– You can also use sentences like: *"I take full responsibility for everything around me."* You can also say: *"I am responsible for everything that is going on in my life."* You should try to say these phrases in an assertive manner; these are powerful reminders of your full responsibility. These phrases are useful especially when you are affected by difficult situations, in which you naturally tend to avoid responsibility. If you have difficulty taking full responsibility you must also imagine how it might be if you were totally responsible; you might even ask yourself: *"How would I act if I were totally responsible?"* Wait for insights and repeat the four Ho'oponopono sentences.

– If you find that accepting your total responsibility is challenging you can ask yourself another question like: *"What is the most difficult part of accepting my total responsibility?"* You must wait for insights and then say this: *"I am sorry for not accepting my total responsibility. Please forgive me for not taking full responsibility for all things going on in my life. I love you. Thank you."* As you use these sentences regularly you will become more prone to take responsibility.

– You can also make a list of things that you believe are

occurring to you, for example *external factors* affecting your life. You must also include on your list the different ways you tend to react to these factors, for example resenting, blaming, judging or any other emotional state. Then you must ask yourself: *"What is going on in me that I am experiencing this?"* Wait for insights and say the four Ho'oponopono sentences many times. When you do this exercise on a frequent basis you will feel less swayed by external circumstances.

– In this chapter it was previously explained that, from Ho'oponopono's perspective, you are responsible for every-thing around you, not only the things affecting you directly. There is a good exercise you can do on your own; look at external events affecting you indirectly: wars, corruption, crime and others. Then you have to explore your responsi-bility regarding these issues by asking yourself: *"What is going in me in relation to these events?"* Wait for insights and take note of them; then say the four Ho'oponopono sentences many times. This exercise helps discover aspects of your responsibility for all circumstances around you.

– It was also explained that you should not react to any situation affecting you whenever possible. As a practical exercise, in order to not react to your life circumstances, you must consciously restrict your impulses as soon as they arise. You must press an imaginary *pause* button to suspend your impulses. When you imagine that you press "pause" you can also ask yourself: *"What is going in me in relation to this?"* Then you must wait for any introspective insights into this and say the four Ho'oponopono sentences repeatedly.

– There is another practical exercise; whenever you face a negative situation in your life affecting you, you must say: *"This situation is part of me"*, *"This circumstance came from me"*, *"I have created this situation"*, *"This has to do with me"*, *"My subconscious memories manifested this"* or any other similar sentences. When you get the habit of using these sentences it

will become easier to assert your full responsibility for whatever comes into your life. When you use these phrases, you can also say the four Ho'oponopono phrases many times.
– You should take responsibility for every negative circumstance affecting you. Mohr suggests a very powerful technique you can use when you face personal problems; you should say: *"Whatever has created this problem, it must have to do something with me. I love the part within me that has caused the problem, I accept it fully, I forgive this part of me, and I thank this part of me. I give this part of me all my love."* You must repeat these sentences as many times as possible and you must feel related to the problem.
– In relation to free will, it was veritably demonstrated that all your actions are initiated on a subconscious level, but they can be censored consciously. There is a very interesting exercise to do at the end of the day, preferably before going to sleep. Find a quiet and comfortable place to sit down and take note of three things that, during the day, you felt the urge to act on, but then refrained from acting on. These things you include on this list must not necessarily be significant or life-changing; you can choose trivial things as well. Then ask yourself, *"What is going on in me in relation to this?"* and wait for some introspective insights, then say the four Ho'oponopono sentences many times.
– From Ho'oponopono's perspective, at the zero state you are likely to be guided by divine inspiration, which is boundless wisdom; your actions tend to be more effortless, spontaneous and creative. At this state you are free from your subconscious memories. You can do a very short exercise; ask yourself: *"What does it mean to be totally free?"* and *"What are the characteristics of limitless freedom?"* Then take note of any insights, and say the four Ho'oponopono sentences repeatedly.

Chapter 6

You Can Delete
Your Subconscious Memories

Ho'oponopono is a tool which, by cleaning and deleting the past errors, it harmonizes us with the soul purpose at present.
– Maria Carmen Martinez Tomás

You have two ways to live your life… From memories or from inspiration. Memories are old programs replaying. Inspiration is the Divine giving you a message. The only way to hear the Divine and receive inspiration is to clean all memories.
– Dr. Ihaleakala Hew Len

1. Different approaches to tackle problems

As explained before, most people try to resolve problematic issues in the traditional way, which implies examining difficulties thoroughly and then working out their solutions. People use their conscious mind to focus steadfastly on their issues and find solutions.

From this viewpoint, you tend to justify the causes of your problems, which sometimes are taken for granted. You also end up being more concentrated on the problems. When you use this strategy, not only are you unable to solve your problems as effectively as possible, you tend to attract much more like problems into your life.

There is well-known saying in Metaphysics which goes *"what you focus your attention on, grows."* In that effect, every time you concentrate on your problems, you tend to manifest more problems. With this traditional approach, you are just dealing with their symptoms, instead of being centered on their causes, which makes it highly unproductive.

When you practice Ho'oponopono, you actually deal with the origins (or causes) of your problems, and not with their symptoms. When you deal with the causes of your problems and remove them, the solutions for your troublesome situations tend to be more lingering. All your problematic situations have definite causes, which are programs constantly playing out in your subconscious mind.

From the metaphysical perspective all the difficulties you encounter in your life are false appearances; they are never the truth. From the Ho'oponopono perspective your problems are creations of your subconscious memories. From both perspectives, the only truth is that you are naturally almighty and unique; you are a being full of unconditional love and limitless power. You were made in the image and likeness of the Divine. You can access your true essence when you get rid of your subconscious memories.

As was explained before, Ho'oponopono is a powerful technique which helps you free yourself from the heavy burden of subconscious programs. These past stories are indelibly written on the blackboard of your subconscious mind; these scripts resemble garbage lying rotten in the back of your mind.

In relation to these subconscious programs, there are several points to take into account:

– These negative subconscious memories cannot be deleted by themselves; their removal is never happenstance. If you don't make the decision to remove your subconscious memories, your status quo (which means your current situation with no change) will remain indefinitely.

– Every time you use the four Ho'oponopono sentences (*"I am sorry"*, *"Please forgive me"*, *"I love you"* and *"Thank you"*) to delete your subconscious programs you are actually being supported by Divinity.

– You don't actually need to know which memories must be

eliminated; this aspect of the cleaning process is the domain of the Divine. In other words, Divinity always knows which memories need to be removed.

– As you delete the memories you enter into a state of surrender. In this instance, surrender means not fighting with your negative circumstances any longer. During the cleaning process you let go of any negative circumstance because your main focus is to remove the subconscious memories from your mind.

– Until you make the firm decision of erasing your past programs, you are actually their accomplice. You are negligent in keeping these detrimental memories; you are implicitly protecting them.

– Metaphorically speaking, when you keep these subconscious programs, you are fathering them and giving shelter in the back of your mind. On the contrary, when you practice Ho'oponopono you render these memories orphaned and homeless.

– When removing your past programs you are deleting the causes of your problems, instead of being concentrated on your problems themselves. Murphy says that: *"Most men try to change conditions and circumstances by working with conditions and circumstances. To remove discord, confusion, lack, and limitation you must remove the cause, and the cause is the way that you are using your subconscious mind."*

– The decision of deleting your subconscious memories is the best choice you can ever make in your life. If you don't take any action to erase your subconscious memories, your negative circumstances will not improve on their own.

– Many people have the natural tendency to be attached to what is familiar to them, even when it is negative. In that effect, when you delete your subconscious memories you are forsaking any attachment to these past programs; you don't cling onto your past any longer, you let it go.

– The only way to overcome the omnipresent power of these subconscious programs over your life is to delete them all. When you do so, you heal the part of you which creates problems in your life, and you erase these programs.

– As you use Ho'oponopono to clean your subconscious programs you become more calm, peaceful and at ease. This is a natural consequence of eliminating programs which generate continuous conflicts in different areas of your life.

– Every time you delete your memories you are taking full responsibility for everything in your life. You are facing your current circumstances instead of escaping them.

– The frequent use of the Ho'oponopono technique helps you transmute your limiting programs into loving energy. The Divine when helping you during the cleaning process dissolves these memories with love energy.

– As you frequently do Ho'oponopono you go from a state of cluelessness and uncertainty to a state of certainty and clarity. You also gain access to divine inspiration, which is limitless wisdom.

– When you delete your subconscious memories you are also erasing the programs you share with other people around you. In other words, when you erase your subconscious programs you are also removing memories which relate you to other people.

– As you clean your subconscious memories you progressively discover your authentic unpolluted essence. Your true nature is generally buried beneath a humongous pile of limiting memories.

– When you delete the memories you change the unpleasant – the negative circumstances in your life – into pleasurable ones. All your negative situations are a product of your subconscious memories, which also keep you distant from Divinity. When you do the cleaning process you are more likely to experience delightful circumstances for you are reconnected to the Divine.

– You have been vesting your subconscious memories in power, in most cases unwittingly. As you do Ho'oponopono you start to reclaim your own power; these memories are stripped away from any power.

– The removal of your subconscious memories can also be considered as a learning process. You learn that your subconscious memories are the cause of all your problems, but you also understand that you must delete these limiting programs to transform your life.

– When you erase your past programming you also transform your perception of reality. As was previously explained, your subconscious programs also distort the way you perceive your reality.

– When you are controlled by your subconscious memories you are likely to behave like a victim of your circumstances; you might even believe that you are disconnected from the Divine. As you remove your memories, you don't victimize yourself any longer and you reconnect to the Divine source, from which you have never been totally severed.

– When you delete the negative memories, you achieve internal freedom because you are liberated from the oppression of your past conditioning. You are not helpless any longer, for you become emancipated from your subconscious tapes.

– Besides, when you remove your subconscious programs you can also achieve external freedom. As you erase these memories, you can act in a freer manner because you are not conditioned by your memories. As you remove your subconscious programming you also become free to receive guidance from the Divine.

– The cleaning process is both destructive and constructive. On one side, the removal of your memories is destructive because you pulverize this programming. On the other side, the clearing process is also constructive (or creative) because, as you remove your memories, you make room for divine inspiration to come into your mind.

2. Other aspects

2.1. All your wrongdoings can be erased

From the Ho'oponopono perspective, when you remove your subconscious memories, *"you make things right"*, which means correcting your mistakes. In order to do so, you do not work directly on your negative circumstances, but you erase the underlying subconscious memories.

Unless you decide to delete your past memories, they naturally perpetuate over time taking over your life. As you remove your limiting subconscious programming, your mind becomes clearer and more pure.

Your problems give you an opportunity to act like a wise alchemist. As you do Ho'oponopono, you transmute these programs into empty space to be filled with divine inspiration.

In the past you might have thought that there was no *delete function* in your complex mental recorder to eliminate your subconscious past records. Nonetheless, you certainly can count on that button, which is the Ho'oponopono technique.

When you clean your subconscious memories you step out of your mental treadmill, made up of countless subconscious programs replaying ceaselessly. Figuratively speaking, eradicating your subconscious programs resembles eliminating noxious parasites attacking your body; Ho'oponopono represents the most effective medication you can use.

Some sages say that removing your subconscious programs is like reformatting the *hard drive* or your bio-computer. As you reset your hard drive, your whole system tends to operate more flowingly; all its internal functions are run in an unencumbered manner. Metaphorically speaking, when you delete your subconscious programs, you also act like a gardener who removes weeds pervading your mental subconscious landscape.

As explained before, Ho'oponopono is also effective in erasing the programs you inherited from your relatives through your DNA. In relation to this, King says that: *"You have the power to override your DNA. Your mindset continuously updates and re-programs your body cells through information and emotions you originate, believe and carry."*

As was previously explained, when you delete your own subconscious memories you also wipe the subconscious programs you share with other people; the individuals you get in contact with directly or indirectly, for example, the ones you see in the media.

However, when you do the cleaning process, you don't have any clue about which specific programs are being removed. The specific programs to be eliminated are always the domain of the Divine.

As was said, since you decided to do the cleaning process you allow Divinity to assist with the removal of your subconscious memories. When you use the four Ho'oponopono phrases, you actually surrender to this unbounded source, which is omnipotent, omnipresent and omniscient.

You do not have to go through the cleaning process only a few times; the cleaning process must be continuous and ongoing. You have countless subconscious memories to be deleted, even when you are not aware of this. The application of this technique is never redundant or useless.

When you go through the cleaning process, some suggest that you should visualize your problems as you repeat the four key sentences. However, others assert it is not actually necessary to visualize anything when you practice Ho'oponopono.

During the cleaning process you can be more aware of your problems when you ask yourself: *"What is going on in me that I am manifesting this?"* The introspective tool was thoroughly explained previously in Chapter 4 of this book.

Your commitment to removing your subconscious memories is not at loggerheads with taking effective actions regarding different areas of your life when necessary. As you clean your subconscious programs, you will notice that your actions tend to be less automatic and more thoughtful, creative and meaningful.

When you remove your memories you should have no expectations on the outcomes of the cleaning process. For example, if you have financial problems, you might be cleaning your past memories because you want to become more prosperous, which implies positive expectations. It was explained that your expectations are detrimental because they are based on your subconscious memories. You should always practice Ho'oponopono and let Divinity act.

2.2. Your subconscious memories have an emotional basis

In the past, you may have asked yourself this question: *"What are really subconscious memories?"* They are just data which are not in accordance with your divine essence. They represent information held in your mind which is not in total harmony with your natural love energy. The disharmony you experience when you hold subconscious memories may take many forms such as: disapproval, restlessness, fear, pain, hate, tension, sadness, etc.

As was explained, all your subconscious memories have an emotional basis; Chopra and Tanzi say that: *"nothing solidifies a memory like emotion."* Whenever you encounter troublesome situations, you hold memories with fearful emotions.

You might argue that, sometimes, your subconscious programs are not necessarily related to fear, for example when you hold grudges against someone or when you are angry, sad or hopeless. Nonetheless, from the metaphysical viewpoint all your negative emotions are fundamentally based on fear, dread or fright.

All the negative emotions are just specific subcategories of the main emotional state called fear. They all have a very low vibratory rate, which tends to attract negative circumstances into your life.

Fear is an emotion which is always in total disharmony with love. When you experience fear you cannot access your core loving essence. During the cleaning process you are pervaded with loving energy from Divinity which removes the memories from your subconscious mind.

When you practice Ho'oponopono you don't just remove your memories, but also the emotional states related to them. Ray says that with the use of Ho'oponopono, *"we clean our feelings and impressions of everything we encounter. Doing so prevents problems from coming into our reality."*

Some people, after having practiced Ho'oponopono regularly, reported they felt fretful, cross, moody or upset for a while. When you eradicate your subconscious memories there is a very profound transmutation which occurs in your mind. As a consequence, some negative emotional states related to your past programs might manifest as residue of the memories being removed.

If you experience any negative emotions after doing Ho'oponopono there is nothing to worry about. These uncomfortable emotional states you might experience will not linger over time. After this temporary emotional turmoil, you are likely to feel in a more peaceful state.

2.3. The deletion of your subconscious memories is like house-keeping

I have to work on my own data, because when I clear that chaos and misinformation, my experiences will reflect balance, harmony and ease, and that will be reflected in the lives of everyone that I encounter.
– Khenpo Gurudas Sunyatananda

In order to illustrate the Ho'oponopono cleaning process, let's take the example of housework activities. When you do the housework chores, such as cleaning and tidying, you don't do them only once. If you don't follow through with these tasks on a continual basis, your house becomes messy. Likewise, your subconscious mind, like a house, must be cleaned on a frequent basis.

This is a regular cleaning process because you have infinite memories held on a subconscious level. You are also continually incorporating new memories at all times. As a consequence, the removal of your memories is never a one-off activity. You should be saying the four sentences as frequently as possible. You should make the use of this cleaning tool a priority in your life.

Moreover you should consider the technique of Ho'oponopono as a vital activity for your life; this activity is as important as breathing. In a practical way, you should use this tool on any occasion, even in the cases where there seem to be no problems in your life. When you do not have any problem you must keep on using this technique in a preemptive manner. You must remember that your memories are always being replayed, even if you are not aware of this situation.

When you do Ho'oponopono you have to trust this tool unconditionally. This powerful technique can wipe out your subconscious memories in a simple and effective manner. You can delete all your subconscious programs, even the ones which cannot be accessed through introspection.

These past programs are likely to be deeply ingrained in your subconscious. It is very common that your memories are deleted in a progressive manner. It takes time to get rid of your past programming. However, with persistence and patience you will reap the fruits of the cleaning process sooner than imagined. You will experience changes in all areas of your life, which will be undeniable for you and others.

You can do Ho'oponopono in advance, which means applying

this tool in relation to specific upcoming situations. You can use this cleaning tool for example when you know that you will have a meeting with some people. In this case you can apply the Ho'oponopono tool while you think about the place and people you will see at the meeting. You can also use Ho'oponopono to clean other future events you arrange in advance, such as trips, reunions, dates, appointments, interviews and holidays, among others.

Martinez Tomás suggests that you can also delete the memories retrospectively. In order to do so, you have to scan all negative experiences you have been through in the past. Once you recollect these negative experiences, you must say the four sentences many times.

Martinez Tomás also recommends that you should make an exhaustive chronological list of the painful experiences and conflicting people you have met throughout your life. You must read the list several times and say the four Ho'oponopono sentences repeatedly.

2.4. When you clean your memories you use divine energy

We can appeal to Divinity who knows our personal blueprint, for healing of all thoughts and memories that are holding us back at this time.
– Morrnah Simeona

It was explained that, when you are taken over by your subconscious memories, your essential connection to the Divine is somewhat obliterated. Likewise, ancient Hawaiian traditions say that you tend to experience illnesses or any other difficulties in your life when your connection with the unlimited source, the Divine, is disrupted. So when you delete these programs your connection with the divine source is naturally restored.

Every time you practice Ho'oponopono you are reconnected to

the love energy from the Divine. The divine love energy can only pervade you when you make the decision to do Ho'oponopono.

The divine energy and your subconscious programs cannot inhabit your mind at the same time. Likewise, Perez says that your mind can only be the servant of one master at a time.

Your conscious is the part of your mind which always initiates the cleaning process. Your subconscious mind cannot delete these memories by itself. During the cleaning process, your conscious mind always acts in a harmonious partnership with your subconscious and also with your super conscious. These three parts of your mind are also assisted by the Divine during this process.

When you regularly repeat these four sentences you grant permission to the Divine to remove the subconscious programming on your behalf. The frequent use of the four Ho'oponopono sentences acts like a password which activates the assistance from Divinity.

As your past memories are erased, you are not attached to them any longer. When the Divine purifies your mind, all the subconscious useless information held in your mind is released for good.

When you commit to cleaning your subconscious programs on a regular basis, you will notice that all your life situations tend to fall into place almost miraculously. All problematic situations are resolved in a spontaneous and effortless manner. Once you remove your subconscious conditioning, your mind becomes a fertile ground to receive divine inspiration.

2.5. Zero point is the final objective of cleaning
When you practice Ho'oponopono, your final objective is to reach the state called zero point or zero state. Some sages say that when you delete all your subconscious data you naturally arrive at this state of void. At zero point you are not snared by your past conditioning because you have removed it all.

You can only experience this state when you do

Ho'oponopono on a frequent basis. Because you have shared subconscious memories with other people, when you arrive at zero point other people around you will too.

This zero state is pure emptiness; your mental clarity is significantly enhanced and you can harness your limitless power, which is your essential birthright. The zero point you achieve is a state of radiant and limitless aliveness.

The zero point is opposite to the state of death which affects you when you are run by your subconscious programs. The zero point is a state in which you will encounter unlimited opportunities and experience continuous growth.

As you delete your subconscious memories, your mind is more prone to receiving divine inspiration; you tend to act in a more creative and meaningful manner. When you are driven by inspiration, you also experience a deep connection with the purpose of your life.

Your subconscious programs constrain your energy. So when you rid yourself from your subconscious memories, you automatically raise your energy. Besides, during the cleaning process you are assisted by the Divine, who envelops you in the all-transmuting love energy, which has the highest vibratory rate that exists.

2.6. Cleaning is the path to evolution

When you delete your subconscious memories you actually walk the path of your personal evolution and development. Lytle says that: *"In transcendence... you replace the negative with the positive... you become more powerful... every problem in your life becomes an opportunity to increase your own personal power."*

From the metaphysical perspective, the negative includes negative emotional states such as hate, sadness, anger, resentment, fear, powerlessness, among others. And the positive encloses uplifting states such as love, gratitude, peacefulness, powerfulness, etc. When you regularly practice Ho'oponopono you remove the negative (subconscious programs) in your mind to create a void to be filled by the positive (divine inspiration).

When you repeatedly do the cleaning process, you are more prone to be aligned with your life mission. You tend to naturally get rid of any meaningless actions in order to only focus on what is of value for you.

When you release your subconscious programs you can harness your natural limitlessness; you feel that you can perform anything that you want, with ease and joy. You will feel more in charge of your life. It is even possible that all your acquaintances and your family become stunned because of all the changes they observe in your life.

With the frequent use of the Ho'oponopono tool you can transcend your past. In relation to this, Tolle says that: *"if you delve into the past it will become a bottomless pit... There is always more..."* This author recommends that you should *"die to the past every moment."* And you do so whenever you delete your subconscious programs through the practice of Ho'oponopono.

When you practice Ho'oponopono regularly your life also becomes more unencumbered. Your life tends to spontaneously improve in all dimensions: health, finance, relationships, career, etc. You will also be able to rediscover the Divine within yourself.

There is a true story about a conversation between the Pope and Michelangelo. The Pope asked this famous Renaissance artist about how he managed to make the statue of David. Michelangelo told him that in order to make that statue he only removed the parts of the rock which were not David. Likewise, when you do Ho'oponopono you chisel away these past chunks (subconscious programs) from your mind in order to uncover your limitless natural radiance.

When you remove your past programming, you also leave all your needless suffering behind, and for good. Likewise, the Buddhist tradition encourages you to look beyond your suffering in order to dispel it.

After doing Ho'oponopono continually, you might face new negative circumstances in your life. These difficult situations are just temporary; they are just part of your inner transformation. These situations represent the residual manifestations of subconscious memories you removed during the cleaning process. All these negative circumstances will vanish over time.

As you use this cleaning tool on a frequent basis, you are also likely to feel lighter and more aware. You will also feel more engaged with every situation in your life, with more access to your inner resources. You will experience a state of powerfulness and plenitude.

3. Subconscious memories and resistance

3.1. General aspects of resistance

It is very common that people place resistance against the removal of their subconscious memories. In some cases, people tend to resist this cleaning process in a very subtle manner; for example, not taking total responsibility for everything that happens in their lives.

In other cases, people can be in denial in relation to their current negative circumstances. They might also resist when they feel guilty or resentful about their life situations. Other people place resistance when they don't admit that their own subconscious memories create everything that happens in their lives. Another way of offering resistance is not doing Ho'oponopono on a frequent basis.

In any of these cases, placing resistance entails implicitly saying *"no"* to what it is. You also try to replace what it is with fabricated delusions. When you place resistance, your opposition makes you experience a state of powerlessness. You tend to dwell in negative emotional states, such as fear, which hinder the removal of your memories.

There is a very well-known metaphysical saying that goes:

"What you resist persists." This principle is totally applicable to your subconscious memories; when you resist them they tend to persist over time. Moreover, all your negative life situations tend to remain unchanged over time. Any type of resistance does not allow you to evolve in your life.

Every time you resist, you cannot take total responsibility for everything going on around you. As was explained, taking total responsibility is one of the main requisites to removing your subconscious programs.

The opposite of resistance is surrender. Resistance only causes you sorrow; instead surrender makes you experience a peaceful and gleeful state. Other differences between resistance and surrender are:

– On one side, when you resist you don't truly realize that you are being driven by your limiting past programming. On the other side, when you surrender you acknowledge this issue and you want to change it; you are committed to practicing Ho'oponopono on a regular basis.

– On one side, each time you resist, you end up being more oppressed by your subconscious programs. On the other side, when you surrender to what it is you are not submitting any longer to your past conditioning because you decided to remove it all.

– On one side, when you resist you tend to be even more attached to your current circumstances; you battle them. On the other side, when you surrender, you understand that, in order to change your outer circumstances, you have to first clean your inner world.

– On one side, when you resist you are prone to act pushily regarding your negative life circumstances. You try hard to manipulate your life circumstances so that they improve. On the other side, when you surrender, you accept your negative life situations and do not try to fix them, at least directly. You know that removing your programs will improve your life with no effort.

– On one side, when you resist, your actions are continually being

dictated by your subconscious programs. On the other side, when you surrender, you erase your subconscious programs in order to be more susceptible to receive divine inspiration.

Many people believe that surrendering means giving up or resigning something. From a spiritual perspective, surrender implies powerfulness and effortlessness. Benner says that:

The English word surrender carries the implication of putting one's full weight on someone or something. It involves letting go – a release of effort, tension and fear. And it involves trust. One cannot let go of self-dependence and transfer dependence to someone else without trust.

When you surrender you are not afraid to accept your own vulnerability. As a consequence, you are also willing to ask the Divine for help with the cleaning of your past programming. This author also makes an analogy between the act of surrendering and floating; when you float you have to put your weight in the water and be confident that it will support you. When you surrender, you completely rely on the Divine.

For this reason, it is important that you eliminate all resistance in your life. You must take the first step to remove resistance by starting with the cleaning process.

It is possible that you are disheartened by the hardship and drudgery affecting your life. When your life is flooded by cumbersome situations, it might seem difficult not to resist them. In these cases, resistance seems to be the default state which naturally emerges.

On those occasions, you can leave resistance behind by remembering that the Divine is always willing to help you with the cleaning process. You must trust this boundless power which supports you with the removal of your subconscious programs.

Every time you surrender, you also cast aside your natural

tendency to control your environment because you truly know that you are wisely guided by the Higher Planes. Surrendering is primarily related to the qualities of trust and reliance on the universal forces. You know in the depth of your heart that Divinity will never abandon you.

3.2. Ho'oponopono and resistance

The way of surrender is like letting God be the sculptor, and letting ourselves be the clay.
– Marianne Williamson

It was previously explained that when you experience resistance you tend to change your current negative circumstances from an outside-in perspective; your main focus is your outer environment. Instead when you don't offer any resistance you use an inside-out approach for your problems, which means that you primarily focus on your internal world.

As mentioned previously, there are countless subtle ways of resistance that most people use. Another manifestation of resistance is avoidance or procrastination of activities that are beneficial for you. For example, you might avoid practicing Ho'oponopono on a regular basis. When you are indefinitely indecisive you are also placing resistance albeit in a very subtle fashion. Another way of resisting is being stuck to an incorrect way of thinking, for example when you tend to avoid your full responsibility.

Every time you resist you are prone to being focused on your negative situations, which makes them appear even more insurmountable. When you release your resistance, you can naturally concentrate on the most effective way to solve the problems, which is removing your subconscious memories. Some masters say that when you release your resistance you experience a life-changing conversion.

Whenever you practice Ho'oponopono you are treading the path of least resistance. With the use of this tool, your life circumstances tend to improve in a graceful manner.

By now, you might be asking yourself this question: *"If the path of no-resistance helps me remove my subconscious memories, why do people get stuck to their limiting programs?"* Many people have serious difficulties in ridding themselves of their subconscious memories because they have invested too much time and energy in these programs, in most cases unwittingly.

Dobelli explains that people get trapped in the so-called *sunk cost fallacy*. This means that when you have been investing a significant amount of time and energy in something in your life, even when it is limiting, you have the natural tendency to continue with it. In that effect, he states that our *"investment becomes a reason to carry on, even if we are dealing with a lost cause."*

Likewise, if you are like most people, you might have held your subconscious memories for a certain period of time. As a consequence, you experience a certain level of familiarity with the subconscious programs. Thus your attachment to your subconscious memories makes it more difficult to remove them.

You might be attached your past programming even when you realize that it is detrimental for your life. It becomes your secure base to explore all the experiences you go through. You have a relationship of proximity with these memories, which makes it impossible for you to imagine living without them; they are an integral part of who you are. This attachment to this programming tends to be subconscious.

You might also be attached to your subconscious memories for other reasons. For example, you might experience fear of the unknown, which makes you resistant to change. In some cases you can also have negative expectations about releasing these subconscious programs which prevent you from removing these memories.

Your subconscious resistance to get rid of your past programs might seem very sensible. This rigid way of thinking is based on the natural need for consistency which all human beings have. People tend to naturally avoid any contradictions in their thoughts and behaviors, even if they are negative.

For this reason, whenever you feel resistance against anything in your life you can ask yourself this question: *"What is going on in me that I am experiencing resistance?"* After this, you should take note of the insights and say the four Ho'oponopono sentences repeatedly.

By repeating these words on a regular basis, your resistance vanishes spontaneously. These phrases have the power of dissolving your resistance. From the Ho'oponopono perspective, your resistance is just another subconscious memory, which can be deleted by using this cleaning technique. The same procedure can be applied in cases when you have resistance to the regular use of Ho'oponopono.

For most people, forming the habit of doing Ho'oponopono frequently might take some time. When you start doing Ho'oponopono, you might go through a transitional period in which your old ways of improving your negative circumstances (for example, working on external situations to fix them) do coexist with the new way of approaching your difficulties (for example, doing Ho'oponopono to remove your subconscious memories).

In some cases, this transitional period might look ambiguous and even chaotic. Nevertheless, if you are patient, determined and committed to this cleaning technique, you will notice that over time you progressively let go of the traditional ways of tackling your troubles and instead practice Ho'oponopono.

Whenever you feel hesitant or uneasy during this transition period, you must remind yourself of the main purpose of Ho'oponopono, which is removing your subconscious programs. You must bear in mind the overarching benefits that this technique brings about for you and your environment. When you are doubtful it is also an opportunity to reinforce your faith in the Divine.

In that effect, you should always remind yourself that Divinity is always assisting you with the removal of your subconscious programming when you do Ho'oponopono.

4. Process of eliminating the negative memories

Negative self-talk will obstruct all high vibrational energy from being channeled through the person. Energy cannot flow through a blocked channel.

– Lisa Marie Gutowski

During the process of removing your subconscious programs, different parts of your mind (conscious, subconscious and super conscious) intervene in a harmonious manner. Detailed outlines of the functions of these three parts of your mind, where their main characteristics will be thoroughly explained, will be covered in Chapter 12. It is also important to remember that, during the cleaning process, you are being assisted by Divinity.

You will find below the main aspects of the cleaning process of your subconscious memories, especially how it is carried out in practice. Nevertheless, even if you do not know these technical aspects, the cleansing process will still be effective.

– When you practice Ho'oponopono, you make the choice of being free from your subconscious memories. You just have to say the four statements (*"I am sorry"*, *"Please forgive me"*, *"I love you"*, *"Thank you"*) repeatedly. This is the essence of the Ho'oponopono cleaning process.

– When you say these four sentences, you actually start with the cleansing process of your subconscious memories. Through the purposeful use of these words, your conscious requests the Divine's assistance for the removal of your subconscious memories.

– Divine always helps you remove your past programs when you do Ho'oponopono. When you say these four phrases frequently you want to transform the subconscious memories crowding your mind into a void.

– When you say these four phrases you are assuming your total responsibility for all problems in your life. Moreover, you take responsibility for everything around you, not only your difficulties. You also know that your current circumstances are just natural manifestations of your subconscious memories.

– When you say the four sentences on a regular basis, you implicitly request your subconscious to eliminate all programs held on that level. From the Ho'oponopono perspective the subconscious also called "the child" is a massive databank full of past programs. This child generally feels uncared for and unloved because of having been filled with countless memories over time.

– Besides saying the four sentences, you can also say to this child that you will always love and care for it. Some masters like Dr. Len say that you can also say: *"I love you"* to your subconscious memories, which are your enemies, in order to remove them.

– During the cleaning process, your subconscious mind will acknowledge the presence of these memories and, as a consequence of this, it will stir them up. Your subconscious mind will also redirect your request of removing these programs to the super conscious level.

– The super conscious is the part of your mind which is in direct contact with the Divine. Your super conscious level will receive the request from your subconscious level, and assess it in order to make it more specific and clear. After this, the super conscious will redirect this request to Divinity.

– Then the Divine also called the creator or *"I am"* will receive the plea from the super conscious mind and will examine it thoroughly. After this, Divinity will send its pure loving energy throughout your super conscious mind. Some masters called this loving energy *"mana."* This energy will, in turn, go through the conscious part of your mind. And lastly, this powerful energy will pervade your subconscious mind.

– This radiant alchemic energy will remove all your subconscious memories effortlessly. Your subconscious memories will be completely neutralized or transmuted by the love energy originally released by the Divine.

– As you delete your subconscious programs over time there will appear a void in your mind which is likely to be filled by inspiration coming from the Divine. When you are arriving at this state of emptiness or void, which is called zero point, you are memory free and you dwell in your divine essence.

5. Practical tips

– There is an exercise you can do on your own. Visualize any problems affecting your life and repeat the four key sentences (*"I am sorry"*, *"Please forgive me"*, *"I love you"* and *"Thank you"*). Some say it is not necessary to use any visualization during the cleaning process.

– When you face any difficulty in your life you can also ask yourself this question: *"What is going on in me that I am manifesting this?"* Then you should wait for any insights about the specific circumstance. You can even take note of the insights, and you must repeat the four Ho'oponopono sentences many times.

– There is another interesting exercise. Sit down in a comfortable and quiet place. Then make some drawings on a piece of paper; allow the ideas to come flowing without thinking too much. After you finish the drawings, look at them attentively for a while. Then ask yourself: *"What is going on in me in relation to this?"* and wait for insights about these drawings. After this, repeat the four Ho'oponopono sentences many times.

– You can also look for a photo of a person who you know in detail. You should choose a person who is currently facing several difficulties. Look at the picture in detail; ask yourself: *"What is going on in me that I am manifesting this?"* You are likely to obtain valuable insights regarding the subconscious memories you share with this person. Take note of these insights and reread them carefully. Then repeat the four Ho'oponopono phrases many times. You can also do this exercise with a picture of yourself.

– Here is another interesting exercise that you can do when you are performing housekeeping activities. For example, you can do this when you clean a room in your house or wash up the dishes. When you perform the chosen activity, you should repeat the four sentences. When you say these phrases, you must be as mindful as possible regarding the housework activity you are performing.

– When you wash up the dishes and as you repeat the four Ho'oponopono sentences, you must be aware of the water drenching the plates and wiping their filth out. You can also be aware of the friction of the sponge with detergent scrubbing that plate intensely. You must be mindful in relation to the chosen cleaning task while you repeat the four sentences. You can apply this mindfulness exercise to any other housework activity.

– There is another version of the previous exercise. When you do a cleaning activity, for example washing up the dishes, you can imagine that the dirt you wipe off the plates represents your subconscious programs. You imagine that this dirt taken off the plates is your subconscious memories which are being deleted. When you perform this activity you must also say the four Ho'oponopono sentences as many times as possible.

– There is another well-known exercise: you must imagine

that you have a house completely filled up with stuff. In this exercise the house represents your subconscious mind and the stuff hoarded there represents your memories. Then you must envision that you de-clutter the place until is completely empty. Then imagine you walk around and try to feel the freedom in your movement. Feel the light of the sun filling the house; sense that the energy of the house is more flowing and peaceful. Then repeat the four Ho'oponopono sentences.

– There is another exercise suggested by Joe Vitale. Imagine that you have a whiteboard, which is full of words covering it up. You cannot distinguish these words clearly. This board represents your subconscious mind and the words are your memories plaguing it. Then imagine that you progressively wipe out the board until it is totally clean. The clean white-board is your zero point, the state in which you are not driven by any subconscious memories. Then ask yourself: *"What is going on in me in relation to this?"* and wait for any insights. Finally, you can say the four Ho'oponopono sentences repeatedly.

– You might have doubts about the effectiveness of this cleaning technique, which creates resistance. Your resistance is just another subconscious memory which must be cleaned. You must welcome this resistance; never fight it or suppress it. Keep on using this technique, despite any state of opposition.

– There is a very interesting exercise you can do when you experience resistance. Make a list of situations that you tend to complain about or you feel guilty about. Include activities you feel obligated to do. You can even comment that you are reluctant to use Ho'oponopono if this is the case. Read the list and ask yourself: *"What is going on in me that I am experiencing resistance regarding this?"* Pay attention to any insights and take note of them. Then say the four sentences many times. When you do this exercise regularly, your resistance will vanish in an effortless manner.

– You must remember that the opposite of resistance is surrender. Every time you surrender, you faithfully rely on the Divine and its valuable assistance. In order to surrender, you can repeatedly say: *"Divinity, I leave all these situations in your hands because I know that you will help me work them out in the best way possible. Thank you very much. And it is done."* Then say the four Ho'oponopono sentences many times. When you practice this exercise frequently, your life becomes lighter and flowing.

– There is another very interesting exercise proposed by Dwoskin. You must sit in a comfortable place and put both hands in front of your chest in a prayer position, with your forearms parallel to the floor. Then one hand must push against the other one, and this second hand has to resist the push of the first one. Then you must switch the hand that pushes and the one that resists many times. As you alternate hands during this exercise, you are more likely to receive more useful insights into this resistance. The purpose of this exercise is to sense resistance in a tangible and physical manner.

– There is a second part of the previous exercise. You must push one hand against the other one and vice versa again. Nonetheless, this time the hand, which in the first part of the exercise was offering resistance to the second hand, must offer no resistance at all. In other words, you must relax the hand which is pushed by the other hand. You must analyze the physical sensations you experience when one of the hands does not offer any resistance to the push of the other one.

– In relation to the two previous parts of the exercise, compare the physical sensations you experience in each case, with resistance and without it. Then you can also ask: *"What is going on in me in relation to this?"* Take note of any insights, and say the four Ho'oponopono sentences as many times as possible.

– There is another exercise also suggested by Dwoskin. In this exercise, you must ask yourself these questions: *"What is going in me when I am resisting?"*, *"Can I welcome feelings, sensations and thoughts about this?"*, *"Can I let this go?"* and *"Can I accept what it is?"* You have to answer this set of questions one by one. Imagine the main aspects related to your resistance; for example, images, sounds, emotions and sensations. Then pose this question: *"Can I let this go?"* and envision that this resistance leaves your body; for example, you can visualize smoke which flies in the sky freely. Then say the four Ho'oponopono sentences repeatedly.

Section II

Procedure to Apply Ho'oponopono

In this section we will explain the main procedure to apply this powerful tool. There will also be a thorough analysis of the four Ho'oponopono sentences (*"I am sorry"*, *"Please forgive me"*, *"I love you"* and *"Thank you"*).

Chapter 7

Main Aspects of the Ho'oponopono Procedure

To use Ho'oponopono is to walk by God's side.
– Maria Jose Cabanillas

1. Purpose of Ho'oponopono

Ho'oponopono is a very straightforward and easy-to-use technique. It is mainly made up of four simple but meaningful sentences:

– *I am sorry*
– *Please forgive me*
– *I love you*
– *Thank you*

These four sentences have the power to right the wrong. This technique uses the power of language as a means of removing your past conditioning. This set of brief sentences has both petitionary elements (for example, the sentence *"Please forgive me"*) and also declarative factors (for instance, the statement *"I love you"*).

These four phrases can be used for all purposes. You can use the same sentences without any need of modifying them according to a specific given situation. This trait makes these phrases very simple to use.

From the linguistic perspective, these sentences can be considered implicit generalizations. People use generalizations in their daily conversations. An example is *"I am a good person."* When you use this sentence you implicitly mean that *"I am always a good person (on all occasions)."* Conversely, the following sentence is not a generalization: *"Sometimes I am a good person"* or

"I am a good person but..." and any similar statements.

The Ho'oponopono phrase *"I love you"* means that *"I always love you"*, *"I love you at all times"* or *"I love you on all occasions."* In that effect, these four sentences always apply at all times and unconditionally. There are no explicit exceptions against the use of these phrases.

Another important feature of these cleaning sentences is brevity, which makes them easy to remember and repeat. These sentences avoid the use of wordy or intricate lexicon; they do not include any unnecessary or indirect vocabulary either.

Besides, these sentences are very clear and straightforward. Some say that you are prone to think more clearly whenever you use these phrases. In relation to this, Dobelli says that: *"verbal expression is the mirror of the mind. Clear thoughts become clear statements, whereas ambiguous ideas transform into vacant ramblings."*

These sentences, albeit apparently simplistic, are truly inspiring, pure and virtuous. Some masters say that these four sentences enclose prized words of blessing. The content of these four phrases is related to very lofty principles or values such as repentance (*"I am sorry"*), forgiveness (*"Please forgive me"*), love (*"I love you"*) and gratitude (*"Thank you"*). The specific meanings assigned to each of these relevant values vary significantly from person to person.

As a consequence, these sentences are empowering and wise. Allen says that: *"wisdom is perceived in the words which are its expression."* The two noble reasons for saying these sentences on a frequent basis are, as follows:

(a) *Cleaning memories held in your subconscious;*
(b) *Making space for divine inspiration to come into your life.*

The main purpose of the use of the Ho'oponopono tool is to go back to zero state, where you have no subconscious memories at all. When you use these sentences your focus should be inner-directed; however, these words are also addressed to the Divine.

In Metaphysics there is a principle called the Law of Compensation which states that: *"You cannot obtain something out of nothing."* In accordance with this principle, in order to clear your mind of subconscious memories you have to repeat the four sentences. Likewise, in order to receive divine inspiration, you have to leave spare room in your mind.

These four sentences can be used in any order. You should use them in the sequence that makes you feel most comfortable. If you use these phrases in a different order the cleaning process will still be as effective. You can only say one of these four sentences or a few of them, instead of using the four of them in a sequence.

When you say these four sentences regularly you will manifest evident changes in all your life circumstances. In order to experience this life transformation you have to be completely committed to using these phrases on a frequent basis.

As explained previously, the cleaning process is never a sporadic or all-out effort, but a gradual and continuous one. In a more graphic way, the cleaning process is like a series of strokes of an axe to fell a tree or a continuous dropping of water to erode stone.

When you practice Ho'oponopono you can repeat these four cleaning sentences either aloud or silently. In both cases, you will experience their transforming effects.

When you use these sentences you might have intrusive thoughts coming up into your mind. Whenever you have detrimental thoughts during the cleaning process you must swiftly redirect your attention to the four sentences. You must avoid getting tense or fretful or distracted by these thoughts when possible.

When you use these four cleaning sentences, you must also observe changes you might experience regarding your feelings and physical sensations.

Satyam says that any signals (images, sounds, or physical sensations) you receive when you practice Ho'oponopono might also prompt you to offer a specific type of reparation for your wrongdoings, more specifically for having held these subconscious memories. This reparation can take different forms, for example saying a prayer, donating things to charity organizations, writing a letter to someone you offended or giving a present to a relative, among others.

In relation to this, Satyam recommends that as soon you receive these insightful clues, you should act on them, offering reparation without any delay. From the Ho'oponopono perspective, the most simple and effective way to offer reparation is to say the four sentences as many times as possible.

When you say the four sentences, you might feel physically unwell, at least for a short time. This physical restlessness is a clear sign of a shift in your overall energy levels. Nonetheless, if you feel too uncomfortable, you must take a shower or have a short nap. After this break you can resume the uttering of the four sentences.

There is a way to check if you did this cleaning process satisfactorily. You must direct your attention inwardly to see if you still have any negative emotions or sensations regarding problematic situations previously bothering you. If so, this means that you have more programs to clean in your subconscious mind in relation to these situations. If not, the cleansing process was performed correctly. In all cases, keep on doing the cleaning at all times, because there are always other subconscious memories to delete.

Many people who use Ho'oponopono say they do not see any tangible results of the cleaning process. You never have to worry; the process is always working, albeit in some cases in a very subtle manner. You must also continue saying these four sentences even in the face of negative situations in your life.

Whenever you practice Ho'oponopono, your subconscious memories are being erased, even if you do not notice this.

2. The power of words

Generally speaking, words can have either a positive vibration or a negative one. The Ho'oponopono sentences vibrate with love and harmony; they are aligned with the highest energy for you. Not only do these four sentences affect you positively but also your environment. There are other interesting aspects to highlight regarding these four sentences:

- *These sentences are like mantras*
- *These sentences relate you to the Divine*
- *These sentences are powerful symbols*
- *These sentences have a transformative effect*
- *These sentences are decrees*
- *These sentences are expressions of your liveliness*
- *These sentences are attention grabbing*
- *These sentences are petitionary and intercessory*
- *These sentences act like prayers*
- *These sentences are carriers of positive energy*
- *These sentences imprint your subconscious mind*
- *These sentences have a transmuting power*
- *These sentences are filled with faith*
- *These sentences are part of your gradual learning through life*
- *These sentences hold no expectations*
- *These sentences are related to non-locality*

2.1. These sentences are like mantras

A mantra is a special sound and a special message that carries the power for healing, blessing and transformation.
Dr. Zhi Gang Sha

The word *mantra* comes from a combination of words in Sanskrit whose specific meaning is *"liberation from your thoughts."* Mantras are also called sacred healing sentences and have a powerful transformative effect. They are instruments designed to attain harmony and peacefulness. Sogyal Rinpoche says that a:

> *mantra is the essence of sound, and the embodiment of the truth in the form of sound. Each syllable is impregnated with spiritual power, condenses a spiritual truth, and vibrates with the blessing of the speech...*

According to Prabhupada: *"a mantra is a transcendental sound vibration with potency to liberate the mind from material conditioning."* Likewise, these sentences liberate you from all your subconscious programs. The incessant repetition of these four sentences has the same effect as mantras. When you repeat these sentences you reconnect with Divinity, who assists you during the cleaning process.

Lastly, there is another interesting point to highlight. Some scientific studies confirm that mantras have a vibration tantamount to planet Earth's, which is 8 Hz. When you repeat these four sentences as mantras, you become more connected to everything that exists.

2.2. These sentences relate you to the Divine

These four Ho'oponopono sentences are relationally based. Specifically speaking, these four phrases are purposed to strengthen your relationship with the Divine; they represent a two-way communication with Divinity. The frequent use of the four Ho'oponopono sentences is the spiritual "salary" you pay Divinity for having its assistance to remove your subconscious memories.

These sentences help you relinquish any state of helplessness. When you are committed to using these sentences, you understand that you were not left to your own devices; you can always resort to the Divine for assistance and guidance. When you use these sentences you are actually receiving support from the Divine.

With these sentences, you grant permission for the Divine to remove your subconscious memories. So these sentences act like secret codes which unlock the access to love energy from the Divine, which deletes your past programming throughout the cleaning process.

From the metaphysical perspective, these sentences only speak the truth, they allow you to go beyond the appearances of negative circumstances in your life, and reconnect to the most powerful source of energy that exists. These four sentences strip you from the fraudulent disguises and dress you up with the robe of divine love energy.

These four sentences bring about the Divine into manifestation. In relation to this, Garlow and Wall say that:

> manifest and manifestation describe times when God is revealed or at work in unique ways. Manifest is from two Latin terms: manus, which means "hand" and it's the root of "manual" and "manicure" and festum which refers to a holiday, festival or celebration. Thus, a divine manifestation might be rendered as "the dancing hand of God."

To put it differently, these sentences are the bridge between your inner world and the Divine. The frequent use of the Ho'oponopono technique has a restorative effect; it helps you restore the full presence of Divinity in you.

As was explained, the divine presence within you is temporarily obscured by your subconscious memories. Dr. Len says that when you use the four sentences you truly acknowledge that Divinity becomes your personal coach during the cleaning process. This divine loving energy is ready to support you with the removal of your subconscious memories but also throughout your personal evolution in life.

These sentences are also an affirmation of your faith on the Divine. You are completely sure that Divinity will assist you with the removal of your memories. The implicit meaning of these four phrases is *"Divinity, please help me clean all memories creating difficulties in my life."*

The Ho'oponopono sentences are also connective; you implicitly admit your connection, not only with the Divine but also with everything that exists. With the frequent use of this tool you can experience the sense of unity with all that exists.

Abd-Ru-Shin states that all your words are actually gifts from the Divine. From this perspective, Divinity is the original word who created everything that exists and you are the image of this High Source. For this reason, all your words are creative; they are actually deeds. Everything that you say always tends to manifest in your life.

You always reap what you sow with no exception; you tend to materialize what you say with no exception whatsoever. As a consequence of this, you must always be very careful and heedful with the words you frequently use in your life; you must avoid any negative or meaningless talk. So you must always give priority in your life to meaningful words, for example, the four Ho'oponopono sentences.

2.3. These sentences are powerful symbols

When you say these four sentences you also become the qualities contained in these phrases. In other words, when you use this tool frequently, you actually become repentance, forgiveness, love and thankfulness. Every time you apply this cleaning technique you embody these four significant values.

Assagioli says that:

> *All words are symbols that not only indicate or point out objects or psychological facts but also possess the power to stimulating and*

arising activities associated with them. They "evoke" and make operative the meanings and idea-forces they signify.

The frequent use of the four Ho'oponopono sentences (*"I am sorry"*, *"Please forgive me"*, *"I love you"* and *"Thank you"*) constitutes the most adequate vehicle to manifest the main aspects evoked with these terms.

From a different perspective, some masters suggest that you should never be too attached to any word you use, because all words are just symbols; they tend to objectify what they name. Words are codes to define tangible or intangible things in a precise manner. So the authentic essence of every single thing that exists can never be accurately depicted with words.

No words can make you feel too close to the objects they name. For example, the real experience of relevant states such as the values contained in the four Ho'oponopono sentences (repentance, forgiveness, love and thankfulness) goes beyond any possible words trying to label these states.

You should be always aware that these sentences don't pigeonhole what you actually experience. All words by nature describe but also limit the real world. Words act like maps you frequently use to move through the intricate territory of reality. From the Ho'oponopono perspective, words are also subconscious memories. You should never be too attached to words but open to explore real experiences, which always go beyond words; they are unnameable by nature.

The discipline called Neuro Linguistic Programming introduces the idea of anchors. An anchor is just a stimulus (for example, a place, a situation, an object, an idea, etc.) which effortlessly elicits a specific state (which includes certain emotions, physical sensations, thoughts and actions) in you. Over time, you learn to automatically relate the stimulus and the certain states you experience because of it.

In relation to this, words can be considered not only symbols but also anchors, positive or negative ones. On one side, you might use some words that rapidly make you feel in a good mood, loving, energetic or relaxed or any other positive state. On the other side, it is possible that some words make you feel de-motivated, despondent, fearful, or any other negative state.

When use an anchor, these states are triggered automatically. From the Ho'oponopono perspective, when the words are used as anchors they actually activate or set off certain subconscious memories, which bring about specific positive states in you.

You must analyze the specific states triggered when you say the four Ho'oponopono sentences (*"I am sorry"*, *"Please forgive me"*, *"I love you"* and *"Thank you"*). In most cases the states you experience from saying these phrases range from neutral to positive ones. It is very unlikely that you experience negative states when you say these four phrases except when they are unconsciously associated to specific past negative experiences.

2.4. These sentences have a transformative effect

Zagrans says that: *"manifestations are physical, emotional and spiritual changes that occur with faith, prayer and connection."* The four Ho'oponopono sentences help you build solid foundations to manifest positive situations in your life.

Nonetheless, when you use these sentences, you should never try to shape future circumstances in specific ways. As was previously explained, when you practice Ho'oponopono you must surrender; you should let go of any control over the outcomes of the cleaning process.

The state of surrender implies accepting the intrinsic uncertainty of future circumstances in an undisturbed manner. You can be at peace with yourself because you know that things will always work out in the best way possible. You are sure about this because you are being assisted by the Divine.

A study mentioned in the book *The Language of Heart* by James J. Lynch confirms that the use of positive words has positive effects on your general health conditions. As a consequence, when you use the Ho'oponopono phrases continually you tend to experience an overall optimization of the different areas of your life, such as health, but also relationships, finances and career, among others.

Dr. Emoto, who is a well-renowned scientist, conducted a very exhaustive research study on water. In this experiment, some people had to say negative and positive words to water. He wanted to test how the structure of molecules of water was influenced by the uttering of different specific words.

Dr. Emoto froze the water crystals and observed their structure through specific scientific instruments, like microscopes. Surprisingly, this scientist discovered that when the water had previously received uplifting words such as *"Love"* and *"Thank you"* or *"I am sorry"* the water structure showed beautiful shapes in their crystals.

He also observed that when water received negative messages such as *"I will kill you"* or *"fool"* its crystals showed deformed shapes; they displayed overt ugliness and lack of harmony. He concluded that the quality of the words uttered has a significant transforming power over water's internal structure. Positive and negative words have different vibratory rates, which modify the internal structure of water in a beneficial or detrimental fashion, respectively.

Likewise, other scientific studies such as one conducted by Korotkov also showed that positive words increase the electrical energy of the water. On the contrary, negative remarks decrease the electricity charge of the liquid. In another experiment a group of healers sent healing to water. The molecular makeup of the water was analyzed with advanced infrared technological equipment. The liquid subjected to healing modified its molecular structure in a significant manner, more specifically its bonding of hydrogen and oxygen.

These experiments have practical implications for your life;

you have to remember that your body is made up mainly of water. Many scientific studies confirm that the fetus of a person is composed of 99% water, but when born the proportion is approximately 90%. Later on in adulthood this percentage is reduced to 70%. In accordance with all these findings, the words you usually say, either negative or positive, actually modify our own internal structure, making it more disorderly or harmonious respectively.

In a similar way, Catherine Ponder says that: *"your words are constantly doing one of two things: building up or tearing down; healing or destroying."* From her perspective, each word produces a chemical change in your body. As a consequence, with the use of positive words, such as the four Ho'oponopono phrases, your body can be healed and invigorated.

McTaggart says that intention affects your physical environment. According to this author intention is a *"purposeful plan to perform an action, which will lead to a desired outcome."* There are countless scientific studies which proved that the sole intention of people bring about physical changes in the environment, even in a remote way, which defies any rational explanation. Your words always have an intention embedded in them. In the case of Ho'oponopono, the intention is obvious: to remove your subconscious memories.

2.5. These sentences are decrees

From the metaphysical perspective, words can be also considered as decrees. From this viewpoint, every single thing that you say tends to turn into manifestation over time. They are your most obedient servants and never come back void. Ferrini states: *"What becomes speech quickly becomes action."*

Some masters say that your words are like a spool of thread you use to weave your ideas; with these threads you make the tapestry of all your life situations. Your words resemble a set of keys which unlock two different safes: one containing all your potential positive circumstances; the other one enclosing negative circumstances. The four Ho'oponopono sentences unlock the first safe.

From a different perspective, your words are just a reflection of your thoughts, which tend to materialize in your life. In relation to this, the Bible says that: *"The tongue of the wise useth knowledge aright; but the mouth of fools poureth foolishness"* (Proverbs 15:2). The four Ho'oponopono sentences are just a composite of positive thoughts, which only bring about good things in your life.

Likewise, Haanel says that: *"words are thoughts and are therefore an invisible and invincible power which will finally objectify themselves in the form that they are given."* This author also says that our positive words are just like comfortable mental palaces in which we can always reside at ease.

2.6. These words are expressions of your liveliness

You might think that Ho'oponopono is boring or de-motivating, because you have to repeat these phrases mechanically over and over. However, Leonard says that: *"the essence of boredom is to be found in the obsessive search for novelty. Satisfaction lies in mindful repetition, the discovery of endless riches in subtle variation on familiar themes."*

In relation to this, some masters suggest that you should say these four Ho'oponopono sentences mindfully, reciting them in a lively, heartfelt and authentic manner. When you do so, you are more likely to become more engaged in the cleaning process.

Other sages recommend that you should never take these four Ho'oponopono sentences too seriously but with a light-hearted attitude. So if you say these sentences in a neutral or mechanical way you will still experience positive effects in your life circumstances all the same.

As you say these sentences, either mindfully or neutrally, you will notice that you are gradually infused with good feelings and thoughts, which will gradually pervade all your activities. These changes will be more noticeable as you use these four phrases on a regular basis.

2.7. These sentences are attention grabbing

As said, the constant use of the Ho'oponopono phrases is a key factor for a long-lasting transformation of your life circumstances. Assagioli says that: *"Repetition acts like the blows of a hammer on a nail and brings about the penetration and fixation of the idea... until it becomes dominant..."*

When you repeat these four cleaning phrases continually they will become part of your subconscious mind; they will actually become positive subconscious memories you hold in your mind. The constant use of these sentences also constitutes one of the best habits which you can create in your life.

The continual repetition of these sentences naturally hooks your attention and, in turn, also increases your interest in these phrases. There is a very well-known metaphysical saying that goes: *"Where you focus your attention, it grows, and where you withdraw you attention it dithers."* From the Ho'oponopono perspective, when you use the four sentences you focus on their relevant values and their qualities tend to grow in your life.

Every time you repeat these four sentences, you tend to be even more concentrated on them. Assagioli states that: *"continued attention tends to increase our interest and interest in turn reinforces the attention, thus creating a positive feedback loop."*

2.8. These sentences are petitionary and intercessory

The four Ho'oponopono sentences are petitionary. Each time you say them you are asking or petitioning the Divine to help you with the cleaning process of your subconscious memories. These phrases can also be defined as intercessory; every time you use these four phrases you request the intervention (or intercession) of Divine Source to delete your subconscious memories. The frequent use of these sentences helps you forge a solid alliance with the Divine.

These sentences are also enablers of change regarding your life circumstances. As seen previously, when you remove your past programs, your life circumstances naturally become more positive.

In a metaphorical way, Goddard states that:

a builder does not erect a beautiful spire or dome to a million dollar cathedral without foundation; he must first have support to hold the spire aloft. He builds walls and cross braces to hold each wall, and each wall is built slowly, stone by stone.

Likewise you must gradually remove your subconscious programs in order to get closer to your pure divine essence, the zero point.

These sentences also have elements of thanksgiving; most especially the phrase *"Thank you."* When you practice Ho'oponopono, not only are you thankful for having the opportunity to clean your negative conditioning, you are also appreciative with the Divine for helping you during the cleaning process.

2.9. These sentences are like prayers

When a man truly prays the delicate tentacles of the soul push themselves out, and explore the infinite in search of God… The human soul seeks the Soul of the universe, until it grips, and is gripped by, the living force of God. The Soul of the universe enfolds our soul, and of an instant the life of God flows into our being enriching and invigorating it.
WJ Dawson

The Ho'oponopono sentences resemble prayers. King says that: *"prayer is conversation delivered in thought form."* Over many centuries, several masters have agreed on the positive effects of frequent prayer. Like a traditional prayer, these four sentences naturally emanate pure energy which is in total harmony with Divinity.

Norman Vincent Peale says that: *"Affirmative prayers release power by which positive results are accomplished..."* He also added that: *"You are dealing with the most tremendous power in the world when you pray."* From this standpoint, every time you use any form of prayer, for instance the Ho'oponopono phrases, you are actually tapping into universal limitless resources.

Likewise, Carnegie says that: *"Prayer gives us a sense of sharing our burdens, of not being alone."* This saying is also applicable to the Ho'oponopono cleaning technique; every time you say the four sentences you are actually connected to the boundless divine source, which helps you with the cleaning process of your subconscious memories.

Research corroborated the sanative power of prayer; it is considered one of the most powerful medicines to cure any ailment. Frequent prayer improved the health conditions of ill people located in distant places, a phenomenon called remote healing.

According to scientific studies, people who pray tend to feel more connected to everything that exists and have more clarity and empathy regarding their own life circumstances. It was also proved that people who frequently pray become less tense and more tranquil.

Most religions in the word consider prayer as one of the most direct and closest ways of contact with the Divine. From the Ho'oponopono perspective, whenever we say the four sentences, we connect to God to delete our subconscious programs.

2.10. These sentences are carriers of positive energy
Your thoughts are always impregnated with energy of different

vibratory levels. Your words are the expression of your thoughts; they carry information in a non-physical fashion. Your words use your prized energy to transmit messages, either to yourself or to your environment. More specifically, your words reshape your internal world and your external environment.

When you use positive words you harness your vital energy in a very effective manner. It is one of the purest means of communication you can ever use.

Your words are crystallizations not only of your thoughts but also your emotions. Your positive words are the consequence of uplifting emotions and thoughts, which radiate positive vibrations and manifest positive circumstances into your life. Your negative words are the result of unsupportive thoughts and emotions which radiate negative vibrations and attract detrimental situations into your life. As the metaphysical saying goes, *"Like attracts alike."*

The Ho'oponopono sentences encode positive words which naturally raise your overall vibration. The intrinsic positive energy of these four sentences not only removes your subconscious programs, but also uplifts your entire vibratory rate bringing about positive circumstances in your life.

When you are committed to using the Ho'oponopono cleaning tool, you will also notice that you become your own best friend. In that state, not only will you feel true love for yourself, but also others.

2.11. These sentences imprint your subconscious mind
The subconscious part of your mind is very suggestible to repetition of sentences. This means that as you use the same sentences on a frequent basis, these phrases tend to be naturally incorporated as memories in your subconscious databank.

It is scientifically proven that, throughout repeated positive suggestions, you can imprint your subconscious mind in a very effective manner. Bristol says that:

Repetition is the fundamental rhythm of all progress, the cadence of the universe... The tap-tap of the same conscious thought causes it to be impressed upon your subconscious mind.

Atkinson also asserts that the continuous repetition of sentences is one of the most powerful ways of suggestion. He highlights that, in the beginning, the mind naturally tends to resist any new suggestions but over time it accepts them unconditionally.

He also states:

The psychological fact involved in this form of suggestion is that impressions upon brain-cells become deepened by constant repetition. It is like sinking a die into a cake of wax – it goes deeper at each pressure. The mind is very apt to accept as true anything that it finds deeply impressed upon its records... Suggestion gains force by each repetition.

So the constant use of Ho'oponopono phrases represents a powerful way of positive self-suggestion.

When you repeat the four Ho'oponopono phrases on a continuous basis, you are just using positive and continual self-talk. As a consequence, these very sentences tend to play out automatically in your mind without your conscious intervention. They become an inseparable part of your subconscious mind.

Metaphorically speaking, these powerful words work like positive seeds planted in the soil of your subconscious mind; over time they bear good fruits in your life. With the continuous repetition of these four sentences, you will have a new mental attitude, which brings about more good in your life.

2.12. These sentences have a transmuting power

Generally speaking, your positive words have an intrinsic power, which can benefit you. They can make you feel well, more at ease, loved or cheerful. Your words when negative can go against you; they can make you feel worthless, unloved or abandoned. Your frequent choice of words will either enrich or impoverish your life.

Some examples of negative words are the ones related to harsh criticism, condemnation, hatred, resentment or any other negative emotional state. These sentences are counterproductive by essence; they don't bring about anything positive into your life.

The four Ho'oponopono sentences naturally have high vibrations because they naturally enclose powerful positive energy and bring about beneficial situations into your life. In relation to this, Schwartz suggests that you should *"deposit only positive thoughts in your memory bank."*

Don Miguel Ruiz says that:

the word is the most powerful tool you have as a human; it is a tool of magic. But like a sword of two edges, your words can create the most wonderful gift, or your words can destroy everything around you.

As a consequence, the four Ho'oponopono sentences always have a positive transmuting power.

According to a story told by Robert Assagioli, there were three stonecutters who were employed for the construction of a cathedral. When the first of the three men was asked what he was doing on that site, he simply answered: *"I am just cutting stones."* Instead the second said: *"I am earning my living."* The third stonecutter answered: *"I am constructing a beautiful cathedral."* Even though these three workers were doing the same activity, their perception of it was significantly different.

This beautiful tale is totally applicable to the Ho'oponopono technique. You can analyze this cleaning tool using the varying perspectives of the three stonecutters. When you remove your subconscious memories with Ho'oponopono, this resembles the perspective of the first stonecutter who said he was *"cutting the stones."*

Nonetheless, when you practice Ho'oponopono, you are not only removing your past programming, you are also reconnecting to the Divine. In that story, this can be compared to the answer from the second stonecutter who said, *"I am earning my living."*

As you remove your subconscious programs you also create empty space in your mind, which tends to be filled with divine inspiration. This aspect can be related in the story more specifically to the third stonecutter who said he was *"building a cathedral."*

There is another point to highlight. In that effect, these phrases allow you to transform your life almost magically. When you commit to using these sentences regularly, you will go:

– *from bondage to freedom*
– *from guilt to responsibility*
– *from worthlessness to preciousness*
– *from illness to continuous health*
– *from scarcity to continual prosperity*
– *from anxiousness to eternal peace*
– *from fear to love*
– *from helplessness to limitlessness*
– *from control to allowance*
– *from resistance to surrender*
– *from darkness to light*
– *from hopelessness to hopefulness*
– *from ignorance to certainty*
– *from struggle to thriving*
– *from cluelessness to clarity*
– *from powerlessness to powerfulness*
– *from meaninglessness to meaningfulness*
– *from disharmony to harmony*
– *from impulsiveness to spontaneity*
– *from repetition to creativity*

– from blame to forgiveness
– from selfishness to selflessness
– from denial to acceptance
– from contentiousness to sociability
– from despondency to happiness
– from purposelessness to purposefulness

The frequent saying of these four Ho'oponopono sentences actually corrects what is wrong in your life, for example aggression, resentment, etc. It is important to remember that all these negative emotional states are manifestations of the memories playing in your subconscious mind.

2.13. These sentences are filled with faith
It is said that for the Ho'oponopono cleaning tool to be effective, it is important to free yourself from any doubts when you use it. You must have unfaltering faith in its positive effects. The well-known spiritual saying which goes *"faith can move mountains"* is completely applicable to the Ho'oponopono cleaning technique.

You might be asking yourself, *"What is the real meaning of faith in this context?"* It is a state of assurance or confidence that you will be assisted by the Divine forces throughout the cleaning process of your subconscious programs.

When you are truly faithful not only do you trust the support from the Divine, but you also pledge unwavering allegiance to this limitless force. With faith you can remain calm at all times, even before the uncertain future scenarios. You don't feel threatened anymore by any uncontrollable or unpredictable factors. You also know that you can harness your innermost resources, whenever you need them.

Napoleon Hill states that: *"Faith is the 'eternal elixir' which gives life, power and action to the impulse of thought."* This author also says that faith is: *"the basis for all 'miracles' and mysteries which cannot be analyzed by the rules of the science."* Moreover, he says that faith *"gives one direct communication with Infinite Intelligence."*

From a metaphysical perspective, faith is an almighty force that brings your innermost desires into manifestation. From Ho'oponopono's perspective, the most important desire you can have in your life is to get completely rid of your subconscious memories.

Faith actually makes you act as if you were a miracle-worker When you are faithful you use this cleaning tool at all times, regardless of any negative situations affecting your life. Garlow and Wall say that:

Faith-filled prayer has an impact. While some miracles are entirely unanticipated, most are prayed for, believed for and – yes – expected.

The four Ho'oponopono sentences implicitly express your innermost desire to work in cooperation with the Divine. Faith also implies determination, persistence and patience. When you are faithful, you truly know that you can endure any difficulties in your life and go through them successfully. When you are faithful you know that, by doing Ho'oponopono, you remove the causes of these very problems, which are your subconscious memories.

Authentic faith is always sterling, which means not renounceable even in moments of intense tribulation. When you are faithful you are absolutely confident that all your negative circumstances will be resolved in the right way. In that sense, Murphy states: *"Faith is your inner knowing or feeling of confidence or trust, containing within itself the mold of expression."* Faith also entails trust; and you have trust because you rely on the assistance from the Divine.

Just by saying the four sentences repeatedly, you implicitly show that you are faithful about this cleaning tool. You would never utter these sentences if you actually did not believe in their intrinsic power, at least slightly.

When you are truly faithful you can also carry on with your life in a tranquil and easy-going manner, even when positive changes don't appear immediately in your life. If you have some difficulties being faithful, your lack of faith is just a subconscious memory, and it can be removed by practicing Ho'oponopono.

Some masters say that it is not even necessary to be faithful when you repeat the four Ho'oponopono sentences because these phrases are effective at all times. You will still experience the positive effects of the use of the Ho'oponopono cleaning tool all the same.

2.14. These sentences are part of your gradual learning through life

Some sages say that your life is like a long trail which you tread along to achieve mastery. As you walk this path you learn throughout several challenging and difficult circumstances which give you the chance to use Ho'oponopono. The continuous application of this clearing tool is part of your learning process through life.

One of the most important objectives in your life is to attain the state of mastery. This applies to any area of your life, even to the practice of Ho'oponopono. Leonard says the best way to achieve mastery is that:

> you practice diligently, but you practice primarily for the sake of the practice itself. Rather than be frustrated while on the plateau, you learn to appreciate it as much as you do the upward surges.

When you start doing a new activity, for example saying the four Ho'oponopono phrases, it is possible that you don't see any tangible results of the application of this tool. This phase is what Leonard calls *"plateau"* and when most people tend be disappointed and discouraged.

Nonetheless, it was also explained that when you do Ho'oponopono on a frequent basis, your life is always transformed, even when changes don't show in an evident manner. Some changes are manifesting on a subtle level. You should show appreciation during the plateau stage and keep on using Ho'oponopono as frequently as possible.

When you begin to perceive positive shifts in your life, this phase is called the *upward way*. In this phase, you experience changes in all your life circumstances because they have built up a certain momentum. This is the natural result of the frequent use of the four sentences.

Mastery of Ho'oponopono always entails you having a big dose of patience. Most people behave impatiently because they are affected by countess challenging circumstances and conditioned by fast consumption trends. So remember that when you use the cleaning tool, your memories are always being progressively erased even when you are not aware of this.

Leonard also says that there are five key factors to master any technique, which can be applied to the use of Ho'oponopono: instruction, practice, surrender, intentionality and the edge. According to this specific framework, when you do Ho'oponopono you need instruction; this means that you have to know how to use this technique properly. You can obtain knowledge about this tool, for example by reading this book or by attending seminars on this topic, among others. In order to master Ho'oponopono you also need regular practice. This means that you must use the technique as frequently as possible.

Another factor to achieving mastery is surrender. As explained, this entails trusting this ancient tool and its positive transformative effect, and relying on the assistance of the Universe during the cleaning process.

The penultimate factor to master Ho'oponopono is intentionality. In that effect, you must have the attitude to apply the technique as frequently as possible. You can regularly repeat the four Ho'oponopono sentences without having any positive intention and you will still enjoy the positive effects of this tool. You must only have the intention to use this tool as frequently as possible; this is the only thing that matters.

The last factor for mastery is playing the edge. This is a paramount factor which entails practicing Ho'oponopono zealously, at all times. When you truly play the edge, you are truly committed and determined to use Ho'oponopono. An additional factor is awareness or alertness, which means being totally conscious of all shifts you experience throughout the cleaning process.

From a different perspective, some authors like Keller and Papasan state that mastery is a process of thinking and taking actions which encloses three main factors: being committed to always doing your best, improving your ways to do things over time and being accountable for the results. In that effect, all these three aspects can be achieved by practicing Ho'oponopono on a frequent basis.

2.15. These sentences hold no expectations

The topic of expectations, which was approached before, will be explored more thoroughly. When you apply the Ho'oponopono technique, you should abdicate any control over the outcomes of the cleaning process. You should let go of any state of anxiety regarding your future situations and let the Divine work things out in the best way. You must remember that your expectations are, in fact, subconscious programs.

Whenever you hold expectations you have specific wishes, desires or wants related to some future circumstances. Your expectations are just your personal projections about future possible scenarios in different areas of your life. Your expectations are always products of your volatile and creative imagination.

With your expectations you try to implicitly control future outcomes. This control might show up in a very subtle manner. In most cases, your expectations naturally lead to disappointment, because your expectations are far from being met in practice.

When you hold expectations you think in a structured manner; you constrain your vision of future outcomes to the specific results you think must occur. These mental projections are usually accompanied by a burning desire for things to unfold in specific ways.

As explained, whenever you hold expectations you prevent the Divine from assisting you effectively. From the Divine's perspective there are infinite ways in which your future circumstances can unfold, as compared to the limited ways you think about when you hold on to your expectations.

For this reason, it is utterly important that you let go of any expectations. When you do so, you are allowing things to occur in their best way possible.

If you are like most people, you have expectations regarding different areas of your life; some of them might be totally unnoticed. For example, you must pay attention to situations in which you say things like:

– *I expect things to be solved my way*
– *I expect my desires to be fulfilled this way*
– *I expect others to...*
– *I expect to receive...*

You can also be using sentences like:

– *I hope things work out in this way*
– *My desire is that things unfold in this direction*
– *My wish for this is...*

In all these examples you are holding expectations about future outcomes. Whenever you hold expectations you are stuck to your subconscious memories, instead of removing them.

As a consequence, you should never have expectations about the application of the Ho'oponopono tool. You should never try to deduce which subconscious memories must be deleted. You should not waste your time guessing how your life circumstances might change as a result of the cleaning process either. The Divine takes charge of the specific memories to be erased.

Besides, you should never ask the Divine how you want your life circumstances to be in the future. Many sages say that Divinity is not your personal concierge. Instead, let Divinity work out your life circumstances in the most appropriate way for you, which might significantly differ from your personal choices or preferences.

When you practice Ho'oponopono you should have an attitude of allowance. You should always surrender and release any control over the cleaning process and unconditionally trust the intervention from the Divine. Every time you say the four Ho'oponopono sentences you are implicitly surrendering to the unbounded power of the Divine. When you welcome Divine's intercession you are more receptive to divine love energy. When you eliminate all your expectations, you are also likely to experience a state of flow, in which things tend to unfold effortlessly.

2.16. These sentences are related to non-locality

The Ho'oponopono technique is related to the principle of non-locality. Ho'oponopono is a non-local tool because its transformative effects extend beyond time and space. For instance, the regular use of Ho'oponopono not only brings about shifts in your own life situations, but also affects other people that are related to you, even when they are not currently in the same place with you.

Besides, the changes produced by the regular use of

Ho'oponopono are lingering; they affect your future circumstances. This tool helps you transform situations related to your past, present and future.

Dossey says that the principle of non-locality: *"implies infinitude in space and time"* and it has: *"shared qualities with the Divine – 'the Divine within' – since infinitude, omnipresence and eternality are qualities that we have attributed also to the Absolute."* As seen before, as you remove your subconscious memories, not only will your life be transformed but also the lives of other people with whom you share subconscious memories.

3. Practical tips to use Ho'oponopono

In this hectic-paced, consumption-oriented and quick-fixing society people tend to become impatient and want to see results as soon as possible. If you are like most people, when you do Ho'oponopono you might want to see extraordinary results in your life very soon or immediately.

You have to understand that you have countless subconscious memories to delete, thus the cleaning process will always be gradual. Besides, any transformation in your life will occur in accordance with Divinity's timing, which might differ from yours.

As a consequence, you must never abandon this technique, even when you have not perceived any results yet; the cleaning process is always working, although on a very subtle level. If you are hesitant or fearful, you can also clean these negative states because they are subconscious memories which can be deleted.

It is said that these four Ho'oponopono sentences should be stated in an authoritative manner. You should never say these words in a begging, imploring or guilty manner. Instead, you must feel deserving to remove your subconscious memories.

From a different perspective, it is said that when you do Ho'oponopono you don't need to use any authoritative tone in these phrases. You can repeat the sentences mechanically and your memories will be removed all the same.

Additionally, you can find below some other recommendations to harness the benefits of this powerful technique more effectively:

– *Practice Ho'oponopono on a frequent basis:* You should repeat these sentences ceaselessly, even when you are not prompted by any negative situation to clean. This does not signify that you must consider Ho'oponopono as a full-time job; use the four cleaning sentences as regularly as possible. Remember that you have an infinite amount of subconscious memories to delete.

– *Create positive cleaning habits:* There are several scientific studies which state that a habit can be formed over 66 days on average by repeating the same activity. As you use these sentences on a frequent basis, you will soon make the use of the tool a positive habit in your life. As you use these sentences steadily they become an integral part of you.

– *Use the four cleaning sentences as you like:* In that effect, you can say these sentences aloud as if you were chanting a mantra; you can also silently say them in your mind. Some people suggest that you can also chant the sentences or whisper them. You can also synchronize the uttering of these sentences with your walking or breathing in order to make the repetition of the phrases effortless and automatic. These four sentences can be said in any language.

– *These sentences always delete the information in your subconscious mind:* It does not matter how you say these four sentences because they will always remove your subconscious programs. Mabel Katz says that the regular use of the four cleaning sentences resembles the "delete key" in your computer. When you use the delete key in your PC you just press it to erase information which appears on the monitor. You don't have to say these four cleaning sentences (or press the delete key) in a passionate or faithful manner for the subconscious memories (or information in your computer monitor) to be effectively erased.

– *Use active voice in the sentences:* You have to notice that these four sentences are worded in an active voice (for example, *"I love you"* and *"Please forgive me"*). These phrases should not be uttered using a passive voice, for example, *"I am loved"* or *"I am being forgiven."* Active voice wording is the best way to demonstrate that you actually accept your full responsibility for everything in your life; you are the cause and not the effect of what happens in your life.

– *Dwell on the essence of these four sentences:* You should reflect on the values expressed in these four cleaning sentences, which are repentance, forgiveness, love and gratefulness. You can also ask yourself: *"What is going on in me in relation to these four values?"* and wait for insights. Then say the four Ho'oponopono sentences many times.

– *Use the sentences in present tense:* The four Ho'oponopono sentences must be used in the present tense (for example, *"I love you"*). You should never use any other tenses such as past tense (for example, *"I loved you"*) or future tense (*"I will love you"*). Every time you say these sentences you must focus on the now, which is the only moment that exists. It is the only moment of power in which you can effectively delete your subconscious programs.

– *Trust this tool:* You must always be confident in this tool. You must remember that whenever you use this cleaning technique you are being assisted by the Divine. When you trust this technique it is easier to use it in a disciplined manner. True trust implies that you surrender to the power of Divinity, which accompanies you during the entire cleaning process.

– *Be unstructured and unworried:* It is important not to be so careful about the details of the process. You should never try to carry out the steps of the cleaning process in a perfect manner; just use the sentences regularly. Furthermore, it is not necessary to use the four sentences; you can use only one (for example, *"I love you"*) or a few of them. You don't even have to follow any sequence for these phrases either.

– *Free yourself from expectations:* You must never expect this technique to solve your problems in specific ways. With expectations you are not being flexible and open-minded but are offering resistance because you want things to only unfold your way. This attitude hinders the whole cleaning process. Be open for things in your life to unfold in different ways; let go of any expectation and let God act.

– *Be compassionate with your difficulties:* When you face difficult situations in your life, avoid blaming or judging anybody, even yourself. Remember that all the difficulties arise in your life so that you can clean your subconscious memories originating them.

– *Focus your attention inwardly:* When you say the four Ho'oponopono cleaning sentences your attention must always be focused internally. These sentences must be said to yourself. You do not need to concentrate on your particular life situations. You should avoid being distracted, even though this is not crucial. In relation to this, Dossey suggests you should say the Ho'oponopono sentences in a *"meditative, prayerful state of awareness."* Nonetheless some masters suggest that you don't need to be fully focused when you use the cleaning sentences; your subconscious memories will be removed all the same.

– *Focus also on specific life situations:* You can also say these four phrases while you think about troublesome conditions you want to change. In this case, you envision the problem you want to solve and then say the sentences repeatedly. However, as was previously mentioned you can repeat these four sentences in an automatic manner, and your subconscious memories will be removed all the same.

– *Be patient and calm:* You must repeat these sentences in an unhurried rhythm and at a calm pace. In that effect, you must never rush when you say these sentences. Many people say you can say the sentences in any rhythm, either fast or slow. When you say these sentences more quickly you do not hasten the cleaning process. Some people prefer to be as calm as possible when using this technique, because anxiety is a negative state.

– *Be relaxed:* Some suggest that you should have a relaxed attitude as you regularly use this tool. With a relaxed attitude you will notice that changes manifest in your life almost effortlessly. You must be relaxed not only physically, but mentally and emotionally. Any states of tension, obsession or hesitation are subconscious memories which must be removed.

– *Be committed:* When you are truly involved in the cleaning process you can access divine assistance without any effort. You will also notice that you become more inspired. In other words, the continuous use of these sentences will make you more prone to act in accordance with divine guidance. This means that you must apply this cleaning tool frequently and in any place.

– *Write a contract:* In order to improve the level of commitment to the use of this technique you can sign a simple written contract with yourself. Its text can be this way: *"I... (include your complete name) am absolutely committed to doing Ho'oponopono as frequently as possible in order to remove my subconscious programming and, in turn, improve my life in all dimensions..."* Sign the contract and keep it a safe place, out of the sight of others. When you have some doubts about the cleaning process reread the contract and then say the four sentences repeatedly.

– *Keep a journal:* You can have detailed records of the regular use of this technique. You can write the four Ho'oponopono sentences and then reread them. You can also take note of your introspective insights regarding your problems and then say the four cleaning sentences repeatedly. Take note of the progress noticed in different areas of your life as a result of using this cleaning tool. Take note of the exercises in this book that you practiced and the insights you obtained. You can also take note of different times and places that you use this tool. You must take this journal wherever you go and keep it updated.

– *Apply this tool to any problematic issue:* You can apply the Ho'oponopono technique to any kind of problem, for example relationship difficulties, work problems, health challenges, career obstacles and financial shortages, among others. In relation to this, DeNoyelles suggests that, every time you face up to a difficulty in your life, you should say: *"Whatever it is that's causing me to feel... (fill in the blank), I Love You. Thank You. Please Come Home to Love."* You can also say the four Ho'oponopono sentences many times.

Chapter 8

I am Sorry

1. Meaning of repentance

The first of the four Ho'oponopono sentences is *"I am sorry."* You can also use other versions such as *"I apologize for all mistakes"* or *"I am sorry for all my wrongs."* You can even use an extended sentence such as *"I am sorry for manifesting these situations in my life. I take total responsibility for all of them."* Any of the sentences carries the same meaningful message; you are expressing repentance for your wrongdoings. With the frequent use of any of these sentences you can effectively trash out all the memories you hold in your subconscious mind.

When you state: *"I am sorry"* you are saying these words to yourself, not to others; your apologies always start and finish in you. Some masters say that you are also addressing these words to the Divine. Even when you are not completely sure of the actual recipient of these words, this fact will not reduce the effectiveness of Ho'oponopono in the least.

When you say the phrase *"I am sorry"* repeatedly some of its possible meanings are:

– You heartily recognize your participation in all the problems affecting you; they are a consequence of your thoughts, emotions, actions and even inactions. You also know that your thinking, emoting, and acting are always originated in your subconscious memories. As a consequence, you can withdraw your mistakes from a place of secrecy, denial and guilt, and put them in the splendorous transmuting light of repentance.

– You not only truly confess that you were wrong in the past, but you also make the resolution to do things in the right way from now onwards. You are willing to make some significant amends in your life by doing the cleaning process on a frequent basis. You know that it is never too late to turn things around.

– You realize that your own attitude can experience an about-face change. You understand that the cleaning process of your memories is the only valuable way of restitution you can use for all your past wrongdoings.

– You admit that you are not comfortable with your current troublesome situations any longer. You are no longer at ease with the subconscious memories originating these problems either. For this reason, you want to remove all memories from your subconscious in order to manifest positive situations in your life.

– You apologize for having accumulated countless subconscious memories, which completely clogged your subconscious mind. You are also repentant for not having cared for your subconscious mind for a long time, leaving it to its own devices. You also realize that because of this your life ended up being totally controlled by umpteen limiting programs. You also know that it is never too late to truly care for your subconscious mind by removing all these memories.

– You truly release any form of condemnation (such as guilt, blame or harsh criticism) regarding your past mistakes. You also drop any resentment or regret (toward yourself or others) related to your past experiences.

– You dwell in your natural boundless mercifulness and compassion; you open your heart fully and cast all its defenses away. You recognize yourself as defenseless before these subconscious memories controlling your life, and request help from the Divine to remove them.

– You admit that you are not perfect, but you understand that you are pure in essence. You also recognize you have committed mistakes in the past and take responsibility for all of them by removing your subconscious programs.

– You can be totally transparent and humble; you admit the existence of memories in your subconscious mind which prevent you from performing your activities in a free and inspiring manner. You don't want to be stuck in this limiting situation; you are determined to do the cleaning process on a frequent basis.

– You realize that your subconscious tapes hinder the full expression of your distinct essential being, which is divine and boundless. Furthermore you realize your past programming hinders your path to evolution; these subconscious memories don't allow you to grow in the way you truly deserve.

– You are truly sorry for the suffering you created in your life because of being controlled by your subconscious programs. You are willing to rid yourself of all memories tormenting you. You are prepared to transmute this lingering grievance with the alchemic divine energy of forgiveness.

– You realize that you are not in a state of equilibrium or balance, but very distant from it. You admit that you have been taken over by subconscious memories, which temporarily sever your link with your divine core. You also want to restore the divine essence in you by progressively peeling away layers of memories accumulated in your subconscious.

– You understand that your negative circumstances cannot be changed permanently using an outside-in approach; you cannot fix your problems by dealing with them directly because you are not addressing their causes. You realize that the only way to transmute any negative situation in your life is with an inside-out perspective, which means removing their origin, which is always your subconscious programs, which is an inside-out perspective.

– You understand that there is an important commonality

among you and other human beings; you are all continually being taking over by copious subconscious conditioning. You also understand that by nature you are, as anybody else, divine and pure. The only thing that you have to do to reconnect to your essence is to remove all these subconscious memories.

– You recognize that in the past you have avoided your responsibility for everything around you in different ways: blaming, escaping, denying, regretting, etc. For this reason, you truly excuse yourself for having held your subconscious programs, which have created all your negative life circumstances.

2. Implications of your apologies

2.1. Apologizing is acknowledging your full responsibility

"I am sorry" is actually a confessionary statement; you are actually apologizing for your wrongdoings. From Ho'oponopono's perspective, your repentance also includes the mistakes of other people, with whom you have shared memories. With this sentence you also request the Divine to help you with the cleaning process of your subconscious mind.

The sentence *"I am sorry"* also entails self-acceptance. With this phrase you unconditionally accept your participation in everything that is occurring in your life. You are fully repentant for everything around you because you know that all the circumstances in your awareness are created by your subconscious programming. You meekly admit that you have missed the mark because you have been taken over by your subconscious programs.

When you say *"I am sorry"* you take one step further; you are willing to make some amends in relation to your troublesome situations by removing all your subconscious programs, which originated them.

As you repeat the sentence *"I am sorry"* on a continuous basis you adopt a different perspective on your life situations; you don't have to blame others (or even yourself) for what is going on in your life. You truly understand that all your life situations are just a natural consequence of subconscious memories.

When you say the sentence *"I am sorry"* you don't have to expose the reasons why you are sorry. The only thing that you have to do is to say *"I am sorry"* to remove your subconscious memories.

2.2. Apologizing is always meaningful and empowering

Most people tend to apologize in a very superficial way. As a consequence, the regular use of sentences like *"I am sorry"*, *"Sorry"* or *"Excuse me"* makes these meaningful words lose their true deep sense. If you are like the rest of the people, you might tend to use the valuable sentence *"I am sorry"* or any other similar one for whatever reason, even trivial motives. The frequent use of this sentence for paltry reasons denaturalizes the prized meaning of the words *"I am sorry."*

Many people also think that apologizing is a demonstration of weakness. According to this perspective, whenever you say *"I am sorry"* you become more fragile and vulnerable. You should avoid being deceived by this baseless idea.

From a spiritual viewpoint, apologizing is an evident signal of your innermost strength. When you repeat the words *"I am sorry"* you show that you truly repent for all mistakes in your life. You admit that all wrongdoings are just consequences of the memories playing in your subconscious mind. With this apologetic attitude you can effectively delete these memories. Apologizing is always an empowering tool which frees you from the bondage of your past programming.

Every time you repeat the words *"I am sorry"* you are handling things in a different way; you are not shunning the problems affecting you. With the frequent use of the words *"I am sorry"* you understand that all your difficulties, mistakes and failures are a necessary part of your learning process through life. These negative situations also indicate that you have subconscious memories to remove.

The sentence *"I am sorry"* is also purgative, expiatory and cathartic. Whenever you say *"I am sorry"* you are becoming liberated from the sorrow related to your past misdeeds or mistakes. You can experience a state of catharsis, which allows you to release any negative emotion trapped in you to restore your natural state of equilibrium. With these words, you can also achieve a state of mental clarity and peacefulness. Some masters say that this phrase has a therapeutic effect on your overall health.

When you say this sentence on a frequent basis, you break the chains that have kept you tied to the past. The frequent use of the words *"I am sorry"* sets you truly free, which is your natural state of being.

From a different perspective, some coaches suggest that there is no such thing as *"committing mistakes."* According to this viewpoint, every time you act wrongly you obtain precious feedback. You can use the feedback from your past experiences, even the negative ones, in order to improve your performance in the future.

Likewise, from Ho'oponopono's perspective, the difficult situations affecting your life always provide you with prized feedback. All negative circumstances in your life only indicate that you have subconscious memories which must be deleted. As a result of this feedback you can regularly practice Ho'oponopono. This feedback allows you to improve your life quality.

For this reason, your repentance during the Ho'oponopono cleaning process represents an about-turn change in your attitude toward life. John Locke says that:

> *Repentance is a hearty sorrow for our past misdeeds, and a sincere resolution and endeavor, to the utmost of our power to conform our action to the law of God.*

2.3. Apologizing is removing unknown memories

Who after his transgression doth repent, is half, or altogether, innocent.
Robert Herrick

When you apologize during the Ho'oponopono cleaning process you don't even have to know the specific reasons of each of your wrongdoings. The only thing that you truly know is that behind each of your negative circumstances there are subconscious memories which created them. You also must understand that the only way to remove these very memories is by doing Ho'oponopono.

Every time you repeat the words *"I am sorry"* you naturally atone for all past mistakes and also show your commitment to the cleaning process of your subconscious programs. Heartfelt apologizing is one of the most appropriate ways to recognize your total responsibility in your life. From Ho'oponopono's perspective, you don't need to repeat *"I am sorry"* in a heartfelt manner; the mechanical repetition of this sentence has the same alchemic effect over your subconscious programs.

Sometimes it might be difficult to discover your own faults. If this is your case, you should say the words *"I am sorry"* regularly all the same; you have countless subconscious memories to delete. You don't even have to know what subconscious programs must be removed. The frequent use of the words *"I am sorry"* rescues you from these merciless captors liberating you for good.

Using an analogy, when you repeat *"I am sorry"* you realize that in the past you signed a secretive binding contract with your subconscious programs, which keeps you in bondage. As you regularly say *"I am sorry"* you cancel this contract in a unilateral way.

With the frequent use of the Ho'oponopono technique you

also sign a more productive covenant with Divinity to remove your subconscious programs. By regularly saying *"I am sorry"* you realize that the Divine is your most trustworthy partner.

2.4. Apologizing is always loving regard

Confession is a powerful tool for reconciliation.
– Rick Warren

From a particular perspective, wrongly called spiritual, repentance has a negative meaning: it implies suffering and contrition. According to this viewpoint, when you are repentant you must necessarily experience sorrow and regret. Sometimes repentance can even entail being punished for all your wrongdoings; you might also experience a state of worthlessness for having committed mistakes.

If you are like most people, you might tend to criticize yourself in many different ways even when you apologize for your mistakes. You might use sentences like *"I should have done…"* or *"I feel bad because I have not…"* or any other one. However, when you use the words *"I am sorry"* during the cleaning process you should avoid feeling guilty, regretful or critical with yourself.

Every time you judge anything in your life you do not take full responsibility. All forms of condemnation imply negative evaluations which do not help you correct your mistakes and do not contribute to your personal growth.

From the Ho'oponopono perspective the meaning of repentance is significantly different. Every time you use the words *"I am sorry"* not only do you truly apologize for your own mistakes, but you also admit your responsibility for all your life situations. Thus apologizing entails acknowledging that all your circumstances are created by your subconscious memories. You also show that you are willing to effectively delete them.

For this reason, when you are truly apologetic you can experience unconditional love regard toward yourself, not criticism and condemnation. The term *love regard* is frequently used by humanist psychologists.

According to this psychological perspective, when you have unconditional love regard toward yourself, you are accepting yourself as you truly are, which allows you to take full responsibility for your life. You can acknowledge your strong and weak points, with no reservation. You evolve as an individual because you access your most precious inner resources and everything seems possible.

3. Practical tips

– As seen before, when you practice Ho'oponopono you use the sentence *"I am sorry."* Or other phrases like *"I apologize for all mistakes"* or *"I am sorry for all my wrongs."* Or *"I am sorry for manifesting these negative situations in my life and thus I take total responsibility for them."* Try to repeat any of these sentences on a frequent basis. You can also use these sentences in combination with the other Ho'oponopono sentences.

– When you practice Ho'oponopono you should always say the words *"I am sorry"* to yourself, and not to others. You should never say sentences like *"I am sorry… (the person's name you want to apologize to)"* during the cleaning process. Your apologies must always start and finish with you. It is also said that you can also address the words *"I am sorry"* to the Divine.

– Be wary of sentences like *"I should have done…"* or *"I feel bad because I have to…"* among others. You might feel guilt for your past experiences or criticize yourself or others for them. If you use these types of sentences, you should utter the words *"I am sorry"* repeatedly. Alternatively you can say the four Ho'oponopono sentences repeatedly.

– Be aware of sentences like *"I wish you could have done…"*, *"I think you should have done…"* or *"I wish you were more…"* With these sentences you are condemning others, albeit subtly. You must take note of occasions on which you use this type of sentence and repeat the four Ho'oponopono sentences many times. Alternatively, you can just say the words *"I am sorry"* repeatedly.

– There is a very interesting exercise related to blame; you must read the news in the newspaper, or pay attention to a news program on television or on radio. Take note of the number of times people blame one another or themselves. Remember that you have shared subconscious memories with these people. Reread these notes and ask yourself: *"What is going on in me that I am experiencing these people casting blame?"* Wait for some insights and say the four Ho'oponopono sentences repeatedly.

– As an exercise, you can also analyze the conversations you have with other people on a daily basis. You must observe the times you are judgmental with others and vice versa. After the conversations, you must take note of the ways that you blame or condemn others and vice versa. You must ask yourself: *"What is going on in me that I am experiencing blame and condemnation?"* Wait for insights and say the four Ho'oponopono sentences many times. Alternatively you can just say *"I am sorry"* repeatedly.

– There is another exercise you can do on your own. This exercise will help you recognize any form of condemnation you might regularly use. At the end of the day take note of the times during that day that you were judgmental with yourself or others. To that effect, you should take note of the occasions you judged or cast guilt on others or yourself. Then ask yourself: *"What is going on in me that I am experiencing this?"* Wait for insights and say the four Ho'oponopono sentences or the words *"I am sorry"* many times.

– There is another simple exercise; whenever you hold a conversation with any person you must observe when you (or they) apologize in a formal or mechanical way. This exercise helps you observe how people from all walks of life apologize without even meaning this. Take note of these apologies; ask yourself: *"What is going on in me that I am experiencing this?"* Wait for insights and say the four Ho'oponopono sentences in a repeated fashion. You can also use the words *"I am sorry"* separately.

– There is another exercise you can do; take note of ten mistakes you made in your life, which can be small or big ones. Read the list many times and ask yourself questions like: *"What is the real meaning of these wrongdoings?"* or *"What is the most important learning that I obtained from each of these mistakes?"* You can also ask yourself: *"What is going on in me in relation to these mistakes?"* Wait for insights and also take note of them; say the four Ho'oponopono sentences many times.

– There is a different way to do the previous exercise. Take note of ten big mistakes committed by other people around you. These wrongdoings can be recent or from a long time ago. Then ask yourself the question: *"What is going on in me in relation to these mistakes?"* Wait for insights and say the four Ho'oponopono sentences many times.

– There is another interesting exercise you can do in your spare time. Take note of ten significant world maladies: wars, unemployment, exploitation, environmental pollution, human trafficking, among others. Select the events that are more poignant to you. They can be recent or they could have occurred a long time ago. Read your notes and ask yourself: *"What is going on in me in relation to these maladies?"* Wait for insights and say the four Ho'oponopono sentences many times.

Chapter 9

Please Forgive Me

The remembering of injuries is spiritual darkness; the fostering of resentment is spiritual suicide... The unforgiving and resentful spirit is a source of great suffering and sorrow... every act of forgiveness brings the doer five kinds of blessedness – the blessedness of love; the blessedness of increased communion and fellowship; the blessedness of a calm and peaceful mind; the blessedness of passion stilled and pride overcome; and the blessedness and kindness of good-will bestowed by others.
– James Allen

1. Meanings of forgiveness

Forgiveness means "giving for" – giving positive, instead of negative, actions. It means giving love, understanding and acceptance where there has been hate, resentment and disharmony. It means changing the attitude of disappointment by cancelling expectations and allowing an attitude of unconditional love.
– Edith Stauffer

One of the four Ho'oponopono sentences is *"Please forgive me."* When you use this sentence you show you are truly sorry for holding memories in your subconscious mind. With this sentence, you are actually performing the cleaning process. The fundamental value contained in this sentence, forgiveness, cannot be easily explained with words.

When you say *"Please forgive me"* during the cleaning process you pardon yourself for all past wrong thoughts, emotions or actions. The sentence *"Please forgive me"* is closely related to the cleaning phrase *"I am sorry"* explained in the previous chapter.

From the Ho'oponopono perspective, forgiveness is not about forgiving other people, but yourself. From this viewpoint, everything going on around you starts with yourself; you (your subconscious programs) are the main creator of every single thing that occurs in your life.

By using the words *"Please forgive me"* you are forgiven unconditionally and automatically, without doing anything else. When you ask for forgiveness you realize that you hold countless subconscious memories that have caused damage to yourself or others. You do not have to concentrate on people that you offended or who have hurt you. You must only center on yourself; you can also be centered on Divinity.

You can only forgive yourself, because all your life circumstances, even the situations in which other people seem to have hurt you, are creations of your own subconscious memories. As previously explained, these programs are the only cause of everything that happens to you in your life. When you forgive yourself, you are assuming one hundred percent responsibility for each of the circumstances affecting you.

When you use the cleaning sentence *"Please forgive me"* you also recognize that, in the past, you did not do anything to remove these programs. With the frequent use of the sentence *"Please forgive me"* you also show that you are committed to deleting these subconscious memories.

2. Other meanings of forgiveness

You can find below some meanings of the phrase *"Please forgive me"* from the Ho'oponopono perspective. Whenever you say *"Please forgive me"*...

   ... you are aware that you have been controlled by your subconscious programs
   ... you are willing to undo all your mistakes and wrongdoings
   ... you delete your subconscious programs in order to make things right

... you are not in denial any longer regarding your life circumstances

... you accept you have been mistaken and embrace your faults to let them go

... you acknowledge that you are totally responsible for everything around you

... you dispel the illusory reality created by your subconscious memories

... you understand that when you remove your programs your life is transformed

... you release any state of tension and restlessness

... you cast away any state of hatred and resentment

... you eradicate any form of blame, grudge or victimhood

... you escape the prison of your subconscious memories

... you can see everything in your life more clearly

... you are open to loving yourself unconditionally

... you understand that you are your best companion

... you perceive your unlimited pureness and innocence

... you are willing to restore your core state of wholeness

... you understand that your essence is memory-free

... you are committed to removing fear from your life

... you are open to being pervaded by pure love

... you know that you are the creator of everything that exists around you

... you eliminate any emotional baggage limiting your boundless potential

... you access love energy which gracefully dissolves any past error

... you transmute your grievance into love

... you are more compassionate with yourself

... you love yourself above all, which allows you to love others

... you accept yourself with no reservations

... you care for yourself unconditionally

... you don't hold yourself down anymore

... you abandon an attitude of perfectionism

... you acknowledge your mistakes in order to amend them

... you destroy all barriers hindering your access to love

... you open your heart fully without being afraid of this

... you learn lessons from your mistakes without feeling guilt-tripped

... you realize that your wrongdoings are indicators of memories to delete

... you befriend yourself and strengthen this tie over time

... you understand that you always work in partnership with Divinity

... you don't deny your current reality by pretending that it is all right

... you embrace your soul fully and caress it affectionately

... you truly repent for having abandoned your subconscious

... you release the burden of the past to heal all your sorrow and pain

... you realize that any type of condemnation is plain useless

... you purify your heart with the light of love

... you realize that when you forgive yourself, you are doing the right thing

... you don't feel guilty or despondent because of your wrongdoings

... you let go of any feeling of being wrong or wronged

... you dwell in your innermost truth, your pure essence

... you look for your own redemption because you deserve it

... you understand that negative emotions are just subconscious memories

... you consider all problems as opportunities to forgive yourself

... you transform darkness into light

... you realize that your connection with the Divine is not obscured any longer

... you are not bound to negativity related to your past errors

... you know that divine love transmutes every aspect of your life

... you understand that your soul can be at peace and in harmony

... you know that the Divine is your natural home

... you realize that you are not broken

... you comprehend that you are essentially good and pure

... you understand that your memories are in the way of your core essence

... you don't punish yourself for your mistakes anymore

... you reconcile with yourself wholeheartedly

... you realize that you are the most amazing manifestation of pure love

... you don't fight with yourself any longer

... you adopt a godlike attitude toward yourself

... you feel that your life is more meaningful and purposeful

... you are not destructive with yourself any longer

... you are determined to improve the quality of your life

... you reestablish your connection with the Divine

... you understand that Divinity assists you with the cleaning process

3. Other aspects of forgiveness

The most important religions in the world are based on the unarguable principle of forgiveness. Likewise, most people acknowledge that forgiveness represents a good value to abide by. Even though forgiveness appears to be a very sensible thing, people still have difficulties with forgiving themselves and others.

Forgiveness is related to an attitude of generosity, compassion and empathy. In relation to this, Ray says that: *"Forgiveness means being in favor of... the process of giving. Giving compassion. Giving understanding... When we forgive ourselves, we naturally forgive all the others."*

Many masters state that when you say *"Please forgive me"* you must always be sincere and authentic. Forgiveness should never be conditional or compromised. For this reason, you never should use expressions like *"Please, forgive me if..."*, *"Please, forgive me even though..."*, *"Please, forgive me but..."* or *"Please, forgive me except for..."* In all these cases forgiveness is subject to specific conditions; if you do not meet these requirements you are not forgiven. From the Ho'oponopono perspective, forgiveness is always unconditional, without prerequisites.

You should adopt a general forgiving attitude in your life, and not only applicable to specific situations. Your request for forgiveness should never be a one-off activity but a continuous process. When you have a steady attitude regarding forgiveness, your pain is naturally released.

From the Ho'oponopono perspective, you can also repeat the sentences *"Please forgive me"* in a mechanical and cold manner. Sincerity and heartiness are not relevant prerequisites for the effectiveness of this cleaning tool.

You can find below some examples of these sentences to use during the cleaning process. This list of examples is indicative; you can use other phrases of your preference.

– Please forgive me for what is going on in me that I have manifested this
– Please forgive me for the memories playing out in my subconscious
– Please forgive me for what is going on in me
– Please forgive me for manifesting this situation through my subconscious memories

You must keep the sentences as simple as possible. With some sentences you ask for forgiveness in general (such as *"Please forgive me"*). In other cases you can be more specific regarding forgiveness (*"Please forgive me for manifesting this situation..."*).

All these sentences start with the word *"Please"* because you ask for forgiveness in a gentle and kind manner. You are displaying that you are truly repentant for your mistakes and you want to be forgiven.

When you use general expressions such as *"Please forgive me"* your request for forgiveness is complete and not partial. You are referring to all your life circumstances and not only to specific situations.

Forgiveness is the most effective remedy to cure all your emotional wounds. Furthermore, when you ask for forgiveness on a continual basis, you can easily release all the negative energy stored in your body-mind system. You also tend to experience a state of joy, peace and love in an effortless manner. Petroff says that: *"Forgiving brings strength and buoyancy because it includes giving up that which weighs us down."* Forgiveness also makes you feel more empowered.

However, if you are not willing to forgive yourself you will continue being stuck in any negative situation affecting you. A negative attitude toward forgiveness is always debilitating. When you have an attitude of non-forgiveness you cannot evolve as a person.

4. Forgiveness implies making things right

When you ask for forgiveness, you are implicitly showing a willingness to reform yourself. You want to return to your essential state of purity. In this state of cleanliness, which is called zero point, you are totally free from your subconscious programs. When you repeatedly say *"Please forgive me"* as a cleaning tool, you are requesting the Divine to help you remove all the information stored in your subconscious mind.

You always have an easy way to know if you need to forgive yourself. When you criticize yourself or others, this is an indicator that you have to ask for forgiveness. Additionally, whenever you get moody or upset before problems you encounter in your life, this is another sign that you should ask for forgiveness.

When you have a forgiving attitude you avoid any form of self-reproach or remorse for your past actions, thoughts or emotions. All your past mistakes were created by your subconscious memories, so there is no need to feel sorrowful or guilty about this.

It is possible that you cannot help feeling guilty or resentful in relation to your past events. In this case, you must realize that these negative emotional states are just subconscious memories and can be removed with Ho'oponopono. You do not have to know which memories you have to delete; the Divine knows that.

It is not the same to say *"Excuse me"* as compared with *"Forgive me."* Whenever you use the first sentence (*"Excuse me"*) you wish that things had unfolded differently as you desire to never commit the same mistake again.

Whenever you use the words *"Excuse me"* their implicit meaning is *"I didn't do that on purpose"* or *"I didn't realize what I was doing."* You can even say any of these two sentences after saying *"Excuse me."*

The justification of your mistakes related to these words does not allow you to accept your full responsibility for your actions. Sometimes when you say *"Excuse me"* you might even feel embarrassed and truly want your mistakes to be forgotten as soon as possible.

Instead, when you say *"Forgive me"* there is no room for excuses; you accept the truth of what it is; you don't try to justify or hide anything. You know that all your circumstances are created by your subconscious memories. You do not downsize, soften or trivialize your wrongdoings because you take full responsibility for them.

You can never ask to be forgiven for something that you consider is not your responsibility. For this reason, a prerequisite for your request for forgiveness is to take full responsibility for everything going on around you.

When you ask for forgiveness (by saying *"Please forgive me"*), you don't want the mistake to be forgotten, as it is in the case of the words *"Excuse me."* Moreover when you say *"Please forgive me"* you fully acknowledge your mistakes; you do not pretend your wrongdoings are to be left behind soon, which tends to happen whenever you say *"Excuse me."*

Your request for forgiveness has significant healing effects, both for your body and mind. Dr. Sha says that every time you are hurt (either by your own actions or by others') your soul, mind and body are affected by negative patterns, which impacts on your energy levels, both on cellular and non-cellular levels, rendering your overall energy imbalanced.

This state of energetic disequilibrium causes all your illnesses. Whenever you forgive yourself you connect to the Divine, whose love light brushes away all negative patterns in you. Likewise, Catherine Ponder states that whenever you experience a health problem of any kind that there is an issue you have not forgiven. She states, *"You must forgive if you want to feel permanently healed."* From a broader viewpoint, whenever you face any difficulty in your life, you must realize that you have something to forgive.

5. Recommendations for forgiveness

5.1. Never judge yourself

Seek not abroad
turn back into thyself
for in the inner man dwells the truth.
– Saint Augustine (400 AD), The City of God

As explained when you use the sentence *"Forgive me"* you address these words to yourself, not to other people. As you regularly request forgiveness, you become more tolerant and understanding with yourself and others. These words will also make you experience a profound state of relief, as if something heavy dropped from your body and mind.

As you ask for forgiveness you also realize that you are naturally fallible. You can also discover that are intrinsically valuable, beyond any of your mistakes. Besides, you are prone to realize that you are a divine being, even with all your mistakes.

For this reason, you should never beat yourself up for your past mistakes, wrongdoings, and shortcomings. When you are hard with yourself this will not make you feel better but temporarily ignorant of your divine essence.

The meaning of the words *"Please forgive me"* implies reparation or restitution. In that sense, the most effective way you can amend your mistakes is doing Ho'oponopono on a frequent basis.

Every time you say the words *"Please forgive me"* you are connected to your most compassionate essence; you can have an understanding attitude toward all your past experiences, even your mistakes and wrongdoings.

When you say the words *"Please forgive me"* you are also being generous, because you give yourself the chance to be forgiven for all your mistakes. Murphy says that: *"To forgive something is to give something for. Give love, peace, wisdom and all the blessings of life to the other, until there is no sting left in your mind."* In that effect, when you regularly use the words *"Please forgive me"* you give yourself true love and compassion.

If you are like most people, you are your most relentless critic; this type of attitude is not constructive at all. Becker states that: *"We have been trained in the art of judging"* but *"Judgement separates us from life."*

Most people tend to make snide remarks about themselves because they have an idea of perfection they want to achieve. This attitude is completely unproductive because when you judge yourself you cannot allow true forgiveness to set in your life. This belligerent attitude only makes you more helpless and vulnerable; you are less likely to solve your problems. Your problems look even more insurmountable.

With all negative emotional states such as blame, holding grudges or resentment not only do you co-opt your vital energy, but you also withhold the love you truly deserve by birthright.

When you are critical with yourself, this attitude keeps your problems unchanged and you tend to manifest more negative circumstances in your life.

In relation to this, Murphy wisely states that: *"Life is not holding grudges against you, and it is always forgiving you."* He also says that:

> *Life, or God, holds no grudge against you. Life never condemns you. Life heals a severe cut on your hand. Life forgives you when you burn your finger. It reduces the edema and restores the part to wholeness and perfection.*

Forgiveness is an essential transforming value always closely related to Divinity. The Divine is essentially and unconditionally forgiving, and so are you. For this reason, you can ask yourself this question: *"If the Divine forgives me unconditionally, should I be harsh with myself?"* With this type of question you will obtain interesting insights.

Dugan says that:

> *forgiveness allows us to step out of the attack/defense cycle by catching ourselves in the act of judging, attacking, or defending, recognizing the problem is not "out there" but in our one mind.*

When you have a judgmental attitude to yourself or others, you tend to be punitive and unforgiving. This is a sign that there are memories which need to be deleted.

5.2. Guilt and forgiveness

> *The quality of mercy is not strained, it droppeth as the gentle rain from heaven upon the place beneath. It is twice blessed – blesseth him that gives and him that takes.*
> – *William Shakespeare,* The Merchant of Venice

As was previously mentioned, when you truly forgive yourself you avoid feeling guilty. Most psychologists say that people develop the emotional state of guilt during their childhood. Over your life you also receive social conditioning that teaches you not only why you should feel guilty but also on which occasions you must do so. From Ho'oponopono's perspective, over time you accumulate umpteen memories in your subconscious mind related to the state of guiltiness.

Even though guilt is considered a negative state it does have a very clear social function, which is to prompt people to act in a sensible manner in their social environment. So guilt acts like an effective internal censor which prevents you from acting in ways that are not adequate. Because you have the capability of feeling guilty you can have a better relationship with people around you.

In accordance with this viewpoint, people who don't experience any guilt at all are considered socially dangerous. There are several examples of extremely guiltless behaviors, for example people who are psychopathic or sociopathic.

For this reason, the internalization of certain moral rules related to your behavior makes sense. This set of internal rules actually allows you to live in society in a harmonious manner. Guilt makes you a civilized individual, who naturally tends to avoid causing harm to others.

However, when you experience an imbalanced sense of guilt, this tends to provoke the upsurge of tormenting thoughts, which tend to harass you constantly. When you feel extremely guilty you are also prone to casting continual harsh criticism on yourself. Sometimes you might also experience restlessness and shame; you can feel despondent and unhappy. When you can truly dwell on forgiveness you tend to feel more at ease and comfortable with yourself.

Tolle says that: *"guilt, regret, resentment, grievances, sadness, bitterness and all forms of unforgiveness are caused by too much past."*

To put it more clearly, guilt is always related to something that happened; it is connected to past situations. You can never change, in the present, the way that things happened in the past; they are essentially irreversible. Nonetheless you can always change the way you interpret your past.

Williams says that in Swedish the same term is used for guilt as for debt. From this perspective, being guilty is like being indebted either to yourself or others in a spiritual way. According to this perspective, guilt is not a very positive state. The quickest way to repay this "debt" is by forgiving yourself unconditionally.

You must understand that, in the past, you always acted in the best way possible according to your resources, mindset and contextual factors. From the Ho'oponopono perspective, in the past your actions were driven by your subconscious memories; you could not have acted otherwise. For this reason, it is not worth feeling guilty for any past circumstances.

Even though you must avoid feeling guilty, you should never deny that you are fallible and thus make mistakes. Without feeling guilty you must always acknowledge your wrongdoings, which implies taking full responsibility for them. From the Ho'oponopono perspective, you recognize that all your past circumstances, even your mistakes, are natural manifestations of memories held in your subconscious mind.

Ferrini says that: *"Chronic guilt is something more than the consistent refusal to take responsibility for recognizing and learning from my mistakes."* When you feel guilty you tend to victimize yourself and give your innermost power away. However, when you do not feel guilty you actually learn from the past. Your wrongdoings are signposts to make amends and become a better person. And you can amend your life with Ho'oponopono.

When you feel truly guiltless you don't need to point fingers at anyone, not even yourself. You understand that you are prone to making mistakes, like the rest of the people. Moreover it is not you who actually commits these mistakes; they are actually caused by your subconscious memories.

When you feel guilty you cannot truly learn from past situations. Guilt is a paralyzing emotional state which does not contribute to your personal transformation.

From the scientific viewpoint, guilt has a very low vibratory rate. On the other side, acceptance is a more constructive state; it has a higher vibration than guilt. In that effect, acceptance is directly related to the concept of taking full responsibility in your life.

Dr. David Hawkins asserts that: *"At this level of awareness a major transformation takes place with the understanding that one is oneself the source and creator of the experience of one's life."* He also says that the state of acceptance: *"is characterized by the capacity to live harmoniously with the forces of life."* Acceptance is a very empowering state, unlike guilt. When you accept things as they are, without feeling guilty, you can take full responsibility.

When you are fully responsible you don't deny your current circumstances but accept them in order to transform them. The best way to transform your life circumstances is by regularly practicing Ho'oponopono.

Guilt is an unforgiving state generally based on victimhood. When you feel guilty you cannot forgive yourself; both things are incompatible. Besides, you tend to suffer a lot. Rinpoche says that: *"Your feeling of being unforgiven and unforgivable is what makes you suffer so."* Forgiveness makes you transcend all needless suffering which ties you to the past. Forgiveness actually acts like an amnesty for all your past mistakes; it releases them and sets you truly free.

Forgiveness always entails compassionateness, which is the opposite to punishment. When you are merciful and kind with yourself, you can accept your mistakes and also the pain caused by them to yourself and others. When you have a compassionate attitude with yourself, you will naturally cover your shortcomings with love to dissolve them all. And this is what you do when you regularly use the Ho'oponopono tool. When you forgive yourself, you escape from a place of immobility and take charge of your life.

5.3. Forgiveness, resistance and surrender

> *Forgiveness is to relinquish your grievance and so let go of grief...*
> *Forgiveness is to offer no resistance to life – to allow life to live*
> *through you... The moment you truly forgive you have reclaimed*
> *your inner power...*
> *– Eckhart Tolle*

Forgiveness is the opposite to resistance. When you forgive yourself you accept your full responsibility for everything going on in your life, which implies not resisting what it is at all. When you place no opposition to whatever occurs in your life, you tap into your most powerful inner resources.

Metaphorically speaking, when you avoid resistance, you act like water going down a mountain. Goddard states when water goes down a mountain it finds its way around to reach the bottom part. In the beginning, the little stream of water works its way out of surrounding rocks and plants. The water offers no resistance to the hindrances it encounters on its way down.

Whenever you are affected by problems you tend to naturally resist them. By resisting your difficulties you are making them even bigger and more tangible. This creates negativity and friction and makes them look more unsolvable. Even paltry situations appear unmanageable.

When you say *"Please forgive me"* you are casting away any form of resistance. You actually look for reconciliation with yourself. Forgiveness acts like a transmuting balm that dissolves all conflicts in your life.

Many people wrongly believe that forgiveness makes you weak. Nonetheless, the truth is that when you forgive yourself you actually become stronger and more powerful. However, when you resist your current circumstances, and this includes not forgiving yourself, you implicitly try to force things to be different, which keeps them even more in place.

Hawkins says that:

For our purposes it is really only necessary to recognize that power is that which makes you go strong, Force makes you go weak. Love, compassion and forgiveness which may by some be mistakenly thought of as submissive are, in fact, profoundly empowering.

He also states that: *"Revenge, judgmentalism and condemnation, on the other hand, inevitably make you go weak... Power attracts, whereas force repels."* From this perspective, the states of surrender and forgiveness place no opposition to what it is; they make you more empowered.

When you don't forgive yourself you tend to suffer a lot in your life. Some psychological schools of thought say that your suffering can sometimes be meaningful. Your painful circumstances help you learn prized lessons from your past and you become more alert before upcoming situations. Your emotional range can become naturally expanded which allows you to be more aware of all your circumstances.

However, it is important to understand that, from the metaphysical perspective, suffering is always a negative state. Suffering beclouds your perception and lowers your levels of energy. It is unquestionably disempowering because it keeps you stuck in the negative situations (past or present). Moreover whenever you suffer you radiate negative energy, which tends to manifest more negative circumstances in your life. To put it simply, suffering affects your overall state of well-being in a very significant manner.

From Ho'oponopono's perspective, suffering is just subconscious memories, which are limiting for your life. As you know, these subconscious programs must be eliminated to arrive at your pure essence. Whenever you have an attitude of non-forgiveness you are, in some way, suffering.

When you cannot forgive yourself you place resistance to what it is. In order to overcome resistance you must surrender to what is going on in your life. And you can truly surrender when you ask for forgiveness.

Whenever you ask for a pardon you are in a state of surrender. In relation to this, Tolle explains that: *"surrender is the simple and profound wisdom of yielding to instead of opposing the flow of life… [it] is to accept the present moment unconditionally and without reservation."* This author also added that: *"surrender reconnects you with your source energy…"* When you surrender your attention is focused inwardly, which allows you to access your most powerful inner resources.

Anthony states that people tend to resist change. From this perspective, *"homeostasis"* is the technical term he used for naming your natural resistance to change. In that effect, the removal of your subconscious memories by doing Ho'oponopono implies a major change in your life. For this reason, when you start doing Ho'oponopono it is likely that you will experience a certain level of resistance regarding the use of this cleaning tool.

All the reasons underpinning your resistance are subconscious. From the metaphysical perspective there is that very well-known saying: *"What you resist, persists."* The most effective way out of resistance is surrender. With this attitude you can remove your subconscious memories.

As explained, when you surrender and truly admit your mistakes with no reservation, this also means that you don't criticize yourself for holding countless limiting programs in your subconscious mind. In that effect, surrender paves the way to authentic forgiveness.

5.4. Obstacles to forgiveness

You may not recognize forgiveness, even when you have experienced it, for what we are seeking to know better is subtle, difficult to define, multi-layered and contains elements of magic. You will – however – feel it in your body.
– Stephanie Dowrick

Many people have big difficulties forgiving themselves or others; for them forgiveness is not an easy task. This happens because people get entangled in reasons for not forgiving; they tend to focus on the motives for their unforgiving attitude.

When you cannot forgive you tend to carry a heavy load of frustration or even humiliation regarding your past negative situations. You might consider that your past sorrowful experiences are utterly unforgivable. Sometimes you might even experience regret, hatred or resentment.

If you have been hurt in the past, it might be very difficult for you to forgive. In these cases, even when you adopt the most positive attitude, you might still feel incapable of forgiving people who have hurt you and be unable to leave all conflicts behind. If you experience this, you should not be disappointed. When you feel unforgiving, you must keep on doing Ho'oponopono.

When you feel that you cannot forgive you must keep saying the sentence *"Please forgive me"* as many times are possible. Your unforgiving attitude is just a subconscious memory. And as any subconscious program it can be deleted when you do the cleaning process.

You also have to remember that when you repeat the words *"Please forgive me"* you are not trying to forgive others, but yourself. You are not even asking others for forgiveness for your mistakes either. From the Ho'oponopono perspective, forgiveness starts and finishes with you.

Whenever you use the words *"Please forgive me"* you address them to yourself and nobody else. To put it more clearly, your main objective of the words *"Please forgive me"* is forgiving yourself.

When you use the sentence *"Please forgive me"* regularly you are forgiving yourself for every single negative circumstance in your life, with no exception. This includes not only situations that you obviously caused but also external circumstances, which seem to be caused by other people.

From the Ho'oponopono perspective, all situations affecting you, even circumstances which you don't evidently seem to be the cause of, are always manifested by your subconscious memories. You are the cause of everything occurring around you; your subconscious programs manifest all these very circumstances.

When you repeat the words *"Please forgive me"* you are actually requesting pardon for every circumstance your subconscious memories originated. With the frequent use of these words, you also apologize for having accumulated countless programs in your mind, which have manifested each of your negative circumstances.

Whenever you find it difficult to say *"Please forgive me"* you must be patient, hopeful and persistent. You should keep on using the Ho'oponopono cleaning tool as frequently as possible. You must understand that even though it might take a lengthier time to fully forgive, as you do the cleaning process you will tend to feel less resentful and more forgiving.

As you say *"Please forgive me"* on a regular basis, you will realize that true forgiveness is always possible, even in the most painful situations. It is important to remember that every time you ask for forgiveness during the cleaning process not only do you remove your subconscious programs but you also release all past grievance.

In other words, when you use the Ho'oponopono cleaning technique you actually heal your wounds. As you use forgiveness as a cleaning tool you see your past negative experiences in the light of compassion and love.

When you say *"Please forgive me"* repeatedly your sorrow is gradually healed. Moreover when you truly feel forgiven, not only do you release the pain from the past, but you also avoid mistreating yourself any longer. In other words, forgiveness makes you abandon any form of punishment toward yourself and also others. When you dwell in forgiveness you cannot be hostile with yourself or other people anymore.

Some say that forgiveness must always be complete without any reservation. This means that you should forgive yourself for every single negative circumstance, with no exception whatsoever. In relation to this, Ferrini says that:

> *Forgiveness is unconditional and impartial. It takes me out of the past into the present... When I forgive I accept what happened in the past, including all the past judgements I made about myself or others, without bringing this material into the present or future. Or if I bring it forward I accept that I bring it forward and release it.*

It was previously explained that forgiveness implies acknowledging your faults. In that effect, when you accept your own faults they naturally become powerless; they do not rule your life any longer.

To put it more clearly, when you truly embrace your wrong-doings not only can you forgive these errors but also you can remove your subconscious memories originating them. In other words, when you have a forgiving attitude toward yourself you can dissolve the subconscious memories which caused your faults.

On the contrary, when you don't forgive yourself for your past experiences, you keep these subconscious memories trapped inside your mind; they continue to dictate your life. When you are unforgiving you are more prone to be stuck in negative emotional states like guilt, resentment or holding grudges.

If you don't forgive yourself your subconscious programs cannot be removed. These tapes will be playing out in the back of your mind and continue manifesting all kinds of negative situations in your life.

To conclude, you should always forgive yourself for all your transgressions. You must have a forgiving attitude with yourself, even if it is not the easiest thing for you. When you have a forgiving attitude with yourself you can leave reproach and judgment aside; you can also be more compassionate and loving with yourself.

5.5. Forgiveness and freedom

Forgiveness is the great masterstroke that helps a person release past mistakes and reset for success.
– Robert Holden

Forgiveness is always liberating because it frees you from your subconscious memories. When you forgive yourself you truly get rid of the burden of your past. Nonetheless, for forgiveness to be effective you should feel no remorse, guilt or grudge. Whenever you experience these negative states you are still tied to the past.

When you don't forgive yourself you perceive reality through the lens of the past. In relation to this, Jampolsky and Cirincione state that:

An unforgiving mind has its own agenda. It includes distorting what is real until it is barely recognizable... Judgments and righteous condemnation are themes for the script of unforgivingness, and we alone write the script.

When you dare to forgive yourself you truly break free from the shackles of the past. When you forgive yourself you are not a hostage to the past any longer. Forgiveness puts your past behind you and for good.

Besides, every time you ask for forgiveness on a regular basis you connect to the Divine. When you say *"Please forgive me"* regularly the limitless love energy of the Divine purifies all your wrongs.

You must consider forgiveness as the best present you can give yourself. Forgiveness represents a present to yourself because it helps you release any negative states (resentment, regret, etc.) and you tend to experience an instant relief. In relation to this, Becker says that:

> *Forgiveness is the key to releasing any emotional baggage we have continued to carry, our outdated and outmoded perspectives, and any other attachment that keep us bound to the past.*

Many people wrongly believe that if you hold on tight to your past faults and remember them continually you are less likely to commit the same mistakes in the future. However, whenever you get attached to your past mistakes, without forgiving them, you are prone to manifest the very same situations over and over.

When you forgive yourself and release all your past wrong-doings, you don't energize them any longer. This not only sets you free from the past but also prevents you from manifesting similar negative situations in the future.

As you forgive yourself, you achieve freedom in two different ways:

(a) You become free from your subconscious memories. This is called the passive aspect of your liberty, which implies that you free yourself from the bondage of your past. Forgiveness helps you put down the load you have been carrying from your past.

(b) You also become free to connect to Universal Sources.

This is the so-called active aspect of your liberty. Forgiveness also sets you free to receive divine inspiration. When you act in an inspired manner, your actions tend to be effortless and spontaneous.

This second aspect of your liberty is in fact revolutionary; you can go beyond any limits known in the past. You are not ensnared by your subconscious limiting programs any longer; you realize that you are essentially limitless, which implies a quantum leap in the quality of all your actions.

When you forgive yourself you can also achieve more clarity in your life. Hale-Evans states that: *"Clarity is freedom from unpleasant thoughts, emotions and states of consciousness… it is freedom pure and simple…"*

5.6. Forgiveness and divine connection

Good nature and good sense must ever join, to err is human, to forgive, divine.
– Alexander Pope

The frequent use of the words *"Please forgive me"* also helps you restore your connection with Divinity. As you surely remember, your natural link with the Divine is transitorily obscured by your subconscious programs.

As you might remember, whenever you say *"Please forgive me"* you ask the Divine to help you delete your subconscious memories. Vitale says that: *"you're not asking the Divine to forgive you; you're asking the Divine to help you forgive yourself."*

From the metaphysical perspective, when you are forgiven your heart is filled with love energy. This means that all your wounds from the past are healed almost magically. Ferrini says that, *"The process of forgiveness starts in your own heart."*

Every time you repeat the words *"Please forgive me"* you attract love energy from the Divine, which dissolves all the memories embedded in your subconscious mind. Forgiveness opens up your path to limitless love.

Many religions say that you are made in the image and likeness of Divinity. One important quality of the Divine is unconditional mercifulness. Thus every time you forgive yourself you display your innermost divine part. When you show lenience toward yourself, you are in total alignment with Divinity.

Stephanie Dowrick says that, *"The need for forgiveness begins with an act of betrayal… separation or loss."* When you are taken by your subconscious negative memories, you are betraying your natural pure essence; you are temporarily separated from the Divine flow. As you forgive yourself and delete your past programming, all residues of your treason to your divine nature are cast faraway. In short, forgiveness frees you from the chains of your merciless mental jailors.

Forgiveness represents a form of reconciliation with your true essence. When you truly forgive yourself you reestablish a close relationship not only with Divinity but also with your true self. Forgiveness is also reconciling because it is opposite to any form of condemnation and helps you resolve all your conflictive circumstances in an effortless manner.

When you forgive yourself you also uplift your overall levels of energy. This happens because forgiveness naturally connects you to divine love energy. Some masters say that forgiveness is just a by-product of love. When you truly forgive yourself, you tend to feel God's love in everything that exists.

With forgiveness not only do you recognize that you are essentially love. You also understand that the most powerful force in the Universe is love. Moreover you comprehend that love is the only important factor in your journey of transformation and evolution. Frankl wisely says that, *"The salvation of man is through love and in love."*

6. Practical tips for forgiveness

The quality of forgiveness must be as limitless as Faith, Love and Hope... repentance and forgiveness are the only ways to alter and correct the mistake.
– Neville Goddard

To forgive is to merely remember only loving thoughts you gave in the past, and those that were given you.
– Marianne Williamson

You can find below further recommendations to harness the almighty power of forgiveness more effectively:

– *Remember that forgiveness is always a choice:* When you choose forgiveness, you tend to be naturally less hurtful and judgmental with yourself or others. It is important to bear in mind that blame, resentment or guilt do not help you change your current circumstances; you are also more prone to being stuck to your problems.

– *Make forgiveness a natural part of your lifestyle:* When you get accustomed to using the words *"Please forgive me"* you gradually feel better with yourself. Holden says that: *"Forgiveness is a decision you make to have a loving relationship with yourself."* Forgiveness makes you a more compassionate and caring person; your relationships with other people tend to improve naturally as well.

– *Relinquish any form of condemnation and pity:* When you dwell in condemnation toward yourself or others, you are radiating negative energy, which attracts only difficulties into your life. Instead when you have a forgiving attitude you are compassionate with everybody, even yourself. Rinpoche says that, *"Compassion is the wish-fulfilling gem whose light of healing spreads in all directions."*

– *Practice forgiveness continually:* You must make forgiveness a positive habit. Think about forgiveness as a continuous process you gradually consolidate over time; it should be one of your priority objectives in your life. When you make this decision, you will find lots of opportunities for asking for forgiveness.

– *Try to be humble:* You should always ask for forgiveness in a humble manner. Remember that the sentence *"Please forgive me"* starts with the word *"Please."* If you have a humble attitude it will be easier for you to accept your responsibility for all circumstances in your life. Instead when you act arrogantly, you tend to be in denial or defensive. Moreover, humility is a graceful quality which helps you reconnect more strongly with the Divine.

– *Release resistance:* You must always observe the situations where you place opposition. Whenever you find resistance in your life, it is a sign that there are issues which were not duly forgiven. You must consider the situations you resist as opportunities to forgive yourself. When you resist, you must ask yourself: *"What am I resisting?"* or *"What haven't I forgiven yet?"* Wait for any insights and say the four Ho'oponopono sentences repeatedly. When you release resistance your energy becomes lighter and your life flows more gracefully.

– *Hold no regret:* You should never experience any guilt or regret for your past negative experiences. The past can never be undone, but it is possible to let go of its burden. As you know you are constantly related to your past through your subconscious memories. Forgiveness sets you free from the bondage of your past conditioning. Forgiveness does not change your past but transforms your present and your future.

– *Get insights from the past:* You can always reinterpret the past in a more constructive way. You must remember that all your negative experiences were created by your subconscious programs. When you realize this, you can adopt a positive attitude toward your past negative circumstances; they are reminders of subconscious memories which must be cleaned.

– *Forgive yourself fully:* Your attitude toward forgiveness should be truthful, not superficial or formal. The process of forgiving yourself represents a heartfelt act of contrition. When you use your rationale to forgive, you naturally tend to overanalyze things, which makes you more prone to be unforgiving. However, from the Ho'oponopono perspective, when you repeat the words *"Please forgive me"* continually you clean your subconscious memories even when you say these words in a heartless manner.

– *Take full responsibility:* You must always take full responsibility for everything going on in your life, which means not feeling guilty. When you accept your responsibility, you do not make any excuses to justify your mistakes but accept them and practice Ho'oponopono regularly.

– *Dwell on other meanings of forgiveness:* Some masters say that forgiving is never condoning or approving mistakes, either yours or others'. Instead, forgiveness entails cancelling these wrongdoings out. Stauffer says that: *"cancelling is the dropping or removing of the requirement that the other person perform in certain way in order to be loved."* In other words, you don't wish that things would have been different; you accept them as they were. When you have this attitude, you can truly transform your reality.

– *Keep a record on forgiveness:* It is important to take note of past situations you have forgiven yourself for. Be as descriptive as possible. You can also include thoughts, emotions and physical sensations related to these past experiences. When you do this exercise on a regular basis, you feel more prone to forgive yourself in the future. You can also take note of the *gains* you obtain in relation to experiences you still have not forgiven yourself for; include the justifications you use for having a non-forgiving attitude. You can also ask yourself the question *"What is going on in me in relation to forgiveness?"* Wait for insights and repeat the four Ho'oponopono sentences many times.

– *Forgive your negativity:* Every time you experience negative feelings, you must let them go with no delay; you must say the words *"Please forgive me"* repeatedly. You can also say *"Please forgive my negative emotions"* many times. From the Ho'oponopono perspective, these negative feelings are just subconscious programs which must be removed.

– *Release your sorrow:* All your pain and grievance is related to an attitude of non-forgiveness. For this reason, when you say the words *"Please forgive me"* on a frequent basis, your sorrow subsides and dissolves naturally. This happens because the memories creating this pain are being eliminated from your mind. When you have a continual attitude of forgiveness with yourself, your mind and heart become more peaceful.

– *Use visualization to forgive:* There is a very well-known exercise related to forgiveness; you must visualize that you are in front of yourself. Look at yourself feeling no guilt or regret. Intend to accept yourself fully. You can envision enveloping this image of yourself with a loving beam of light, which dissolves any negative state within you.

– *Remember that forgiveness is healing:* The frequent practice of forgiveness helps you eradicate any type of tension, physical, mental or emotional. When you get used to forgiving yourself, your mood becomes naturally uplifted. You tend to experience a noticeable overall state of well-being. According to Dowrick, forgiveness also boosts your immune system and makes you less prone to despondency.

– *Visualize yourself forgiving and being forgiven:* Dr. Sha suggests a very simple exercise; you must envision that you can talk to the soul of the person with whom you are in a conflictive relationship. You must imagine that you tell this soul about all the difficulties you both went through in the past. Then tell this soul that you truly want to forgive this person and vice versa. You must also ask the Divine to send love and forgiveness energy to strengthen your relationship with this person.

– *See the people you hurt:* There is second version of the previous exercise suggested by Dr. Sha. Visualize all the people you hurt and also the ones you hurt in this past. Imagine that all these people are inside your abdomen. Then you must forgive them and also ask them to forgive you. Say *"Please forgive me"* to people you have hurt and also *"I forgive you"* to the ones who have hurt you. Imagine that these people are bathed by a luminous ray of love coming from the Divine light as you repeat *"God's light"* many times.

– *Beware that nothing is unforgivable:* Always bear in mind that everything can be forgiven, even your most terrible mistakes. All wrongdoings were created by your subconscious memories, which can be removed. Remember that the Divine is always forgiving and as you are made in its image and likeness, you should forgive too.

Chapter 10

I Love You

Our illusion of separation from Love is the root of all our suffering.
– Alaya DeNoyelles

1. General aspects of love

If a man be gracious and courteous to strangers, it shows he is a
citizen of the world, and that his heart is no island cut off from other
lands, but a continent that joins to them.
– Francis Bacon

One of the four Ho'oponopono sentences is *"I love you."* Love is
the common factor shared by the most diverse spiritual and
philosophical perspectives. Moreover, the term *love* is present in
all languages in the world; the positive meaning of this word is
widespread.

The ongoing lack of love in the world is also noticeable:
racism, exploitation, human trafficking, wars, murders,
corruption, and other worldwide maladies. Nonetheless, love
can never be destroyed or eradicated because it is the most
powerful energy that exists. It is naturally all-pervasive and all-
encompassing of everything that exists.

In relation to this, Ayne says that:

Love is the mortar between the individual stones of people, tribes,
culture. Love makes the building and holds it up, when we unite in
the open wonderment and awe of our differences, our similarities.

Likewise Benner says that: *"Creation is an outpouring of love – an*
overflow of love from heaven to earth."

Love has the highest vibration; its transmuting power can dissolve negativity almost instantaneously. There is countless scientific evidence regarding the positive effects of love energy. Love energy not only healed people but also improved conflictive relationships and situations.

If you are like the majority of people, love might have different specific connotations, most of them positive. For the metaphysical perspective, the word *love* can easily be related to these meanings:

Mindfulness - Respect - Kindness - Lightness - Beauty - Knowingness - Thankfulness - Forgiveness - Empathy - Strength - Unity - Brotherhood - Smoothness - Faith - Vitality - Spirituality - Freedom - Compassion - Integration - Essence - Easiness - Gentleness - Presence - Limitlessness - Radiance - Solace - Awareness - Magnetism - Truth - Empowerment - Authenticity - Spontaneity - Sweetness - Harmony - Bliss - Open-heartedness - Grace - Pleasure - Nobleness - Assistance - Acceptance - Effortlessness - Humbleness - Healing - Peace - Completeness - Purpose - Meaningfulness - Aliveness - Integrity - Connection - Sharing - Trust - Enlightenment - Cooperation - Tenderness - Life - Surrender - Harmlessness - Generosity - Humaneness - Allowance - Liberation - Care - Nourishment - Tenderness - Selflessness - Salvation - Oneness - Gregariousness - Celebration - Inclusiveness - Virtue - Service - Stillness - Resourcefulness - Meaning - Wisdom - Mercy - Courage - Childlikeness - Plurality - Tolerance - Alchemy - Positivity - Gratitude - Repentance - Interconnectedness

Some masters say that you are not only made of love but you are essentially love. Moreover everything around you is also consti-tuted of the same very energy. Lake says that:

Love is the motivating force in life that creates, sustains, enhances,

*and gives meaning to life. There is nothing else here but love
because Life is love. We are love.*

When you say *"I love you"* on a regular basis you are actually
connected with Divinity, which is the inexhaustible source of
pure love, and which helps you remove your subconscious
programs. In addition, every time you say *"I love you"* you accept
yourself with no reservation, and this includes your subconscious programs.

Love is an intrinsically harmonizing energy which helps you
remove any dissonant vibration in you. Even though love is a
very subtle energy it has very tangible positive effects in your
life. When you say the words *"I love you"* on a frequent basis you
create empty space in your mind in order to be filled with divine
inspiration.

Metaphorically speaking, every time you say *"I love you"* you
sift through a layer of gravel to reach prized gold. In this graphic
example, the gravel is your past conditioning stored in your
subconscious mind, and the gold is just your pure essence, which
is divine by nature.

Whenever you experience love you naturally cast away any
form of judgment or hostility to yourself or others. When you say
the words *"I love you"* on a regular basis, you replace all the
limiting energy within you (for example, states of low vibration
such as hatred, sadness, contentiousness, etc.) for pure love
energy. Becker says that: *"Love changes everything yet love itself
never changes."*

You can use the sentence *"I love you"* on its own or combined
with the other three sentences which are *"I am sorry"*, *"Please
forgive me"* and *"Thank you."* You can also use sentences such as:
"I love myself the way I actually am", *"I am a loving being"*, *"I am
love"*, *"I am worthy of love"* or *"I am lovable"*, among others.

When you say *"I love you"* you can also visualize a fountain in
the middle of your chest which outpours pure love and pervades

everything around you. Nonetheless, when you do the cleaning process regularly you don't really need to visualize anything to delete your subconscious memories.

It is interesting to highlight that newborns are naturally open to receive love energy; when they don't have enough love they struggle to survive. Love force is as important as food for their personal growth.

All people can naturally supply themselves and their environment with love from within themselves on demand. However, as people grow older they gradually develop blockages which hinder their natural way of receiving and giving love. These blocks related to love are the result of bad relational experiences with family members, friends, lovers and other people.

In some extreme cases, people end up cutting themselves off completely from everybody; they become loners. Even in these cases, people never lose their natural ability to express and receive love; they just exclude this skill temporarily.

There is a statement in *A Course in Miracles* which wisely goes: *"The task is not to seek for love, but to seek all of the barriers you have built against it."* The regular use of the words *"I love you"* helps you dissolve all your hindrances which temporarily sever you from love.

Some anthropological, psychological and sociological schools of thought assert that expressing love is a learned skill. People learn this from different sources, for example family conditioning, friendship and romantic relationships and other influences (church, school, etc.).

Bauman says that your capacity for love and self-love is directly correlated to the love you have received from others over your life. Likewise Leo Buscaglia says that: *"you can only give what you have... If you have love, you can give it. If you don't have it, you don't have it to give."* From this perspective, in order to love yourself and others you need as a prerequisite to have been loved in the past.

From a different perspective, some sages say that you are naturally equipped with love; it is not a skill you develop; it comes from birth. This energy is always in you and cannot be destroyed. This energy is an intrinsic part of your DNA. Holden coined the term *"loveability"* which represents your natural *"ability to love and be loved."*

2. Metaphysical and scientific perspectives on love

It is only with the heart that we can see rightly: what is essential is invisible to the eye.
– Antoine De Saint-Exupery, The Little Prince

Indeed, love is essential for our species' survival because it involves self-sacrifice. It helps us to put others before ourselves and this is what actually keeps us going as a species. From the genetic and biological standpoint, love certainly does make the world go around.
– Dr. Raj Persaud

From the metaphysical perspective, love is not contrary to hatred, as many people might suppose; love is opposite to fear. Love is always an opening and expansive energy; on the contrary, fear is always a contractive energy, which can take many forms such as resentment, pain, guilt, sadness, worrying, among others. Many masters state that love can remove any negative emotional state. It is a natural curative tool and puts your mind in poise, order and harmony.

Fredrickson says that whenever you feel threatened or unsafe, which are just expressions of fear, you cannot experience authentic love. On those occasions, your survival mechanism is naturally activated and overrides any possible loving state.

Love energy is naturally connected with the depths of your heart. Some masters say that love is the language spoken by your heart. Love allows you to go beyond your current limitations; it helps you evolve as a person.

Love also implies a feeling of togetherness; when you experience true love there seems to be no boundaries between you and the world. When you choose to be a loving individual, you tend to be naturally more compassionate with yourself and others; you develop a more profound bond with everything that exists.

Katin says that: *"Love has many imposters: physical attraction (hormones), sentimentality, phony caring, imitativeness, tough love, punishing out of love."* When you explore these states more deeply you discover that they are just vulgar forgeries of love.

From a scientific perspective, Dr. Hawkins concludes that love (along with joy, peace and enlightenment) is one of the most powerful and benign energetic states that exists. He also says that when you experience this high energetic state you naturally show interest not only in yourself but also others.

Additionally, he states that:

> *Love is a way of being. It is a way of relating to the world that is forgiving, nurturing and supportive... Love focuses on the goodness of Life in all its expressions and augments that which is positive. It dissolves negativity...*

From this perspective, love also allows you to understand the essence or wholeness of any life situation in a more profound way.

In accordance to his scientific perspective, there are many other states which are, energetically speaking, far below love such as: reason, acceptance, willingness, neutrality, courage, pride, anger, desire, fear, grief, apathy, guilt and shame. According to these findings, whenever you experience a highly energetic state, such as love, you naturally counteract the energy of thousands of people who experience lower energetic states, for example fear, grief, shame and others.

There are many studies which confirm that love has positive effects on your health conditions. Shimoff and Kline say that:

> *when you experience love, the heart and the brain in concert with the endocrine and nervous systems release "love chemicals," including endorphins, oxytocin, and vasopressin, which strengthen the immune system and increase resilience...*

These authors also add that: *"Love brings our biochemistry into balance."*

There are other scientific studies which certify that people who are prompted to experience intense love bring about positive changes in their DNA. Some specialists assert that love also enhances your natural wisdom and creative skills. Maturana states that: *"Love expands intelligence and enables creativity. Love returns autonomy and, as it returns autonomy, it returns responsibility and the experience of freedom."* Some spiritual sages assert that love helps you connect with your innermost wisdom; love naturally erodes any state of uncertainty or lack of clarity.

HeartMath is an organization which researches the functioning of the heart from an overarching perspective. This institution has discovered that when you truly experience love in the area of your heart, you enter a state of coherence, in which your body systems act more harmoniously. As a consequence, you can access your inner resources more easily.

Fredrickson says that:

> *Love, as it turns out, nourishes your body the way the right balance of sunlight, nutrient-rich soil, and water nourishes plants and allows them to flourish. The more you experience it, the more you open up and grow, becoming wiser and more attuned, more resilient and effective, happier and healthier. You grow spiritually as well, better able to see, feel and appreciate the deep interconnection that inexplicably ties you to others.*

She also states that the loving energy changes the architecture of your cells and improves your general state of well-being.

There is also solid scientific research on the influence of love on plants. In a study there were two groups of people who formed part of the research. The first group of people lovingly talked to plants and caressed them on a frequent basis. The second group provided plants with the minimum care, such as water, but they treated the plants in a nonchalant manner.

The findings of this experiment were utterly shocking; the results showed that over time the plants which received a loving treatment grew stronger and bigger, as compared to the plants that were treated indifferently. In this study it was proved that love acts as an enlivening force.

3. Other meanings of love

The original state for all beings is Love. Our troubles are due only to our covering over this natural state... Love is the balm, the salve that soothes and heals everything and all... Love is a tremendous power. One discovers that the power behind love, without question, is far more powerful than the hydrogen bomb. All love including human love has its source in divine love.
– Lester Levenson

True love is never shallow or superficial but deep, rich and meaningful. Borysenko states that: *"Love is a verb not a noun. It can only be experienced when it is flowing."* On a different note, Erich Fromm states that love is a learnable capability which is paramount for life. Some spiritual masters state that love is the most important nourishment for your soul.

Love also represents your most important mission in life. Some suggest that love is just your natural way of being. This mighty energy cannot be easily described with words. Despite this, you can find below some other meanings for love as follows:

– *Love is your true essence*

– *Love is the most effective way to remove your subconscious programming*

– *Love is an indestructible force which nullifies all negativity*

– *Love is the capability to value everything in your life*

– *Love is lingering inner peace and compassion*

– *Love is being aware that you are connected to everything that exists*

– *Love is the only answer to all your problematic experiences in life*

– *Love is energy that enhances the beauty of everything around you*

– *Love is inexhaustible energy*

– *Love is something not perceptible by your senses but truly felt with your heart*

– *Love is the unstoppable flow which makes you embrace all your best qualities*

– *Love is the supportive force helping you surmount your difficult times*

– *Love is the easiest way to shorten the distance among people*

– *Love is the magical balm that vivifies and strengthens your relationships*

– *Love is the constituent substance of everything in the Universe*

– *Love is silent wisdom whispered by your heart, always comforting and soothing*

– *Love is pure thoughtfulness and mindfulness*

– *Love is your shortest and quickest path to Divinity*

– *Love is the celebration of the divine essence in you*

– *Love is a signal of your core aliveness*

– *Love is absolute surrender to what is*

– *Love is what makes your life meaningful and complete*

– *Love is unconditional openness and utter innocence*

– *Love is what transmutes hatred to yourself or others*

– *Love is a multiplying energy; when you give it, you get even more of it*

– *Love is a transmuting energy which helps you be more compassionate*

– *Love is casting aside any state of defensiveness*
– *Love is feeling safe and comfortable even when exposed and vulnerable*
– *Love is what props and enlivens everything that exists*
– *Love is an all-encompassing expression of all forms of life*
– *Love is an indescribable and unspeakable state of being*
– *Love is pure gleefulness pervading your mind and body*
– *Love is the most important primary need for any human being*
– *Love is pure selflessness*
– *Love is willingness to be loved and give love with no condition*
– *Love is expansive energy facilitating all your activities*
– *Love is the mediator prompting you to make friends with yourself again*
– *Love is the most empowering inner resource you count on*
– *Love is poise and serenity in your life*
– *Love is the only underlying purpose of your life*
– *Love is the main compass in your life pathway*
– *Love is a deep sense of meaningfulness*
– *Love is a sign of your absolute limitlessness*
– *Love is the evident manifestation of your almightiness*
– *Love is a direct enabler for receiving divine inspiration*
– *Love is the most important cornerstone on your way to enlightenment*
– *Love is what all civilizations, ancient and modern ones, have looked for*
– *Love is the graceful force contributing to the betterment of humankind*

4. Unconditional love

The first step to take is to become aware that love is an art, just as living is an art; if we want to learn how to love we must proceed in the same way we proceed if we want to learn any other art, say music, painting, carpentry, or the art of medicine or engineering.
– Erich Fromm

4.1. Main aspects of unconditional love

To love unconditionally is a life wager. In love we put ourselves on the line and there is no going back. It is at this brink that many things seem to collapse. Within arms' reach they faint at the thought of never returning. It is the less travelled road.
– John Powell

Unconditional love is always unlimited; it is totally opposite to conditional love. The former is the supreme form of love; it is also called true love, real love, abiding love, universal love, infinite love and also deep love. It is also impartial and with no reservation. When you feel unconditional love you are truly connected to the Divine.

This type of love implies your natural and spontaneous choice to love everyone you encounter in your life, irrespective of who they are or what they do. With unconditional love, you are a loving individual before any circumstance, no matter if it is positive or negative.

In relation to this, Powell says that:

The essential message of unconditional love is one of liberation: You can be whoever you are, express all your thoughts and feelings with absolute confidence. You do not have to be fearful that love will be taken away... There is no admission price to my love, no rental fees of instalment payments to be made.

Unconditional love has no hidden agenda to follow and no secret terms to abide by.

Unconditional love is by nature fully accepting and non-judgmental; you hold no negative feeling toward yourself or others. Whenever you feel unconditional love you effortlessly accept others (and yourself) with no reservation, without trying to change them.

When you give people unconditional love, you do not expect any reciprocal treatment from them in return. Unconditional love is supportive and selfless. Expressing unconditional love can be a very challenging task for most people. Fromm wisely says that: *"To love one's flesh and blood is no achievement… Only in the love of those who do not serve a purpose, love begins to unfold."* You should not have to make any effort to experience unconditional love.

With unconditional love you are not concerned about the outcomes of your love. You don't set any conditions to yourself or others. Baer says that: *"Real love is always a gift freely given and freely received."* In other words, unconditional love is pure generosity.

With this type of love you tend to use phrases such as *"I will always love you…"* or *"I will love you no matter what happens."* It is about loving for no reason.

When you love people unconditionally you avoid controlling them; you just intend to affect them positively. With this type of attitude, you accept and respect others' differences. Holden says that: *"Unconditional love creates a holding environment in a relationship that makes it safe for you to be yourself."* With unconditional love you do not need to make any impression on others.

When you feel unconditional love, you can see all the good in people around you and also in yourself. This type of love is never related to specific contexts (for example workplace, home, friend meetings, etc.) or special relationships (such as the ones with the members of your family, lovers, friends, etc.). On the contrary, unconditional love is all encompassing and expanding. When you experience unconditional love you can pour it onto anybody, at any time.

Unconditional love never means accepting any kind of behavior from others, for example, deprecatory judgment toward you. You can be a loving individual as you set solid boundaries to others in order to avoid being mistreated. Dr. Hawkins asserts that the only type of love which is authentic is unconditional love. From this perspective, unconditional love is changeless and totally independent of external circumstances.

This type of love is compassionate and forgiving. Some other relevant qualities of this type of love are kindness, care and supportiveness. It is naturally linked to gratitude because it is focused only on the good aspects of people and circumstances around you.

Unconditional love is one of the most elevated types of energy; any form of negativity dissolves with no effort. Little children are a natural manifestation of innocence and unconditional love. They don't have to pretend that they are love beings; they naturally dwell in their loving state of being.

From the Ho'oponopono perspective, unconditional love is your true essence. You can be temporarily disconnected from your love essence, especially when you are taken over by your subconscious programs. As you remove your subconscious memories, you gradually reconnect to your true loving nature, the Divine within you.

4.2. Other characteristics of unconditional love

Love is not primarily a relationship to a specific person; it is an attitude, an orientation of character which determines the relatedness of the person to the world as a whole, not toward one "object" of love. If a person only loves one other person and is indifferent to the rest of his fellow men, his love is not love but a symbiotic attachment, or an enlarged egotism.
– Erich Fromm

You can find below other aspects of unconditional love. The present list is not meant to be exhaustive:

a) Effortlessness
When you feel unconditional love, it surges spontaneously, flowingly. When you experience unconditional love, your life

circumstances tend to unfold in a graceful manner.

b) Limitlessness

When you have an attitude of unconditional love, you realize your natural almighty essence. You truly understand that there are no limits regarding what you can achieve in your life, because you are the Divine in essence. The only thing that prevents you from harnessing your unlimited potential is your subconscious programming.

Unconditional love is the powerful force which helps you experience the so-called *"miracles."* Another fundamental trait of unconditional love is speediness because it accelerates the manifestation of your innermost wishes.

c) Trust

Unconditional love is based on unconditional trust. When your trust is conditional you tend to confide in people until they disappoint you. Instead, unconditional trust is always magnanimous, all-encompassing, benevolent and even naïve.

When you trust unconditionally you have no reservations or expectations on other people. With unconditional love, you feel compelled to share your most prized resources (knowledge, time, emotions, etc.) with others for no reason, just because you trust them. You also feel better every time you help others.

d) Cooperation

This type of love is opposite to competition but closely related to cooperation. You tend to assist people who need help, regardless of their specific condition and their relationship with you.

You never express unconditional love exclusively to a few people; instead it is overarching. Most successful cooperative relationships or business ventures are founded on unwavering trust, which always implies unconditional love.

e) Enlightenment
Villani says that: *"Enlightenment is the realization that you are simply who you are."* When you love unconditionally you understand that you are the image of the Divine. You truly get in contact with your true core, which is essentially pure love.

f) Meaningfulness
Unconditional love is a profound state with a lot of meaning. The true meaning of unconditional love is never assigned by your rational mind but your heart. Unconditional love means sharing, forgiveness, selflessness, and assistance. Unconditional love also means glee; when you love unconditionally not only do you experience joy but you also make others experience it as well.

g) Compassion
When you love unconditionally you avoid discriminating, judging or condemning anyone or anything. On the contrary, you tend to be more compassionate, warm and nourishing with everything and everyone around you. You can fully express your love to anyone, irrespective of their thoughts or actions. This type of love is kindness; Villani states that: *"Kindness is the currency of love, of life... Kindness to others is the natural way to lighting you and them up."*

h) Care
When you love unconditionally you want the best for others; moreover, you try to help them in the best way possible. This type of love is altruistic and generous by nature. Stauffer states that: *"The attitude of unconditional love involves actively helping, while expressing tenderness, compassionate understanding, unselfish intent and wise judgment."* Whenever you help others your assistance comes from the depth of your heart; Fromm says that: *"love is the active concern for the life and the growth of the ones which we love."*

i) Detachment

Unconditional love is *unconditional* because is not needy; you do not cling to specific people, things or circumstances. You hold no expectations about others either. You are more prone to appreciate the value of every situation and the people you encounter in your life. Unconditional love is also detachment because you realize that there is no need to control anything. You trust that everything will fall into place in the best way. You become more spontaneous and less structured; you can harness your inner resources more easily and progress despite any difficulties.

j) Focus on the present

Unconditional love is fully connected to the present moment. For example, when you experience unconditional love, you don't have any expectations about people you give love to. When you feel unconditional love toward other people, you don't dwell in their past behavior either.

When you love unconditionally, you are willing to express your love because this is what you feel at present. You truly surrender to the present moment in order that you can grasp the magic of each situation.

k) Interconnectedness

Whenever you love unconditionally you feel that you are connected to all that exists. With unconditional love all boundaries between you and the rest of the people seem to disappear miraculously. From this perspective, you comprehend that you are never on your own in your life; all your actions constantly impact on others and vice versa.

l) Inclusiveness

Unconditional love is always impersonal; you don't express it only to specific people. Your unconditional love never has a particular object of love; it is universal with no distinctions or preferences.

Instead, the other types of love, thoroughly described in Appendix F, have special and exclusive people to whom you give love.

When you love unconditionally you realize that all people truly matter in life, not only the ones that you know. From a wider perspective you can also focus on mankind in general, as a whole. Fromm states that: *"Just as love for one individual which excludes the love for others is not love, love for one's country which is not part of one's love for humanity is not love, but idolatrous worship."*

4.3. Final comments on unconditional love

You might be asking yourself: *"If unconditional love is so positive, why don't people experience it more?"* There are many relevant factors that prevent people from experiencing unconditional love. For example, some people truly believe in the notion of separateness, which implies that you are not interrelated to others.

Most people cannot acknowledge that they are essentially part of the wholeness. So they tend to act in a selfish and self-reliant manner, without caring about what happens with other people.

The social conditioning you are constantly immersed in also sets countless invisible rules against unconditional love. Most widespread and accepted values in our social context are egocentrism, carelessness, manipulation, resentment, domination, discrimination, bigotry and defensiveness, among others. All these negative qualities are opposite to unconditional love.

The entrepreneurial world also discourages the attitude of unconditional love with values such as: competition, exploitation of workers, unstoppable consumerism, win-lose agreements, one-upmanship and struggle to succeed, among others.

In relation to this, George states that:

The commercialization of the belief that love can only be found through personal achievement, the acquisition of products, or in an exclusive relationship, only makes love small, elusive and distant; when in truth, it is unlimited, huge and instantly accessible.

From the Ho'oponopono perspective, there is another reason which prevents people from experiencing unconditional love: your subconscious programs. When you are taken over by subconscious memories, as you generally are, you are more likely to experience conditional love, which will be thoroughly explained in the following point. As you practice Ho'oponopono on a frequent basis, you become more prone to express unconditional love.

5. Conditional love

When you experience conditional love, other people must meet your conditions to be loved. This characteristic makes this type of love very rigid, controlling and utterly selfish. This is the type of love you are more likely to experience when you are ruled by your subconscious programs.

When you experience conditional self-love, you only love yourself when you act correctly, fulfil your goals or meet your own expectations. On the contrary, whenever you make mistakes or miss the mark you tend to withhold love to yourself.

When you have an attitude of conditional love to people, you only give them love if you consider that they truly deserve it, which implies a manipulative attitude. The requirements or conditions you impose on people in order to receive your love vary significantly from person to person.

With conditional love, you try to stifle people's natural freedom. You don't allow them to be as authentic as they should be. Your love, when conditional, is never given freely to others. You are naturally impaired to express love at all times. This type of love tends to be very constrictive and calculating.

Besides, when you experience conditional love to others, you tend to expect reciprocal treatment from them. Conditional love resembles a commercial transaction of love; both parties are expected to provide each other with goods of similar value.

Conditional love toward others is generally related to possessiveness, a power struggle and jealousy, which are all forms of fear. Every time you experience fear, you tend to become defensive and try to keep things and people under your control.

Conditional love to others always implies a certain level of attachment to them. Some psychological schools of thought state that people tend to get attached to others when they feel helpless, isolated or separate.

Conditional love is naturally based on manipulation, sometimes on a very subtle level. It is important to highlight that romantic love, which in many cases tends to be addictive, possessive, conflictive and obsessive, can be considered a subtype of conditional love.

When you have an attitude of conditional love you tend to use sentences like: *"I will love you if..."* or *"I will love you when..."* or *"I love you because..."* It is important to realize that in all these sentences you implicitly refer to conditions to be met by using words such as *if, when* or *because.*

Lastly, conditional love is also related to some disgusting behaviors such as attacking and victimizing yourself or others. When you love conditionally you might also tend to act in a dishonest and untrustworthy manner. You might also tend to cling on to others in a needy way.

6. Love spectrum

Only by acts of selfless kindness, unconditional forgiveness and limitless compassion is love felt. Only by the intention to benefit "the other" before the self is love made real and realized. And yet, even this is only possible when it is not a deliberate act, but when motive is innocent.

– Mike George

Shimoff and Kline highlight four distinct states in the love spectrum. From this perspective, there is a first state called *"no love"*: you tend to dwell on resistance, anger, grief, and hate. You are in state of defensiveness; your divine loving essence is totally obscured by negative emotions, which take it over, at least transitorily.

There is second state called *"love for bad reason"*, which cannot be considered a positive form of love, either. You tend to manipulate others for your personal needs. You seek being loved in order to eliminate the void in you. As a consequence of this, *"love for bad reason"* always implies neediness and dependence.

Thirdly, you can experience *"love for good reason."* This state entails a deep sense of appreciation for others and it can also include reciprocal affection. You try to contribute to others' lives in some way. With this type of love, you don't give love to others freely; there is always a motive for expressing your love. These reasons are likely to change over time. Both *"love for bad reason"* and *"love for good reason"* are forms of conditional love. The only difference is that in the former the reasons are negative and in the latter the motives are positive.

And lastly there is the state called *"unconditional love."* This is the purest way of love because you don't need any motive, neither bad nor good, to express your love to others. When you love unconditionally you are not dependent on any situation or people. This type of love is expressed to all people, in an unconstrained manner.

It is important to understand that unconditional love is the most wonderful way to experience joyfulness and liberty. You are fulfilled just because of the fact that you can bring love to others with no reservation whatsoever. You cannot be judgmental with others because unconditional love is essentially benevolent. There are other types of love besides unconditional love, which are explained in Appendix F.

7. Other topics related to love

The hunger for love is more difficult to remove than the hunger for bread.
– Mother Teresa

Love today and tomorrow your past will be filled with love.
– Harold Becker

7.1. Love removes your subconscious memories

Love is the key to healing. Many doctors now agree that the majority of man's ills come from congestion and from poisons stirred up by negative emotions. Love relaxes and harmonizes man's emotions. Love attunes the individual to the healing power within himself.
– Catherine Ponder

Dr. Sha says that: *"love melts all blockages and transforms all life."* When you do Ho'oponopono and say the words *"I love you"* on a frequent basis you are being liberated from the ruthless domination of your subconscious memories.

When you repeat the words *"I love you"* you are implicitly seeking assistance from the Divine. With these words, you are asking Divinity to help you remove your subconscious memories. As you regularly say *"I love you"* the Divine pervades your subconscious programs with transmuting love energy to dissolve them as if they were lumps of sugar in water.

Some suggest that, in order to eradicate your subconscious memories, you should imagine that your memories are being bathed with love energy as vividly as possible. However, you don't actually need to do any visualization to remove your subconscious information; just repeat the words *"I love you"* frequently.

7.2. You are the main source of love

> *Love is the hidden ground upon which we are dancing. This love is the essence and expression of what oneness is... Love feeds all our basic desires, including our desire to be connected, to be known, to be safe, to be happy, to be successful and to be free...*
> *... Love is our purpose, love is our delight, and love is our salvation.*
> – Robert Holden

Love is the most valuable and powerful resource you were born with; you are essentially made of love. Whenever you experience authentic love it naturally comes from the very core of your being. Nobody and nothing can ever take it away from you. Love is as close to you as your own breath.

Many people, because of being hurt in the past, tend to protect themselves from experiencing true love. These people only tend to feel love on a superficial level. No matter what type of wounds you carry from the past, authentic love can never be absent in you.

The only thing you have to do to access real love is to acknowledge this in your true nature in order to tap into it. In relation to this, Ayne says that:

> *Without becoming intimately acquainted with the pilot light of love burning at one's center, the furnace of full engagement in life cannot be ignited.*

There is another relevant point to highlight. Remember that most religions in the world say that you are made in the image and likeness of the Divine, which is almighty love. When you repeat the words *"I love you"* you connect with the divine love energy already within you. Besides, love is never dependent on others; the origin of your love is always you.

Subconscious memories can temporarily obscure your access to your source of love but you can never be completely disconnected from it. As you remove these programs, you can fully access your loving core.

As any high type of energy, love can be cultivated regularly; in order to do so, you must resort to love whenever possible by saying the words *"I love you"* on a regular basis. With these words, you naturally radiate love energy everywhere.

The frequent use of the words *"I love you"* takes you back to the fact that you are not loveless but a loving and loveable being. When you say *"I love you"* you are celebrating the love that you are.

From the metaphysical perspective, the most paramount objective in life is not to love yourself and others but instead to *"be love."* Love is what makes your other objectives more relevant. Moreover love is the only quality that makes your life journey worthwhile.

Love can only be related to an inside-out approach. This means that you must never look for love outside of you but only within you, where it actually resides. From this perspective, you are a natural fountain of love, which never depletes.

There is a very interesting exercise; you can imagine that you breathe love in and out in the area around your heart. This visualization technique is very effective; when you use it you will experience love energy in a tangible bodily manner.

You can also imagine that this loving energy pervades all your body, not only around your heart. As you practice this exercise you will become more revitalized and your mood will turn more positive.

7.3. The importance of self-love

Love is changeless. It asks not questions and makes no judgement. It is always gentle and tender. It is always unfolding, extending and expanding beyond all limitations... Love will enter immediately into any mind that truly wants it, but it must want it truly.
– Gerald G. Jampolsky and Diane V. Cirincione

All disease, all unhappiness, come from the violation of the law of love. Man's boomerangs of hate, resentment and criticism, come back laden with sickness and sorrow.
– Florence Scovel Shinn

Many people believe that self-love is being conceited or narcissistic. However, self-love implies self-acceptance, which means that you must love yourself the way you are, at any moment; and every single thing that you do, with no exception.

Many people naturally develop an attitude of self-loathing. They tend to condemn themselves in a merciless way, worse than any pain which could be inflicted by others. Field says that: *"Lack of self-worth is just another expression of not loving ourselves."*

Sometimes people tend to feel hate toward themselves in a very subtle manner. Some blatant examples of self-hatred are:

- *obsessive negative rumination*
- *self-condemnation*
- *overworking*
- *denial of pleasure*
- *underutilizing your skills*
- *passive aggression*
- *continuous hesitation*
- *merciless looking for perfection*
- *comparing with others*
- *lingering addictions*
- *deep depression*
- *sense of helplessness, among others*

When you first came into this world you did not have any of these traits of self-loathing, which were incorporated over time as part of your social programming. All attitudes of self-hatred are subconscious memories, and hence can be removed by doing Ho'oponopono.

Instead when you have an attitude of self-love you treat yourself with kindness, patience and gentleness, even when you go through difficult moments. You cast aside any negative emotional states such as fear, hatred or resentment.

You can love yourself more easily when you acknowledge your distinct valuable traits. You are more likely to express love to yourself when you realize that your true core is divine. When you truly love yourself, you are more prone to love other people in the same way.

It is really necessary that you start loving yourself unconditionally, if you have not done so yet. Holden says that: *"Self-love is, in essence, a loving attitude from which positive actions arise that benefit you and others."*

When you love yourself your actions tend to be more real and spontaneous than ever before. You don't have to feign to be someone else any longer. With this attitude you access your sacred core, which is concealed beneath masks and roles you use in your social environment. You can actually grasp the truth beyond the false.

From the Ho'oponopono perspective, when you regularly say *"I love you"* you are practicing self-love. With the use of this sentence you go beyond all appearances, which are manifestations of your subconscious negative programs.

Self-love naturally brings more harmony and awakening into your life; you tread the trail of your personal evolution. With self-love you never put yourself down through criticism, blame or regret but you always see yourself in the best light.

If you ever travelled by plane, you probably know that in a case of decompression of the plane cabin you must put your own oxygen mask in place before you proceed to help other people with their masks. Likewise, you can only love others if you truly love yourself first.

As you practice self-love regularly you are more prone to feeling elated with no apparent reason. When you have an attitude of self-love you tend to value yourself more, which prompts your positive feelings.

When you love yourself, you don't need to compare yourself with others. You understand that you are a unique being, as everybody is. You also know that you have a very important commonality with the rest of the people; your essence is divine love like theirs.

Self-love is never about feeling superior or wiser than others; this is just vanity or conceit. Instead, feeling love for yourself is appreciating the being you are, and respecting others at all times.

When you experience true love, you acknowledge your inter-connection to every single person and thing around you. As a consequence of this, you truly know that when you practice Ho'oponopono, not only do you improve your life but also others'.

The quickest way to love yourself is to become your best friend; a person who you wholeheartedly help and care for whenever needed. You must realize that you can never be too far away from yourself.

When you truly experience self-love you also have a higher respect for yourself, regardless of others' opinions. You also realize that you do not need to please others at your own expense.

As you love yourself authentically, you achieve a lingering state of peace, freedom and general well-being. With self-love, your energy levels rise and naturally dissolve any negativity in your life. In other words, your overall vibration reaches higher levels than ever before.

When you love yourself you tend to attract more positive things into your life. Furthermore with self-love, your problematic situations tend to be solved in an effortless manner. When you are filled with love you see life full of love.

If you find it difficult to love yourself you must observe any resistance you might experience against self-love. You can even ask yourself: *"What is going on in me that I am placing resistance against self-love?"* Take note of any insights and say the words *"I love you"* repeatedly. With these words, you can delete the memories underpinning your resistance to self-love.

It is really important that you love yourself for no reason, whenever possible. Your love toward yourself must never be conditioned by your achievements, status, health conditions or wealth. You must love yourself just because you are naturally loveable. You don't have to explain this to anyone, not even to yourself. When you have this attitude, your energy will rise in a miraculous manner.

You must always remember that self-love is your innermost birthright; it is the fuel which keeps you alive and the purifying water that washes away all impurities within you, as well. Field says: *"love your life and it will love you back."*

7.4. Love and difficult circumstances

... the love of the plant for water causes it to send forth its roots until the loved thing is found... the love of a flower for the sun causes it to grow away from the dark places, so that it may receive the light... Nothing but intense love will enable you to surmount the many obstacles placed in your path.
– William Walker Atkinson

There is no difficulty that enough love will not conquer; no disease that enough love will not heal; no door that enough love will not open; no gulf that enough love will not bridge; no wall that enough love will not throw down; no sin that enough love will not redeem. It makes no difference how deeply seated may be the trouble; how hopeless the outlook; how muddled the tangle; how great the mistake; a sufficient realization of love will dissolve it all.
– Emmet Fox

Many masters say that a lack of love is the cause of all difficulties in your life. From the Ho'oponopono perspective all negative circumstances in your life are generated by memories playing out under the level of your consciousness, which is temporarily severed from your love essence. Every time you repeat the words *"I love you"* you obtain the following benefits:

– You fill your life with love energy. With the frequent use of the words *"I love you"* you become a more loving person; you feel more empowered and proactive.
– You raise your vibration. Love energy shifts your overall vibratory levels and you are more prone to manifest more positive things in your life. This high vibration also pushes any detrimental situation away from you.
– You request assistance from the Divine. As explained in this book, with the regular use of the words *"I love you"* you receive support from Divinity during the cleaning process.
– You remove your subconscious negative memories. With the continuous use of the words *"I love you"* you effectively clean long-term ingrained memories almost miraculously.
– You rid yourself from your negative circumstances. In this book you saw that, once you removed these subconscious programs, all your difficulties tended to disappear with no effort.
– You create a void in your mind for inspiration. When you remove your subconscious programs, you create free space in your mind, which is to be filled with guidance from the Divine.

Fromm said that love is the most appropriate answer for all problems of humankind. You must think about this for a while. If you analyze this seriously, you may notice that every time in the past when you faced up to a dire situation, your negativity never helped you solve the problem, but kept you more stuck to it.

For this reason, when you are challenged by difficulties the most important thing you can do in that situation is experience love; feel love in the depth of your heart. You will feel more empowered to solve them because you connect to the most powerful energy that exists.

When you experience love energy you tend to have more clarity regarding your troublesome circumstances, which allows you to access your inner wisdom. As you experience true love, you realize that everything is possible and achievable.

In simple words, love naturally dissolves your negative emotional states. This in turn makes your difficult circumstances much easier to solve. Furthermore, love makes you feel more invigorated, peaceful and optimistic to face life challenges dexterously.

When you fill your actions with love you cast away any shadow in your life. Love works like an antidote against the poison of adversity. Love truly helps you resolve any unfinished business once and for good. Moreover, love magically compensates for all your shortcomings and failures.

7.5. Love and resistance

Every person is a gold mine; most of us just don't take the time to dig.
– Anonymous

If you are like most people, every time you face difficulties, your automatic reaction is likely to be resistance. You can resist your problems in different ways, for example fighting, denying or manipulating, among others. Sometimes, you truly wish these problems had never existed.

However, when you have a loving attitude regarding your problems you offer no resistance to them. Whenever you experience love despite your problems you tend to fully accept your difficult circumstances, which is the first step you can take to surmount them. You also take full responsibility for your life, which is one of the main requirements to deleting your subconscious programs.

Most oriental philosophies state that when you face a challenging situation you must always surrender to it. You naturally let go of any negative feelings related to your difficult circumstances and accept things as they are without becoming emotionally overwhelmed.

Resistance only keeps things stuck in the same place. Some masters say that resistance is just a specific form of fear. From this perspective, when you have a loving attitude, you not only surrender but you also let go of fear.

When you surrender and accept what it is, your negative circumstances tend to improve almost effortlessly. This happens naturally because you got rid of resistance, which was what actually kept you stuck in these problematic situations.

Surrender is not becoming resigned or inactive before your problems; you are faithful that things will work out in the best way possible. When you surrender you also know that you are always being supported by Divinity.

Furthermore, when you experience a state of surrender, you are more prone to practice Ho'oponopono regularly and become more susceptible to receiving divine guidance. If you truly surrender before your difficulties you are more prone to feel immense peace and powerfulness.

7.6. Love and the Divine

The universe is preserved because Love is at the Heart of it.
– James Allen

As seen, Divinity is pure love so whenever you say *"I love you"* you naturally reconnect to the Divine. The words *"I love you"* are sacred reminders of the presence of Divinity in you.

Some ancient philosophies wisely state that pure love and the Divine have the same meaning; they are interchangeable. From this perspective, feeling love is just feeling the Divine.

The Divine is incommensurable and omnipresent. Divinity is not only the source of pure love but the origin of everything that exists. It is all-pervading love energy which not only makes the planets gyrate but also makes every single being breathe. Byrne says that: *"the force of love is the intelligence of life and the universe."*

In relation to this, George states that: *"Ultimately love has no opposite. It is the very fabric that holds together all that exists at all levels. Love is like an invisible matrix that connects everything and everyone."* The Divine (or Love) is infinite and inexhaustible; it is always multiplying itself. It is pure wisdom and unbounded harmony, which is the same state you experience when you feel unconditional love.

With unconditional love, you can truly feel your connection with the Divine. For this reason, it is necessary to practice unconditional love whenever possible in order to perceive that everything which exists in your life is divine.

With unconditional love you also become more susceptible to the assistance from the Divine. When you have a continuous attitude of unconditional love you can easily recognize the Divine within you, as well.

Moreover when you have an attitude of unconditional love you feel your visceral connectedness with everything that exists. All apparently invincible boundaries which seem to separate you from others start to crumble naturally; you feel that we are all one.

A Course in Miracles recommends that, in order to connect to the Divine, you should concentrate on love energy on a frequent basis. That text says:

Put your faith in the Love of God within you; eternal, changeless, and forever unfailing. This is the answer to whatever confronts you today. Through the Love of God within you, you can resolve all seeming difficulties without effort and in sure confidence.

In a very similar tone, the great metaphysician Emmet Fox suggested a tool named the Golden Key. According to this technique, every time you face a problem, such as relational difficulties, financial challenges or others, you must exclusively focus on the Divine instead of concentrating on your problems.

You can think about its main characteristics, such as omnipresence, unconditional love, omniscience, almightiness, truth and wholeness, among others. From this viewpoint, when you constantly think about the Divine, the divine love energy will dissolve all your problems almost magically.

7.7. Be loving at all times

To be without Love is to be stagnant, lifeless, in pain. To be within Love is to be happy, energetic, vibrant, radiant and inspired.
– Nicola Jayne

Love is a magnificent, empowering and transformative energy. Moreover, love is the most important creator in the world, the linchpin of everything that exists. Byrne states that:

It is the positive force of love that inspires you to move and gives you the desires to be, do or have anything. The positive force of love can create anything good, increase the good things, and change anything negative in your life.

For this reason, you must make love energy the main fuel of your activities.

When you do things in a loving way, you are more likely to

succeed in your life. Likewise, Holden says that: *"love is the heart of success."* You must always consider love as your most important guidance to achieving all your goals in life. Holden states that: *"Love is the ultimate coach… let love guide you. Let love inspire you."*

Love is an energy which helps you evolve in your life path. Benner says that: *"Love is the fulfilment of everything that makes us human."* Furthermore, from a spiritual perspective it is said that planet Earth can be considered as your school of life; one of the most important lessons you can learn is to be true love.

Love should always be one of the main purposes in your life. Becker says that: *"We live to love just as we love to live."* This also means that all your life goals become meaningless when they are not solidly based on love.

There is a very easy way to have a loving attitude with yourself; start by taking note of your most evident positive traits, which are generally taken for granted. If you have difficulty assessing your best features you can try to imagine how an external observer will perceive you in a very positive light. You will notice that you have a more loving attitude toward yourself. You will also realize that you perform your activities more gracefully and effortlessly.

Frankl says that: *"The salvation of man is through love and in love… Love is the only way to grasp another human being in the inner core of his personality."* He states that love also helps you discover potentialities and essential traits, not only in yourself but also in other people.

Whenever you use the words *"I love you"* on a frequent basis they naturally remind you of your good features. With the frequent use of these words, you are actually imprinting in your mind the idea that you are a loving person.

Many people erroneously believe that if they behave lovingly they will become more vulnerable, but the opposite is true. When you have a loving attitude you naturally cast away your useless defenses, the ones you generally use to protect yourself; you become less restrictive and more empowered.

When you have a loving attitude, your perceptual lenses become clearer and your perception is widened. Becker says that: *"When you open your heart, you open your eyes to a new reality."* You can see yourself as part of the wholeness; you also understand that everything in the Universe flows in a perfectly orchestrated manner.

When you don't experience love, your life tends to become empty and meaningless. When you cannot feel love you realize that this void cannot be filled by anything else, except love.

Love is the most important energizer in your life; love naturally sweetens everything around you. With a loving attitude you can see beauty and harmony everywhere. Martin Luther King Jr. wisely said:

> *Hatred paralyzes life; love releases it. Hatred creates confusion; love harmonizes it. Hatred darkens life; love illuminates it.*

8. Practical tips to be more loving

> *What we think is less than what we know; what we know is less than what we love; what we love is so much less than what there is; and to this precise extent, we are much less than what we are.*
> *– RD Laing*

You can find below some tips you can use to have a more loving attitude in your life:

– *Dwell on your loving past:* You can always relive past loving moments, for example people treating you lovingly. Recall them to lift your mood. You can also recollect occasions in which you naturally behaved as a loving individual, either with yourself or others.

– *Pervade everything with love:* Your current well-being primarily depends on the amount of love you feel and, in turn, spread over your environment. Williamson says that: *"love in your mind produces love in your life."* In order to be happier and healthier you must feel that you are full of love. Visualize that this love energy overflows from you and impregnates your entire being. Imagine that you are giving love to everything and everyone around you. Envision that you are linked to the Divine through a strong love thread.

– *Be open to be loved:* Avoid closing your heart to love. Repeat aloud this sentence *"I am ready to receive all the love I deserve; I am ready to receive all the forgiveness"* as many times as possible. Imagine that your heart and mind are filled up with love. Another sentence that you can use is *"I am ready to give love to anyone at all times."* In this case, you can imagine that you are linked to every person you meet through luminous love rays.

– *Imagine being loved by everything that exists:* Love not only helps you develop a more intimate bond with yourself but also with everything that exists. Some masters suggest another very interesting exercise. When you walk down the street you must imagine that all people and things around you are shooting you with countless *"beams of love."* Imagine that these rays of love pervade your entire body. Philena Bruce suggests that you should *"imagine the Universe is a loving parent."*

– *Practice forgiveness:* You cannot fully love yourself or others if you constantly dwell in resentment, guilt and blame. To be a loving individual, you must also be a forgiving one. Forgive others but also yourself because forgiveness is the natural by-product of a loving attitude. Stauffer says that: *"Forgiveness requires that we be aware of the error of withdrawing love from others. There must be a willingness to correct this error in order to restore inner harmony."*

– *Feel blessed for all the good things that you have:* Love is naturally related to thankfulness, which is one of the most energetic states. When you are truly grateful you radiate high vibrations as in the case of love energy. For this reason, you must always be thankful for all positive things in your life, even little ones. Some masters even suggest that you be thankful for having subconscious memories, because they give you the chance to remove them and, in turn, improve your life.

– *Remember that love implies continual practice:* You must make the decision to be a loving person at all times. Express and receive love in a regular manner and consider love as your most precious inner resource, which can be accessed at all times. This might appear at first a bit challenging and even unnatural but, as the time goes by, you feel more comfortable with this attitude. Consider love as the compass which guides all your actions. In relation to this, Fromm shrewdly said, *"Love is an activity, a power of the soul... love is an orientation."* Love must be practiced; as you regularly dwell in this positive energy you will get more expert at it.

– *Be caring with yourself, others and your environment:* You must remember that compassion is a very positive value, which is closely related to unconditional love. When you are compassionate, you cannot be judgmental or critical to yourself or others because your energy is naturally positive. With compassion you truly understand that everybody is essentially love, even yourself. Whenever you behave compassionately you can see beyond negative appearances. You can say to the Divine this sentence: *"Please help me see everything with the eyes of love"* frequently.

– *Be a universal servant:* According to Dr. Sha, our main purpose in this world is to offer universal service, which includes unconditional love and forgiveness. When you offer service to others, you knowingly contribute for others' lives to be better. Whenever you help others, you are actually giving your love to them. On a similar note, Shimoff and Kline say that: *"The purpose of life is to expand in love."* Whenever you serve others you are adding prized value to their lives. With your assistance their lives become easier and more enjoyable. Muhammad Ali says: *"Service to others is the rent you pay for your room here on earth."*

– *Be generous:* When you are generous you are also a universal servant; you are obliging and support everyone around you. There are different ways through which you can be more generous, for example: donations, other charitable actions, volunteering, mentoring activities, random acts of kindness, tithing, and philanthropy, among others. Through these actions you can also express unconditional love.

– *Never try to withhold love:* If you are like most people you might have been affected by loveless experiences in the past. Despite this, you should never prevent yourself from giving love to others. Moreover, you should give your love to others freely, without any condition or resistance. You should focus your love not only on yourself but also on other people around you. Authentic love is never selfish or self-centered. Elbert Hubbard says that: *"The love we give away is the only love we keep."* Unconditional love is essentially expansive and multiplying. Byrne says that: *"Every single time you give love, through your feelings, sounds or actions, you add more love to the field around you."*

– *Look for models of unconditional love:* In order to be more loving in your life, you can also study the biographies of spiritual masters such as Jesus, Gandhi, Buddha or others to obtain insights into the principles underpinning unconditional love. You can also take into account more simple examples of unconditional love, such as little babies and domestic pets, which both radiate pure love energy around themselves.

– *Analyze your past actions:* There is an interesting exercise that you can do on your own. Find a comfortable place in which you can be relaxed and make a list of past events in which you did not behave in a loving manner. Include as many details as possible. Visualize these past events and ask this question: *"What is going on in me that I am experiencing this?"* Then wait for insights and say the four Ho'oponopono sentences repeatedly.

– *Visualize that you behave lovingly:* It was previously explained that you must recall past experiences in which you behaved in an unloving manner. After this, re-imagine that on these same occasions you instead behaved in a very loving manner. Then repeat the four Ho'oponopono sentences many times. You can also say the words *"I love you"* repeatedly.

– *Use your heart to purify the negative:* Visualize that you are breathing in and absorbing all negative experiences in your life. Imagine placing this negativity in your heart, which transmutes these negative aspects with its radiant love. Sunyatananda suggests that once you have absorbed the negative energy you must imagine that it is burnt in an imaginary oven located in the base of your spine and converted into love energy. After this, you must spread this high vibration energy all over your environment. You can also imagine this energy bringing about countless positive experiences in your life.

– *Remember that love only attracts love:* When you have a continual loving attitude, you naturally tend to manifest positive circumstances in your life. This happens because love has the highest vibration that exists, which draws back to you only positive situations. Whenever you experience love, you repel any negative circumstances in your life. Atkinson states that: *"Thoughts of Love will attract to us the Love of others; circumstances and surroundings in accord with the thought; people who are of like thought."*

– *Ask yourself questions about unconditional love:* Ask yourself questions about different aspects of unconditional love, for example, *"What is the experience of unconditional love about?"*, *"What are the main qualities of unconditional love?"*, *"How can I know when I experience unconditional love?"* and *"How should I behave when I feel unconditional love?"* With these types of questions, you can obtain very useful insights about this type of love. If you practice meditation regularly, you can ask these questions just before entering the meditative state. In all cases, after asking these questions, you must say the four Ho'oponopono sentences or the words *"I love you"* repeatedly.

– *Spread love over your loving beings:* Dr. Sha suggests a very interesting exercise you can do on your own. Imagine that all your loved beings are located inside your own abdomen, and imagine that you pervade them with a beam of love energy. Then visualize that the sun, the moon and every little thing that exists in the Universe is also located in your abdomen. Lastly, envision that your abdomen is pervaded with love energy.

– *Impregnate your problems with love:* This is an interesting technique you can use whenever you are challenged by difficult situations. Think about troublesome issues affecting you and ask yourself: *"How can I love this problem?"* Then imagine a love beam of light going through the top of your head and pervading your body. See the problematic situation being bathed by love light. Avoid being taken over by any negative emotion.

– *Do some random acts of kindness:* Random acts of kindness are little but prized deeds in which you benefit others, even strangers, for no reason and without expecting anything in return. You help other people in a warm and heartfelt manner. These acts are pure expression of unconditional love. Dowrick says that:

> – *Any act of selfless giving expands your world outwards... it breaks that illusion of your aloneness... It takes your attention away from you, even momentarily... It affects the crevices of your mind.*

Make these acts one of your positive habits. An example of a random act of kindness is helping elderly people cross the street. Set the goal of performing, at least, one random act of kindness per day. Some serious scientific studies confirmed that when you give to others genuinely, your mood and your general health conditions tend to improve in a significant manner.

Chapter 11

Thank You

Whenever you realize it or not, every single time you experience happiness, underneath it all you're in a state of appreciation. No matter what you're excited about, that feeling means that you're thankful for something.
– Sandra Anne Taylor

O Lord, that lends me life, Lend me a heart replete with thankfulness!
– William Shakespeare, Henry VI, Part 2, Act 1, Scene 1

No matter who you are or how confused you are about life. There is one prayer that will provide the key to your tranquility and it is simply to say 'thank you.'
– David Baird

1. Importance of gratitude

A thankful heart cannot be cynical.
– AW Tozer

Through history countless sages, philosophers, humanitarians and great men from different origins have recognized the importance of gratitude. Likewise, most relevant religions and spiritual teachings in the world truly believe in the transformative power of thankfulness.

The opposite of gratitude is ungratefulness. Whenever you are ungrateful, you are not truly accepting or valuing life. When you are unappreciative you are only focusing on the negative aspects of your life. You tend to feel fear, regret, worry, hatred, anxiousness or other negative emotional states regarding your life circumstances. In short, ingratitude is just a reflection of a state of unhappiness.

When you are unthankful you also tend to be excessively driven by expectations. You are likely to say things like *"I wish I could be..."* or *"I wish that situation had been different."* Whenever you use these types of sentences not only are you rejecting your life experiences but you also crave for better ones.

You are prone to be unappreciative if, in the past, your expectations have been frustrated. So you believe that things are likely to be the same in the future, which renders you ungrateful.

Other examples of an ungrateful attitude are complaining or moaning. You are not being appreciative whenever you tend to compare yourself with others. In these examples, ingratitude represents intense resistance to your current life situations.

The most common signal of ingratitude appears whenever you judge anything in a negative manner. With this attitude you do not understand that all situations even the most detrimental ones have positive aspects, albeit sometimes carefully hidden. You cannot be judgmental and appreciative at the same time, because these two attitudes are incompatible. You always have the choice to adopt the attitude which is more constructive for you.

Many people argue that it is very difficult to be grateful before life's dire problems. However, whenever you are ungrateful this attitude does not help you solve your problems but it keeps you more stuck to them.

The principle of Newtonian Physics asserts that every action has an equal reaction. This is an immutable law which always applies. Remember the metaphysical principle called Law of Causality, which similarly states that every cause has its respective consequence.

In relation to this, Byrne says that:

The very action of gratitude sets off the reaction of receiving. And the more sincere and the more deeply grateful you feel (in other words, the more gratitude you give) the more you will receive.

To put it simply, when you are truly grateful (cause) you remove your subconscious memories and, in turn, transform your life into a more positive one (consequence).

You can even be thankful for facing difficult circumstances because they make you aware that you have subconscious memories to remove. You can also be thankful for having the opportunity to use the Ho'oponopono technique. Besides you can be appreciative because of receiving the assistance of the Divine during the cleaning process of your subconscious data.

Gratitude is always related to a state of mindfulness. Whenever you say *"thank you"* you purposely acknowledge and value all things and experiences you have in your life, which implies being mindful.

2. Ways to express gratitude

Appreciation is the hinge that swings open the door of love.
– Mindy Audlin

The simplest way to express thankfulness is to use the simple statement *"Thank you"* which is one of the four Ho'oponopono sentences. You don't have to say *"Thank you"* to anybody in particular, just to yourself. Some suggest that you should also say these words to Divinity or however you want to call this almighty force.

You might also be asking yourself, *"How can I be more appreciative?"* The answer to this question is, simply: you should say the brief sentence *"Thank you"* as many times as possible.

You can also use a more complete statement, for example, *"Thank you for... because..."* to identify the object of your appreciation and the reason why you are appreciative. You can also use other statements such as *"I express my gratitude for… "*, *"I am grateful for…"*, *"I show my appreciation for…"* or similar ones.

Many masters say that you should always be unconditionally grateful. In other words you must be willing to give thanks at all times, for no specific reason whatsoever.

It was mentioned previously that you can address your appreciation to the Divine. In this case, you can use specific sentences, for example: *"Thank you, Divinity (God, the Universe, etc.), for cleaning all the subconscious memories manifesting negative circumstances in my life"* or *"Thank you, Divinity, for resolving all my life situations"* or *"Thank you, Divinity, for bringing the best to my life"* among others.

Rosenberg says that your messages of gratitude should always be as specific and concrete as possible. From this perspective, whenever you are grateful to other people (or God) you must precisely communicate the things they did for you and express the emotions you feel because of this. In addition, you must also disclose the needs of yours they met.

An example of a gratitude sentence can be *"Thank you, God, for making my life wonderful, I feel exhilarated and I am full of love."* In this example your feelings are mentioned by using the word "exhilarated." You also express the needs of yours which were satisfied, in this case *love*.

From the Ho'oponopono perspective, you can also thank Divinity for helping you to remove your subconscious memories. You can also express your gratitude to the Divine for the inspirational insights you are about to receive.

You should never feel that expressing gratitude is mandatory for you. Many parents naturally press their little children to be thankful with other people. As a consequence, when they grow older they tend to express their gratitude in a false manner.

Sometimes the words *"Thank you"* are devalued; many people say *"Thank you"* without even feeling it. These words are used just as a social formality or as matter of curtesy. In many cases people are not truly thankful.

Real thankfulness only comes from the core of your being; you feel it in your heart. Whenever you use these words, you should acknowledge their true meaning. However, when you do Ho'oponopono, you do not need to say *"Thank you"* heartily. If you say these words mechanically the removal of your subconscious memories will be effective all the same.

3. Main meanings of gratefulness

Gratitude is all-encompassing, it can transform our lives into ones of great meaning and ultimately, joy.
– Lenore Skomal

Thankfulness has countless meanings; it is possible to say that gratitude is:

– A way to pay back for all the experiences you went through in your life
– A positive focus on all your life circumstances
– A very enlightened way of living
– An overt way of celebrating life
– A sign of your authenticity and humanness
– Your acknowledgement of your connection to all that exists
– Your recognition of your greatness
– Your valuable feedback to the Divine regarding your life situations
– Pure love energy dissolving all negativity within you
– An expanding enlivening force which uplifts your mood effortlessly
– A state of pure peacefulness and serenity
– A signal of your personal development and evolution
– Your alignment with your purest essence
– Your admiration of the beauty in everything around you
– A potent magnet which attracts positive things in your life

– The path to access your most prized inner resources
– A soothing balm for all your negative feelings
– A relief of your physical and emotional tension
– The best present you give yourself and others
– An easy way to experience unconditional love
– An open doorway to receiving multiple gifts from the Universe
– The opposite to deprecating what you experience in life
– A sign of maturity, thoughtfulness and mindfulness
– The opposite to any form of negative judgment
– A sincere expression of love to yourself and others
– A regenerative, nurturing and vitalizing power
– A sense of clarity regarding all your experiences

Smith says that: *"Gratitude is unconditional appreciation for everything."* When you go through positive experiences you highlight all their enjoyable aspects. Instead, when you face negative experiences, you appreciate the lessons that you get from them. Thankfulness is just a way of recognizing that you are blessed by many life presents.

When you are grateful, difficulties represent prized opportunities to introduce some changes in your life. As explained, each negative experience you go through gives you the opportunity to clean your subconscious memories.

It is very important that when you face a negative situation you ask yourself: *"What are the positive traits of this circumstance that I can be appreciative for?"* You are likely to obtain very useful insights.

When you are appreciative and centered on positive attributes of everything around you, you are fully present. When you are in the now you cannot be taken by past memories, and you also avoid being misguided by expectations. By being appreciative you also raise your levels of energy, which in turn help you to attract more positive things into your life.

Moreover, when you are appreciative you can release any

negativity, which puts you in a better position to face your life challenges. Patent says that: *"embracing any creation in deep appreciation removes the disguise and frees the energy to be reclaimed as what it really is – unconditional love... Appreciation is the ever expanding energy of valuing."* Some masters say that when you appreciate you increase the value of what you are grateful for.

Whenever you give thanks you are also displaying positive aspects of yourself: love, compassion, peacefulness and empathy. If you have an attitude of gratitude you naturally radiate high vibrations, which draw more abundance into your life.

In relation to this, Childre, Martin and Beech say that: *"Positive thoughts and feelings add energy to our system. An optimistic perspective, a feeling of appreciation, or a gesture of kindness, for example, are energy assets."* These authors state that the so-called *"heart feelings"*, which include love, compassion, forgiveness, appreciation and non-judgment, are contributory to your overall state of well-being. They also highlight that: *"Appreciation has a way of smoothing out life's lumps and bumps. It puts things into perspective, reducing the heaviness and density of stressful thoughts and feelings."*

There have been several scientific studies about gratitude, such as one conducted by Emmons and McCullough. During this study two groups were compared; the first group kept records of all the things they were grateful for, using a gratitude journal. The second group did not keep any record at all.

The first group experienced more positivity and optimism than the second group. Besides, the first group had a better performance regarding the achievement of their personal objectives. According to this study when you express your gratitude you tend to have a more positive attitude, which improves your state of well-being.

Becker pinpoints that: *"Gratitude is a wonderful way to experience this world through peace, freedom and joy."* There are other scientific studies which confirm that when you have a grateful attitude, your immune and cardiovascular systems are strengthened.

You can never be too grateful; gratitude always has a multiplying effect in your life. As you have a continual thankful attitude, you will notice more miraculous shifts in every area of your life.

Gratitude is one of the easiest ways to access your inner power. Moreover, when you are thankful you are more likely to be benefited by blessings from the Divine. Murphy says that: *"the thankful heart is close to the riches of the universe."*

The word *appreciation* has two main meanings, which are deeply interconnected. The first meaning is *"to be grateful or expressing gratitude."* The second meaning of this word is *"to increase the value of things."* Whenever you appreciate things and situations in your life, you make them more valuable.

In addition, thankfulness is like a sacred bridge you cross in order to reunite with Divinity. When you are grateful you know that Divinity is always caring for you. Your heart is totally attuned with the Divine.

You should be thankful as frequently as possible. Thankfulness does not cost you anything but its benefits are significant. When you adopt a continuous grateful attitude, you are less likely to have negative emotions and thoughts, because you are exclusively focused on positive aspects of your reality.

4. Main reasons for gratitude

Gratitude unlocks the fullness of life. It turns what we have into enough, and more. It turns denial into acceptance, chaos into order, and confusion to clarity. It can turn a meal into a feast, a house into a home, a stranger into a friend. Gratitude makes sense of past, brings peace for today, and creates a vision for tomorrow.
– Melody Beattie

From Ho'oponopono's perspective, you can be grateful for many different reasons. In that effect, when you say *"Thank you"* repeatedly you are being grateful for:

– *Facing negative circumstances:* These negative situations make you realize that there are subconscious memories which must be removed.

– *Taking full responsibility:* Your problematic situations are of high value because they prompt you to take one hundred percent responsibility for each of your life situations. These difficulties also goad you to remove all the memories you have stored in your subconscious mind.

– *Removing subconscious memories:* You should also be thankful for having discovered that your life is taken over by your subconscious programs. Gratitude represents a very overt way to show your joy because you can let go of all these programs. When you are grateful you can also use a sentence like: *"Thank you for cleaning all subconscious memories which manifest all problems in my life."*

– *Receiving the support from the Divine:* Every time you say *"Thank you"* you are demonstrating that you unconditionally rely on Divinity for the deletion of your subconscious programs. Petroff says that: *"Appreciation awakens us to the reality that Divinity is conspiring for us and aiding our spiritual growth."*

– *Knowing that your problems will be solved:* You are also grateful, even in the cases when you are harassed by difficulties, because you know that all your problematic issues will be resolved in an effortless manner, once you delete the subconscious data originating them. You are thankful in advance before the problems are solved.

– *Increasing your levels of energy:* When you say *"Thank you"* and remove your past programming you tend to naturally radiate better energy. This increase in your energy levels also helps you attract good things into your life.

– *New positive situations about to come:* When you say *"Thank you"* on a frequent basis you are also grateful in advance for all positive transformations about to occur in your life. You clearly understand that any positive change you might experience in your life is the natural consequence of having removed your subconscious programs. Wattles says that: *"faith is born of gratitude. The grateful mind continually expects good things, and expectation becomes faith."*

– *Receiving divine inspiration:* When you say the words *"Thank you"* repeatedly, you are also grateful for having the chance of receiving inspirational messages from the Divine. Every time you say *"Thank you"* you also create space in your mind to receive inspiration from Divinity.

5. Other reasons for thankfulness

There are many other things that you can be grateful for in your life. For example, whenever you say *"Thank you"* you can also be thankful for:

– *Your specialness and uniqueness*
– *The skills and capabilities you have acquired all over your life*
– *All useful information you have access to*
– *Every good experience you have been through in your life*
– *The difficulties you overcame in the past*
– *The challenges you will face in the future*
– *Every service (education, medical assistance, etc.) or product (books, food, clothes, etc.) you have been enjoying in your life*
– *The places you visited or are about to visit*
– *Your career and way of living*
– *The little or abundant money in your life*
– *Each of your possessions (house, car, etc.)*
– *The fact you are alive*

– Your mental, emotional and physical health conditions
– Our beautiful planet and everything that exists in the Universe
– Your knowledge about the Ho'oponopono technique
– All relationships in your life which provide you with important lessons
– All people that makes this world worthwhile

In relation to people, you must be grateful for every person who appears in your life. You should consider all the people in your life as precious gifts; these people are just reflections of you. When you encounter people who are malevolent or with difficulties, they help you realize you have subconscious memories to delete.

You should take everything into account as valuable in your life. You can even be grateful for minor things, like the hot tea you drank in the morning. Never put limits to the appreciation that you can express.

If you have difficulties being more thankful, think about the little blessings you receive every day. When you do not know what to be thankful for you can ask: *"What should I be grateful for?"*

You should not take anything for granted in your life, for example, the facts that you can breathe or have a good sleep. They perfectly count as objects of your appreciation. Buddha says:

Let's rise up and be thankful, for if we didn't learn a lot today, at least we learnt a little, and if we didn't learn a little, at least we didn't get sick, and if we got sick at least we didn't die; so, let us all be thankful.

6. Practical tips for gratitude

If the only prayer you have ever said in your life was thank you, that would suffice.
– Meister Eckhart

Most people experience a shortage of thankfulness: Your most important goal must be having an appreciative attitude at all times and for any reason. You can find below a list with a few recommendations on being more grateful in your life.

– *Realize the real value of gratitude:* You have nothing to lose, but a lot to win, by being grateful. Gratitude is always free and brings a myriad of benefits into your life. Look for things or situations which make you feel alive, exhilarated or at peace and then be appreciative for experiencing them in your life.

– *Be thankful for negative experiences:* You should be grateful even when you face negative situations in your life. You should avoid being defensive or closing down when you face up to difficult circumstances. The best way to accept your negative situations is by being appreciative. Remember that these circumstances make you aware that you have subconscious memories which you have to delete; they are blessings in disguise.

– *Find a motive to be grateful:* You can always find a reason such as being alive or having people who care for you, among others. You can find these *treasures* at all times, even when you are affected by difficulties. Ferrini states: *"Gratitude is the choice to see the love of God in all things."* There is a very simple exercise you can do in your spare time; say the word *"yes"* to the Universe to express your gratitude to all that exists. As you do this exercise, your energy will rise and your negative life circumstances will be transformed into positive ones.

– *Have a steady focus on appreciation:* Sometimes your thoughts can be unhealthy. Whenever your mind wanders over negative things, you must refocus on positive things you can be grateful for. For example, you can switch from worrying or moaning to showing appreciation for things you have or experience. When you do this exercise on a frequent basis, you will make a habit of it. You can also say: *"Despite this, I am thankful for..."* or *"Nonetheless I can express my gratitude for..."* When you concentrate on positive aspects of your life you are more prone to attract like situations.

– *Focus also on the past and the future:* You can also be grateful for things, experiences, people, and places you enjoyed in the past. You can also give thanks for your past negative experiences especially for the lessons you obtained. You can also be appreciative for experiences that will come to your life in the future. You can also be thankful for specific opportunities you know are about to come into your life, such as nice people you will meet or delightful places. Whenever you are grateful about your upcoming events, you energize them positively.

– *Avoid criticism:* Whenever you act like a harsh critic of your life you tend to concentrate primarily on its negative aspects, which attract even more detrimental situations into your life. The most effective way out of this is to focus only on things that give you pleasure or make you feel positive emotions. Bear in mind that you cannot be appreciative and judgmental at the same time; they are incompatible states. Each time you focus on things that you love or enjoy this renders you in a receptive mode, which makes you manifest more positive things in your life.

– *Choose to always be grateful:* Whenever you are grateful you are making the best decision in your life. As previously mentioned many scientific studies confirm that thankful people are more optimistic and less prone to despondency. Carnegie says that: *"gratitude is a 'cultivated' trait."* You must understand that once you start being more appreciative you will gradually find more reasons to be grateful.

– *Be grateful for all relationships in your life:* You must always be thankful for all relationships you develop in life. Focus not only on the main relationships such as with relatives, friends and lovers, but with others such as colleagues, acquaintances and strangers. All of these ties make you realize you have subconscious memories to remove. Remember that you have shared subconscious memories with all the people you are aware of.

– *Don't refrain yourself from having a thankful attitude:* You should always be unconditionally appreciative with anybody, even with people you are at odds with. Byrne suggests a very interesting exercise you can do on your own. Look for pictures of three people with whom you have a conflictive relationship and mentally say to them several things you are grateful for. Your gratitude must be expressed in a silent, but also heartfelt manner. If you cannot find anything to be grateful for in relation to these people ask yourself: *"If I was truly thankful with these people, what would I be appreciative for?"* and repeat the four Ho'oponopono sentences many times.

– *Acknowledge others' contribution to your life:* You should be grateful for goods and services you get from others. When you do so, you are implicitly acknowledging that you are interconnected with the rest of the people. For example, when you are grateful for having a beautiful house, you must also realize that this abode was the result of the work of many people, such as architects, bricklayers, suppliers of material, etc. All things or services that you enjoy are the result of numerous people that contributed to making this available for you. Patent says that: *"Self-appreciation is appreciation for the Oneness, the God presence that we are."*

Section III

Other Aspects Related to Ho'oponopono

In this section there will be thorough explanations of the functioning of the mind. There is a chapter about the Zero Point and inspiration. This section includes numerous exercises related to Ho'oponopono. There is also a chapter about meditation and Ho'oponopono.

Chapter 12

Structure of the Mind

The mind in its pure state is like a mirror cleansed of dust, will then reflect undistorted images… allowing to go beneath the surface and perceive the essential spiritual quality of all life's experiences.
– AC Bhaktivedanta Swami Prabhupada

1. General aspects of the mind

Our greatest failures as well as our grandest triumphs were merely pictures in our minds at first. Nothing can happen until someone thinks of it.
– Audrey Craft Davis

Like the perspective of traditional psychology, the Hawaiian masters conceive that the human mind is divided into three parts:

– subconscious mind
– conscious mind
– and super conscious mind

From the Ho'oponopono perspective, these three parts can be considered as if they were the three members of the family:

– the child (which is subconscious mind)
– the mother (which is the conscious)
– and the father (which is the super conscious)

It is important to remember that it is in the subconscious mind (the child) where all your past programs are stored. It is also necessary to recall that these memories are the only cause of any negative circumstances you face in your life.

You should consciously develop a loving relationship with the child. Your subconscious mind tends to be cooperative when your conscious mind (the mother) treats it with affection. Most people dismiss their child for a long time, which weakens this relationship.

When you do Ho'oponopono, the mother (conscious mind) asks the father (super conscious mind) to heal the destructive programming held in by the child (subconscious mind). This request to the father is made throughout the child.

When these family members have a harmonious relationship among them, you tend to feel unbounded peace and you are more likely to receive inspirational insights from the Divine. In practice there are no definite and clear-cut boundaries among these three parts of the mind. Despite this, each of them has distinct functions.

2. Subconscious mind

The Subconscious Mind experiences vicariously, mimicking and echoing memories replaying. It behaves, sees, feels and decides exactly as memories dictate.
– Dr. Hew Len

2.1. General aspects of the subconscious mind

The initiation of the preparation to culminate in a freely voluntary movement arises unconsciously in the brain preceding the conscious awareness of wanting or intending to act now by about 400 msec or more.
– Benjamin Libet

It is also called the subjective mind, deep mind, or low self. From the Ho'oponopono perspective it is called Unihipili or *the child*. Its analytical capacities are not fully developed, as compared with the conscious part.

Bristol says that:

> *the powers of the subconscious are many: intuition, emotion, certitude, inspiration, suggestion, deduction, imagination, organization, and, of course, memory and dynamic energy.*

It is considered as the mental stage where your most significant mind processes are performed.

There is a very important difference between conscious and subconscious mental processes; in the latter ones there is an absence of awareness as compared with the former ones.

On one side, the subconscious mind is generally characterized as unfathomable. It can also be considered like a secretive chest where all your darkest impulses are hidden. On the other side, the subconscious mind can also be conceived as your source of life and creativity. The subconscious part of your mind has the following characteristics:

a) Storage of your past programming

> *The subconscious psychic activity, powerful in itself, is reinforced by a still more potent and infallible memory which leaves the feeble and limited conscious memory far behind...*
>
> *Everything occurs as though the multitude of daily experiences had as their end or their result an uninterrupted enrichment of subconsciousness during the whole life. No remembrance, no vital or psychological experience is lost.*
> – Gustave Geley

It resembles the hard drive of a personal computer keeping all the programs accumulated all over your life. As explained these subconscious programs are influences received (or downloaded) from your social environment as the so-called social conditioning.

All over your life you have accumulated thousands of these memories.

Wilson states: *"There is a vast storehouse of primitive, infantile thought that is kept out of consciousness because it is a source of psychic pain."* From the Ho'oponopono perspective, your subconscious mind is related to your childhood.

Bristol says that the subconscious mind:

is a repository of spontaneous past impressions of man and nature and a memory vault in which are kept the records of facts and experiences... for safekeeping and future house... It is beyond space and time, and is fundamentally a powerful receiving and sending station with the universal hookup.

As explained, your subconscious mind includes every bit of information even the one you inherited from your ancestors.

Claxton says that:

in the modern view of adaptive unconscious... a lot of interesting stuff about human mind – judgement, feelings, and motives – occurs outside of awareness for reasons of efficiency, and not because of repression.

Most of the information you need for your survival is processed by your subconscious mind. If all the information stored below the level of your conscious emerged to your awareness, it would be impossible to process it effectively.

Your subconscious mind acts like a precise recording device which can store everything that goes into it. Your subconscious appliance does not have any power to discard or dispose of the memories recorded. You can only delete these recordings by doing Ho'oponopono. All your subconscious memories are constantly played out, as if they were true at all times. There are some points you should take into account regarding the imprinting of information on your subconscious mind:

– Your subconscious mind cannot differentiate real experiences from imagined ones. All things are stored in your subconscious mind. Your subconscious is very susceptible to any suggestions, for example visualizations or affirmations; it feels more comfortable working with imagery and metaphors rather than rational concepts.

– Your subconscious mind does not discriminate if you are talking about a topic in a joking or earnest manner; no information is discarded. Your subconscious mind cannot differentiate past, present or future either.

– The subconscious part of your mind is easily affected by repeated sentences and metaphors. Ho'oponopono's technique is so effective because you have to repeat the four sentences as frequently as possible, and by doing so, you are embedding these phrases in your subconscious.

– Many of your subconscious memories are reformulated over time. Nonetheless other subconscious programs tend to adopt a rigid structure. When new information is incorporated in your subconscious mind which is contradictory to the data held there, the former is likely to be adapted to fit in with the latter one.

Your subconscious mind never rejects or argues with the information provided by your conscious mind. Scovel Shinn says that: *"The subconscious is simply power, without direction. It is like steam or electricity, and it does what it is directed to do; it has no power of induction."*

Your subconscious mind is not judgmental nor does it reason, but instead it is impartial regarding information received. As explained, most of the information which imprints your subconscious mind is not even detected by your conscious mind.

Jungian psychology also says there is a collective subconscious made up of universal patterns of thoughts which affect the emotions, thoughts and actions of any individual. These arche-types are related to various cultural aspects and traditional, collective myths and visions. Your subconscious mind also includes this collective subconscious. McKenna states that the collective subconscious: *"contains experiences shared by all human beings and is part of your biological inheritance."* These are meaningful concepts and symbols shared with the rest of the human race, for example the concepts of hero, the idea of God, the maternal figure, among others.

As seen previously, it is very difficult, if not impossible, to directly access the information held in your subconscious mind. Levenson says that: *"The biggest difficulty is the subconscious mind. We have related things to the subconscious mind, stored them there, and thrown away the key."* As was previously explained, the use of introspection can give you some clues about the information kept in your subconscious mind.

Bailes says that the subconscious mind is the *"loom that weaves thought into thing."* You are always attracting things, people and circumstances into your life which are in accordance with the memories held in your subconscious mind. Murphy states that: *"what you impress on your subconscious mind is expressed on the screen of space as conditions, experiences and events."*

It is important to remember that the main objective of the Ho'oponopono cleaning technique is to remove all the memories held in your subconscious mind. However the subconscious does not know how to get rid of these memories by itself. You always need to start this cleaning process on a conscious level.

b) Source of emotions

We know less than we think we do about our own minds, and exert less control over our minds than we think.
– Timothy Wilson

Your subconscious mind is not rational or lineal but emotional by nature. It is the spring fountain of all your various feelings, which in many cases you tend to experience in a conscious way. The state of emotional awareness is known as emotional intelligence.

However, not all your emotions are felt in a conscious manner; your subconscious mind tends to hide some of your emotional states and thoughts, especially the ones which could be harmful for you. The different mental defenses were explained in detail in Chapter 3.

When your subconscious mind intervenes in any decision-making process, it does not have the capability to decide if something is right or erroneous for you. Instead, your subconscious mind just plays out the information stored in it. Your subconscious mind is essentially reactive; all your reactions are based on the data stored in your humongous subconscious database.

Your subconscious mind is also willing to learn, when your conscious mind gives it instructions in a caring way. Lastly all the past memories engraved in your subconscious mind have a very intense emotional charge attached to them. So when you use Ho'oponopono, you also dissolve the emotional states related to these memories.

c) Other functions of the subconscious mind

The unconscious is mental processes that are inaccessible to consciousness but that influence judgments, feelings or behavior... the mental processes that operate our perceptual, language and motor systems operate largely outside of awareness, much like the vast workings of the federal government that go on out of the view of the president.
– *Timothy Wilson*

Your subconscious mind has a very important capability to store and process massive amounts of information, as compared with your conscious mind. Your subconscious is constraining by nature; it always acts in accordance to the information it holds. Your subconscious mind is working 24/7 even when you are asleep.

Besides, your subconscious mind and your conscious mind are continually interacting with one another. For example, your subconscious mind in interaction with the conscious level participates in perception and interpretation of your environment as well as in decision-making and learning processes. Sometimes, your subconscious and your conscious work cooperatively; other times they seem to be at odds.

As mentioned previously, all your intentions are originated in your subconscious mind, which means your past programs. Libet says that:

> we may view unconscious initiative for voluntary acts as burbling up unconsciously in the brain. The conscious will then select which of these initiatives may go forward to an action, or which ones to veto and abort so no act occurs.

This author added that: "The unconscious appearance of an intention to act could not be controlled consciously. Only its final consummation in a motor act could be consciously controlled."

There are some other aspects of your subconscious mind to highlight, as follows:

– Your subconscious encloses all your beliefs, values and assumptions, your personal life biography and your different automatisms (skills and abilities). It also stores your general knowledge, your lexicon (also called semantic memory), your motivations and desires, among other elements.

– The subconscious part of your mind is in charge of all functions related to your survival. For example, your subconscious is in charge of the management and monitoring of all your body functions and reflexes. It also deals with immunity processes against threatening external agents and regulates the vital energy in your body.

– All your automatic or routine activities are taken over by your subconscious mind in order to be carried out effortlessly and virtuously. Every time you are multitasking, some of the activities involved are performed by your subconscious.

– Your subconscious mind is the source of repetitive unintentional thoughts such as obsessive ruminations, unintentional judgments, stereotyping, among others.

– The subconscious is the part of your mind where all things you like and dislike, also called preferences, are formed. These preferences are the main bases for your decisions in life.

– All your creative skills are naturally cryptic and performed beneath the level of your consciousness. Libet states that: *"cognitive, imaginative and decision-making processes all can proceed unconsciously, often more creatively than in conscious functions."* The subconscious mind is also the fountain of your intuitive insights. Murphy also states that: *"Your subconscious is in touch with infinite life and boundless wisdom, and its impulses and ideas are always lifeward."*

– In situations of emergency, your subconscious mind takes over and tends to always privilege your survival. On these occasions, your subconscious mind puts you into one of these three different modes: fight (it makes you combat the threatening force), flight (it prompts you escape the threatening factor), or freeze (it paralyzes your actions and thoughts so that you have no reaction at all).

– Wilson stated that the subconscious acts like a pattern detector regarding your environment, which behaves in a very quick and automatic way. Conversely your conscious mind is more prone to check facts more slowly and thoroughly. Claxton states: *"What becomes conscious, in any moment, emerges from an unconscious appraisal of the situation."*

2.2. Tips to harness the potential of your subconscious

Practically all of your mind is unconscious to you, just like all of an iceberg is underneath the surface of the water.
– Gary Renard

Finally, you can find below some tips to make better use of your subconscious mind.

– Remember that everything imprinted in your subconscious tends to manifest in your reality. Your subconscious is like a silent butler who continually but secretively tries to fulfil your innermost desires. Anthony states: *"The subconscious is a system of checks and balances. It always makes sure our image of reality comes true."* It is very important to do Ho'oponopono on a frequent basis in order to remove your subconscious memories.

– Bear in mind that the subconscious mind is always obedient to the information it stores. For this reason, some masters recommend that you should always be the zealous guardian of your words in order to prevent negative data from entering your subconscious mind unwittingly.

– Your subconscious mind tends to work more effectively when your brainwaves are theta or alpha. In theta and alpha states your brainwaves become slower; thus you can record information more easily on your subconscious level. You can achieve these states through hypnosis, deep meditation, yoga or simply sleeping.

3. Conscious mind

The Conscious Mind has a choice. It can initiate incessant cleansing or it can allow memories to replay problems incessantly.
– Dr. Ihaleakala Hew Len

3.1. General aspects of the conscious mind

Consciousness is the experience of experiencing, the knowledge of knowing, the sense of sensing.
– Tor Norretranders

The conscious mind is also called *Uhane*, surface mind, middle self, intellect or objective mind. From the Ho'oponopono perspective the conscious is called *the mother* and it is the rational part of your mind. It is the most evident sign of your humaneness.

The conscious is the part of your mind you use at all times during your waking state, for example when writing, walking, and reading, etc. It has a higher vibration than the subconscious mind.

Your conscious mind has multiple functions. Bristol states that the:

conscious mind is the source of thought... it gives a sense of awareness in our normal waking life; the knowledge that we are ourselves here and now; the recognition and understanding of our environment; the power to rule over our mental faculties; to recall the events of our past life; to comprehend our emotions and their significance... The chief powers of conscious mind are reason, logic, form, judgement, calculation, conscience and the moral sense.

3.2. Conscious mind and perception

Whenever you pay attention to specific things you are allowing information about them to inhabit your conscious mind. You can become conscious about things perceived either by your external senses (touch, sight, etc.), or inner senses (imagery, inner dialogue, etc.).

From the psychological perspective, your conscious mind is in charge of the perception of your environment. Your conscious mind interacts with the material world, your environment, throughout your senses. You use your rationale to interpret and describe everything that you sense.

However, when the conscious mind perceives the world it does so based on the programs held on your subconscious level. From Ho'oponopono's perspective all mental processes are always taken over by your subconscious memories. Your conscious mind acts before stimuli from the environment according to the memories held on your subconscious level. In other words, when you perceive your world there is a continuous interaction between your conscious and your subconscious.

Your conscious mind is the gateway through which information from the external environment enters your subconscious mind and gets embedded in it. However, information from your environment can also be introduced to your subconscious bypassing your conscious mind.

The conscious part of your mind makes you experience the different qualities of your physical world in a unique and personal way. Consciousness is always a private and subjective experience. The term *subjective* means that you are the only one who can comment about your own experience, which makes it more difficult to conduct scientific analysis of it.

The conscious part of your mind tends to process the information of the environment much more slowly, as compared with your subconscious level. Your conscious mind also has a very limited capacity as compared with your subconscious.

3.3. Conscious mind decisions and free will

The conscious mind is also called the choosing mind by some psychologists. However, your conscious mind continually takes information from the subconscious to make decisions in your daily life. As seen before, several scientific studies confirmed that all your actions are actually originated by your subconscious mind; your conscious can only impede or proceed with them.

As seen before according to these scientific discoveries, your free will, generally related to your conscious mind, does not actually initiate your *voluntary* actions. Your *free will* can only control the final result of your actions; you can consciously restrain or perform your acts which are always initiated subconsciously. Some sages argue against the idea of freedom in human beings because their choice is always conditioned by their subconscious minds.

Your conscious mind has the capability of evaluating, reasoning and setting goals in your life. However, the programs held on your subconscious level constantly impact these capabilities.

Your conscious mind is the rational part of your mind and it resembles a computer processor. Your conscious can be analytic, which implies examining the parts of a situation, person or thing; it can also be synthetic when it focuses on the core aspects of a situation.

Your conscious mind can use deductive reasoning (from general aspects to specific ones), and inductive (from particular aspects to general ones). In all cases, your conscious is affected by the programs stored in your subconscious.

According to psychologists, one of the main functions of the conscious part of your mind is to select stimuli from the humongous amount of information surrounding you. Your conscious mind also organizes and processes the data from your environment that goes into the subconscious.

Norretranders (citing Dietrich Trincker) states that:

of all information that every second flows into our brains through our sensory organs, only a fraction arrives in our consciousness... That is to say, only one millionth of what our eyes see, our ears hear, and our other senses inform about appears in our consciousness.

3.4. Other characteristics of the conscious mind
There are other relevant aspects of the conscious mind such as: awareness of thoughts, feelings and physical sensations and awareness of you as a person, also called self-awareness. Besides,

your conscious mind naturally tends to dismiss gaps in the perception. Your conscious mind makes you perceive things as if all aspects of your experiences were integrated.

Your conscious mind is not attached to a specific time. This means that you can use your conscious mind to focus on the present, future or past in a very swift manner. For example, when you worry you are focusing on the future and when you are regretful you are centered on the past.

When you are fully present and totally aware (or conscious), you can detect some automatic patterns carried out by your subconscious mind. This happens when you are focused on the now.

From the Ho'oponopono perspective, the *mother* or conscious mind can also send love and appreciation to the *child* or subconscious. It is very important that a relationship of trust between your conscious mind (the mother) and your subconscious (the child) is developed and strengthened over time. Many sages say that this relationship is the most important one in your life.

3.5. Consciousness and flow

There is a state called the *zone* or *flow* which has been studied by many scientists for decades. In this state you are fully focused on the present moment and you completely surrender to the activities at hand.

In this state you have what psychologists call *tunnel vision* which allows you to concentrate on your activities with undivided attention and makes you effortlessly productive. You are prone to experience a lot of pleasure when you carry out your activities.

In the zone you naturally cast aside any negative emotional state such as fear or trepidation. You also avoid controlling things; you let them unfold flowingly. Many specialists highlight that you also tend to lose the notion of time and space. When you are flowing, your mind's performance is fully enhanced. Your conscious mind reaches its full potential and works in harmony with your subconscious.

Some psychologists define flow as a state where there are no boundaries between your conscious mind and your subconscious. During the state of flow, your mind can process larger amounts of information and you are more capable of making better decisions.

Csikszentmihályi defines flow as an optimal experience. He states that when you are in the flow *"physic energy flows effortlessly. There is no need to worry, no reason to question one's inadequacy... one does stop thinking about oneself."*

He also highlights that:

> *attention can freely be invested in a person's goal because there is no disorder to straighten out, no threats for the self to defend against... people become so involved in what they are doing that the activity becomes spontaneous, almost automatic; they stop being aware of themselves as separate from the actions they are performing.*

From this perspective, in order to reach a state of flow your tasks should be neither too easy nor too difficult.

This author also introduces the concept of psychic entropy. This occurs when your conscious mind is affected by disruptive information, which comes from your environment (such as noise, visual distractions, etc.) or from within you (memories that are held in your subconscious which are playing out loud). When you are in the zone, you don't experience psychic entropy.

3.6. Ego and conscious mind

> *Ego is the darkness that imprisons the light of love.*
> – Mike George

> *Ego is our self-love turned into self-hatred.*
> – Marianne Williamson

According to Watson the ego is: *"that part of ourselves with which we consciously identify... who we think we are – our subjective identity."* Some say that your ego is the creation of the conscious part of your mind. However, psychologists state that ego is related to both your conscious and subconscious mind.

According to some philosophical perspectives, your ego is just an illusion; your ego has a strong identification with your body, position, belongings, name, race, preferences, history, religion, nationality, etc. These characteristics do not truly represent the real you, nor your core essence. From the Ho'oponopono viewpoint, all these personal features are just subconscious memories.

Your ego is also attached to different roles you have in your life, such as parent, son, sibling and friend, among others; you generally derive your own identity from all those traits. Your ego tends to become naturally protective regarding these attachments. George says that your ego creates *"disturbance of the energy of your consciousness when the object of attachment is damaged, threatened, moved or lost."*

Whenever you speak from your ego you tend to use phrases beginning with *"I."* Some clues about your ego can be reflected on your continual mental chattering. When you do introspective activities you can also gain some insights into your ego.

Your ego is always defensive and selfish; it usually tries hard to keep your individuality and uniqueness. Besides, your ego is very demanding and it is always attempting to command your life. Your ego continually wants to be center of the attention, either for positive things or negative ones.

Love states that: *"All of us have an ego – that part of ourselves that is totally focused on our needs, desires, thoughts, feelings, talents, drama or wants in the world."* There are other characteristics of your ego as follows:

– As you create your ego, you gradually deposit stories (memories) related to it on your subconscious level. Every experience that you had, either sorrowful or pleasant, is being integrated into your ego. Besides, your ego is constantly affected by your belief system. Your ego continually strengthens the memories embedded on your subconscious level.

– When you are ego-centered it is difficult to concentrate on the present moment. Your ego generally makes you perceive things through the perspective of your past experiences. Likewise, from the Ho'oponopono perspective, your perception is always influenced by your subconscious past programs. Even your projections regarding the future (for example, expectations, plans, worries, etc.) are based on the past.

– From the ego's perspective, you are always separate from the rest of the people. In other words, your ego naturally denies your interconnectedness with all that exists and makes you act accordingly.

– Your ego is always based on fear and it is constantly trying to preserve itself. Your ego is scared of losing some of its characteristics, such as status, beauty, intelligence, health, among others.

– Your ego is always self-centered; it is constantly seeking others' attention either in a positive manner, by showing off your uniqueness, or also in a negative way, for example playing the role of the victim.

– Some masters state the ego is only subconscious memories constantly playing out, and nothing else. Your ego does not exist as such and you can get rid of your ego by doing Ho'oponopono.

– Your ego likes drama, problems, and problematic issues. It seems very difficult for your ego to be completely at peace. Besides, your ego is always judging you or others and is also related to states of grudge, blame, guilt and resentment.

– When you approach relationships from an ego's perspective, you tend to be possessive and manipulative. When you are egocentric you can only experience conditional love, which means that you always love for a reason.

– Some oriental philosophies state that your ego is related to your false identity; your authentic identity is never linked to ideas, labels, or specific characteristics of yours. George states your natural identity is a *"no-identity."* Likewise Ho'oponopono says your core essence is the state in which you are not ruled by any subconscious memories – called zero point.

– Your ego is never dwelling in the truth. The book *A Course in Miracles* says: *"the ego is a man-made attempt to perceive himself as he wished to be, rather than as he is."*

– Your ego hinders your connection with the Higher Planes. Your ego also prevents you from harnessing your prized inner resources.

4. Super conscious mind

The higher mind transcends all doubts and confusion. It's spacious and clear like cloudless blue sky.
– Jason Chan and Jan Rogers

The superconscious mind is the God Mind within each man, and is the realm of perfect ideas. In it, is the 'perfect pattern' spoken of by Plato, The Divine Design; for there is a Divine Design for each person.
– Florence Scovel Shinn

The super conscious is also called para-conscious mind, Higher Self or higher mind. This transcendental part of your mind is also called your divine part, God-self or higher consciousness. Your super conscious has a higher vibratory rate than the conscious mind.

From the Ho'oponopono perspective, your super conscious is also called Aumakua or *the father*. Long says that your super conscious is your *"parental guide spirit."* It works in the subtle realm and represents infinite wisdom, all-knowingness and perfection.

The super conscious is connected to universal flow, also called the Divine. This part of your mind is also the main channel through which you receive divine inspiration. From the Ho'oponopono perspective your conscious mind can never get in contact with your super conscious directly but through your subconscious.

Long says that: *"we are allowed free will, and that the High Self will not interfere with our doings, no matter how we muddle our lives... unless we ask it to come to our aid."* The super conscious mind will not cooperate in the cleaning process unless your conscious mind explicitly asks for this through your subconscious. And you do so by saying the four Ho'oponopono sentences repeatedly.

Your super conscious is naturally free from any memories; it is always beyond your social conditioning. Your super conscious is eternal, flawless, timeless and limitless; it is your holy or divine part. It is essentially enlightened and it has no boundaries. Some even say that the super conscious is the pure reflection or presence of God in you; Ray says the super conscious is the transformative station between you and the cosmos.

When you are in contact with your super conscious part you can access the unbounded source, your godly self. Besides, your super conscious usually oversees your conscious and subconscious. From the metaphysical viewpoint, the super conscious is also known as the observer; your daily actions, thoughts and emotions are carefully observed by your super conscious mind.

Your super conscious is also related to qualities such as humility, authenticity, joy, compassion, contentment, peacefulness, among others. For Jeffers the super conscious is: *"the place within that is loving, kind, abundant, joyful"* and *"when you operate from the Higher Self you feel centered and abundant – in fact, overflowing... you create 'miracles' in your life."* Ray also highlights that when you get in contact with your super conscious you tend to increase your creativity and commitment to your projects.

When you are truly attuned with your super conscious, you are able to contribute to your life and others' more significantly. You feel more caring, appreciative and peaceful with anybody around you. Besides, you tend to be more deeply involved in all your life activities.

Lastly when these three parts of your mind work in harmony, you can harness your innermost limitless power. When these three parts cooperate you can also effectively delete all your past subconscious programming.

Chapter 13

Zero Point and Divine Inspiration

1. Zero point

It is hard to imagine being afraid of a number. Yet zero was inextricably linked with the void – with nothing. There was a primal fear of void and chaos. There was also a fear of zero. Most ancient peoples believed that only emptiness and chaos were present before the universe came to be...
– Charles Seife

1.1. Main aspects of the zero state

To be empty, completely empty, is not a fearsome thing; it is absolutely essential for the mind to be unoccupied; to be empty, unenforced, for then only can it move into unknown depths.
– Krishnamurti

Many scientific studies have confirmed that most of matter is formed of empty space. In that effect, atoms, which are the constituent stuff of everything that exists, are made up of energy vibrating at different rates, but they are fundamentally emptiness. Likewise, there many spiritual philosophies which state that all phenomena in the Universe are in fact void. Ramesh Balsekar says that: *"the source of everything is potential nothingness."* Only a very tiny percentage of everything in the Universe is made up of solid matter.

This state of vacuum is naturally unnameable and indescribable. Seife states that:

Zero is powerful because it is infinity's twin. They are equal and

*opposite, yin and yang... Zero was inextricably linked with the void
– with nothing... Zero has no substance...*

Likewise, when you get rid of all your subconscious memories
you arrive at the zero point, which is a state of emptiness. Some
traits of this state are: all-encompassing love, serenity, insight-
fulness, spontaneous empowerment, clarity, limitlessness,
blinding radiance, pure order and justice, vastness of prized
resources, unstoppable expansiveness, countless possibilities,
pure naturalness and effortlessness, among others.

The zero point is your very essence; it is totally incompatible
with your subconscious memories. In the zero point you are fully
connected to the Divine, which can be named in different ways
such as: God, the Cause, Love, the Providence, the Universe, the
Universal Mind, Divinity, the Principle, the Primal Substance,
the Divine Intelligence, the First Cause or the Higher Planes,
among others. As explained previously, Divinity is the imper-
ishable living presence and the numinous essence underneath
everything that exists.

When you are in zero state, you are also dwelling in your own
divine essence. You must remember that, according to most
religions, you are made in the image and likeness of the Divine.

By nature, Divinity is ineffable, omniscient and omnipresent.
The Divine is also limitless, shapeless and ageless. Lytle states that:

*The Universal Mind is the intelligence that created the universe and
keeps it functioning. The human mind is part of the Universal
Mind. When we use our human minds to gain access to it, we can
turn universal power into personal power.*

At the zero point you are fused with the Divine; you can experience
a state of wholeness, which allows you to access unfiltered and
timeless wisdom. You have clarity and deep understanding.

Even though the zero point is naturally empty, this primordial state has everything you need. This point is your natural creative place; you can be infinitely innovative. Your actions are just what they are essentially meant to be. The zero point is the natural springboard for your personal growth and evolution.

It is interesting to remember that at the zero state you are provided with divine inspiration. Your actions tend to be naturally purposeful and flawless. When you are guided by the Divine everything is possible, even the most unlikely feats. This point is a godlike state in which you are connected to infinity and perfection.

Some masters say that little babies experience this state of emptiness naturally because they have no disruptive or confusing data running in their subconscious minds. In other words, their subconscious minds are still unpolluted, only filled by love energy.

As was previously explained in this book, all people over their lives accrue massive amounts of data in their subconscious minds which overshadow their natural zero point. For this reason, Ho'oponopono practice is critical to arrive at the zero point. Vitale says that in: *"the zero state... nothing exists but anything is possible. In the zero state there are no thoughts, words, deeds, memories, programs, beliefs, or anything else."*

1.2. Your experience in the zero state

A zero in quantum mechanics means that the entire universe – including the vacuum – is filled with an infinite amount of energy: the zero-point energy.
– Charles Seife

You are meant to be at one with God. It's that simple you were created by God. You are made of the same stuff as God, only pressed out into this world. Man is God pressed out into flesh.
– E. Bernard Jordan

There are some traits that can merely describe this state, which will be enumerated below. You can use these characteristics as a way of checking if you have arrived at this state.

In the zero point...

... you are in contact with the Creator, which is pure love and beauty

... you have broken free from the chains of the past

... you are in your natural state, free from any conditioning or mental categories

... you realize that there is no more data playing in your subconscious mind

... you are, you truly are, your essence beyond your thoughts, emotions and body

... you truly feel that the Infinite Mind removed all your mental garbage

... you dwell in unconditional love

... you feel like arriving home; you feel safe and at peace

... you experience absolute clarity about everything going on in your life

... you experience a heavenly state of well-being and bliss

... you removed all fear-ridden thoughts

... you are in a state where everything is possible

... you receive all the blessings that you are naturally entitled to

... you truly realize that you are the perfect image of the Divine

... you allow the Divine to lead your way in life

... you know that Divinity is always guiding you

... you experience the end of suffering and pain

... you enjoy true freedom and boundless joy

... you go back to your outstanding default state, your factory setting

... you recover your childlike state of innocence and pureness

... you can tap into inexhaustible resources to succeed

... you have unfaltering confidence in the divine infinite supply

... you experience continual expansiveness in every area of your life

... you perceive your environment through a divine lens

... you have no hesitation because you trust your life purpose
... you experience natural glee and lingering easiness
... you realize there are no boundaries; everything is interconnected
... you connect with the endless and refreshing water spring within you
... your heart is immaculate
... you sense the brightness and purity of all that exists
... you feel that your spiritual essence flourishes in liberty
... you realize that you are just a conduit or a channel of the Source
... you are continually illuminated by the beaming light of Divine
... your problems dissolve naturally
... you know that the Divine is the only source of all inspiration
... you are in the state where no more questions are needed
... you know there are no limits because you can harness your unbounded power
... you realize that the Divine is your caregiver for all your endeavors
... you do not have intentions or goals because you fully rely on divine guidance
... you become a potent and prolific miracle-worker
... you dwell in a place of eternal awakening and enlightenment
... your mind is totally nude because it was stripped from all limiting memories

In relation to the zero point, Seife says that:

All that scientists know is the cosmos was spawned from nothing, and will return to the nothing from whence it came. The universe begins and ends with zero.

2. Divine inspiration

Without even realizing it, there is always one of two things driving our thoughts, actions and deeds: inspiration or ego. Inspiration comes from Pure Awareness and the Super-conscious Mind, and

always supports the process of rediscovering our True Nature. Ego uses and replays old memories, fears and experiences and the other erroneous "data" to create a distorted reality, resulting in imbalance, disharmony and dis-ease.
– Khenpo Gurudas Sunyatananda

2.1. Main aspects of inspiration

You need not leave your room. Remain sitting at your table and listen. You need not even listen, simply wait, just learn to become quiet, still and solitary. The world will freely offer itself to you to be unmasked.
– Franz Kafka

Vitale says that there are different stages of evolution in the life of any human being. During the first phase you are prone to behave like a victim, and blame others or even yourself for your negative life circumstances. In this stage, you tend to be reactive instead of proactive. From the Ho'oponopono perspective, in this phase you cannot take full responsibility for what is going on in your life.

In the second phase you feel that you are in control of your life; you believe that you can introduce significant changes in your reality. In this phase you also tend to use some powerful tools such as visualization and affirmations in order to affect your reality. From the Ho'oponopono perspective, in this stage you can take full responsibility for whatever is going on in your life.

In the third stage, which Vitale calls awakening, you naturally surrender to the Divine; you let yourself be guided by divine inspiration. You don't feel the need to set objectives or use tools such as visualization or affirmations. You don't feel prompted to have expectations about future circumstances. With the continuous practice of Ho'oponopono, you can dwell in this stage.

The real meaning of the word *inspiration* is *in spirit*; this term comes from Latin and means *"inspire, inhale, or breathe in."* In other words, inspiration is something you receive from the Divine, namely guidance. Receptiveness is a very important requirement to be benefited by inspirational directions. From the Ho'oponopono viewpoint, you become more receptive to inspiration as you remove your subconscious memories.

In ancient Greece, it was believed that the muses were always inspiring scientists and artists. Throughout history there were many luminaries in art, science, commerce, and politics which overtly stated that their most brilliant ideas and creations were just dictated by God or Divinity.

When you are inspired, the unlimited power of Divinity is truly working through you. When you are inspired you are flowingly linked to the living source, with no interferences. With inspiration, your innermost capabilities show up in a spontaneous manner. All negative emotions or unconstructive feelings are left aside.

Dyer says that when we are inspired: *"an idea takes hold of us from the invisible reality of Spirit."* When you are truly inspired your self-imposed limits fade away and your thinking expands spontaneously. You are not bound to limiting memories. Some masters say that inspirational messages are nudges from the Higher Planes.

Throughout your life you are constantly receiving directions or advice from other people. For example, parents, friends, colleagues, employers, neighbors, mentors, counsellors and other people. You have been receiving directions from books and magazines, seminars and courses, the Internet and many other sources. Guidance is omnipresent all over your life. Nonetheless, inspiration is totally different; it comes exclusively from Divinity. And as you know by now, the Divine is the most powerful source of wisdom.

You are always prone to being guided by Divinity even if you are not aware of this. You are never alone in life. However, you are more likely to receive divine directions as you remove your subconscious memories.

Inspiration is just prized information that the Universe wants you to know, which is beneficial and meaningful for your life. When you follow inspirational messages you are more likely to fulfil your dreams in an effortless manner.

Some people are reluctant to believe that they can actually be rewarded by inspirational messages. You, like the rest of the people, are naturally entitled to receive directions from Divinity. The Divine loves you with no conditions, as you truly are. Many say that you do not actually have to do anything to deserve inspiration. However, your propensity to receive inspiration increases as you use Ho'oponopono.

You must humbly believe that you deserve to receive inspiration. You must realize that the Divine is the most caring and trustworthy teacher of yours. Divinity has limitless wisdom which can benefit all dimensions of your life. With this prized knowledge all struggle and hardship are left behind for good.

However, some sages state that the Universe cannot help you without your permission; you must be willing to receive divine assistance. You explicitly allow the Divine to provide you with inspiration as you remove your subconscious programs. It is also important to highlight that you can rely on divine support at any moment, not only when you face dire situations. You must bear in mind that Divinity will never disappoint you.

You cannot compare the wisdom from the Divine with the limited knowledge you hold in your mind. The Divine provides you with unpolluted guidance, which encloses the greatest power than exists. Cameron says that you must:

Learn to accept the possibility that the universe is helping you with what you are doing. Become willing to see the hand of God and accept it as a friend's offer to help with what you are doing.

When you are truly inspired, you see yourself as Divinity's faithful servant; you are like a conduit through which divine wisdom is channeled. You become a co-creator who works in partnership with the Divine.

2.2. Some evidence of inspirational messages
When you are truly inspired, your physical energy might increase significantly. It is possible that you also feel a sense of connection with all that exists; you can even feel intense unconditional love. You might also experience a state of flow regarding the performance of your actions. You are also likely to feel compelled to act in a certain way, with no rational explanation. Your actions are likely to be performed in a graceful fashion, as if they were guided by an invisible loving hand supporting them.

Another important sign of receiving inspiration is a sense of limitless knowingness, which drives you in a very specific direction. When you are inspired, sometimes you do not even have solid arguments supporting your actions.

When you feel inspired you are likely to have limitless faith in the purpose of your actions, which helps you to act in a determined manner. Even though your actions might look baseless, they are solidly founded on divine directions. These directions will help you in your challenging endeavors.

When you receive divine inspiration, you might feel as if you were taking an order from Divinity that you have to deliver with no hesitation whatsoever. You are more prone to getting detangled from your ego, whose actions are usually based on fear and defensiveness.

Every time your actions are inspired, you naturally release any tension or opposition. When you are driven by inspiration you become fully expanded and with a sense of powerfulness.

Becker states that: *"Inspiration is the timely awareness of opportunity."* From the metaphysical perspective there is a saying that goes *"When the student is ready the master appears."* When you are inspired you become the student ready to grasp the lessons from the master, which is the Divine.

When you are inspired you are actually cooperating with the Divine; you work in close alliance with it. You are also aware of the presence of Divinity within you. Some masters say that you act like a midwife of the divine flow; the best of you appears reflected in the results of your actions.

There were many scientific studies conducted on inspiration, especially one which was directed by Dr. Tobin Hart, of the State University of West Georgia. This scientist interviewed many people from different walks of life and some of them said that when they were inspired they felt connected with the whole. They also experienced a state of unity with all that exists. They also experienced surrender, extreme clarity and openness. Some of the interviewed said their lives would be senseless and boring if they could not receive inspiration.

This scientific study concluded that even though you cannot produce moments of inspiration on demand, some activities such as prayer or meditation make you more likely to receive inspirational messages.

2.3. Inspiration and Ho'oponopono

One does not discover new lands
without consenting to lose sight
of the shore for a very long time.
– Andre Gide

There is a very well-known oriental tale related to the topic of inspiration. Once upon a time there was a Zen master who was kindly visited by one of his disciples. This adept asked the master about the path to wisdom. The master did not say a word; instead, he poured some tea in the student's cup. When the cup was full, the tea began to overflow the cup; it trickled down ceaselessly. Then the master wisely quipped: *"When the cup is full there is no place for new knowledge."*

From Ho'oponopono's standpoint, this short story is very meaningful. You cannot access inspiration (wisdom) if your mind (cup) is full of memories (tea). According to this perspective, your actions can only be driven in opposite ways: they are prompted either by the Divine or by your limiting past memories.

For this reason, as you delete your memories by saying *"I am sorry, please forgive, I love you, thank you"* on a continuous basis, you make space in your mind to receive inspirational messages from the Divine. This space to be filled with inspiration was previously occupied by these memories. As stated this empty space is called *the zero state.*

Garlow and Wall say that inspiration can be also called *"word of knowledge."* From this perspective, this knowledge represents divine impressions you can receive either in your mind or your body. To put it more clearly, these inspirational messages can be transmitted through voices, images or physical sensations, among others.

You can receive inspiration from different sources, even the most unexpected ones. Sometimes these divine messages can indicate places to go, actions to take, things to research about or certain people to contact. In many cases, the inspirational insights convey information which is beyond your rational discerning processes. This trait of inspiration might prompt you to distrust, at first, the validity of the information received.

When you receive inspiration, you tend to come up with ideas which you could not have imagined otherwise just by using your traditional rationale. Sometimes divine inspiration is even beyond your current level of understanding.

All inspiration you receive has one important purpose, which is to support your self-development. These messages allow you to contribute to the world in a very distinct way.

For this reason, you have to decide if you want to actually

receive inspiration or instead continue being driven by your subconscious memories. This is one of the most relevant decisions you can make in your entire life. If you make the decision to receive divine guidance, you have to do Ho'oponopono frequently.

Some masters say that you can never be completely sure if the directions you received were sent by the Divine (which means inspiration) or from your imagination (which means your subconscious memories). In case of doubt, you should ask Divinity about this; you can pose questions like *"Is this really inspiration?"* and then wait for an answer.

Other useful questions you can use are: *"Does this information contribute to the well-being of other people besides me?"* or *"Is this what you want me to know?"* All these questions should be addressed to the Divine.

There is another clue to know if you are driven by divine inspiration. Effortlessness in your actions is a key characteristic of inspiration. In relation to this, Geley states that a person:

is quite aware whether he is inspired or not. If he is, the work proceeds easily, almost without check, to his complete satisfaction, or even exultation. If he is not, he experiences fatigue not only of mind, but of body also; he makes false starts, and his wearisome and painful efforts are accompanied with a sense of powerlessness and discouragement. Inspiration does not come from effort; on the contrary, it comes often when least expected, and especially when the mind is at ease; not during the times of connected work.

Other factors related to knowing if a message is actually divine inspiration are:

– Alignment of the message with your life purpose
– Benevolence or malevolence of the message

When you are in doubt about the messages received you can also say the four Ho'oponopono sentences for a while. If, after having done this, the message is still coming up to your mind, this direction is very likely to come from Divinity. However, you can never be one hundred percent sure that the messages you receive are inspirational.

It is important to analyze if your intention is closely related to inspiration. In relation to this, Vitale says that every time you intend to do something you are driven by your subconscious programming. He states that intention is not really relevant because it always works like a fool's game or an ego's toy. From this perspective, your real source of powerfulness is divine inspiration.

Every time you act in an uninspired manner, which means based on your subconscious programming, you tend to repeat yourself in several different ways; nothing fresh comes out of you.

2.4. Requirements to receive inspiration

When you feel inspired, what appeared to be risky becomes a path you feel compelled to follow.
– Wayne Dyer

Even though you are likely to receive inspiration in unexpected ways and moments, there are some conditions that can improve your chances of receiving inspirational messages from the Divine, such as:

a) Receptivity
You are more likely to receive inspiration from Divinity when you are as receptive as possible, which implies deleting your subconscious memories with Ho'oponopono.

Inspirational messages are also very common when you experience states of tranquility and peacefulness. In other words, tension and fretfulness hinder your access to divine guidance.

Rudolf Steiner says that you are more receptive to guidance from the Higher Planes when you regularly listen to other people's messages in a selfless and non-judgmental manner. When you eliminate your prejudice and criticism to others you are more susceptible to receive divine directions.

b) Sterling faith

You are more likely to receive inspiration when you have unconditional faith in the support from the Divine. You must realize that you are always connected to the Universal Source even when this connection is temporarily obscured by your subconscious memories.

When you have faith you release any control over the circumstances, and let Divinity guide you along the way. You truly know that the divine intervention has its own way to work things out.

If you have faith, you are clear of hesitation, which allows you to act like a channel from divine messages. In relation to this, the book *A Course in Miracles* says:

> *Revelations come from the above or the superconscious level. Revelation induces complete but temporary suspension of doubt and fear. It represents the original form of communication between God and his souls, involving an extremely personal sense of closeness to Creation... Revelation unites Souls directly with God.*

c) Non-resistance

You are more likely to receive divine inspiration when you are not offering any resistance to what is going on in your life. Many masters state that resistance is a useless attempt to eschew the present which is uncomfortable and difficult to inhabit fully. As we have seen in this book, there are subtle ways of placing resistance such as complaining, moaning or criticizing.

Instead, whenever you have an attitude of non-resistance not only do you say yes to life, but you are open to receive divine directions, even those which might challenge your discernment.

In order to not place resistance, you should try to be flexible whenever possible. This means that you should cast away any structured strategies regarding different areas of your life. Some masters suggest that you should not have any strategy in your life; Divinity is always providing you with the best plan. From this perspective, the main steps of your strategy are to be revealed throughout inspiration.

When you are truly flexible, you become open to any other possible alternatives beside the obvious ones. You can face uncertainty without feeling overly uncomfortable. You also realize that the most appropriate resources you need for every situation in your life will always turn up in the most appropriate manner. This attitude gives you peace of mind especially before challenging circumstances.

You must also remember that you, as a unique individual, are part of a plan which is greater than any paltry goal you can set. This divine strategy is perfect; it has no errors or mistakes and all resources are available for you in the most adequate way. In this divine strategy, all situations make complete sense, even the ones disguised as difficulties.

Whenever you receive inspiration, you are provided with information useful for you to contribute to this divine plan. From this perspective, each time that you receive and act on inspiration you become a facilitator of God's innermost desires on Earth.

d) Confidence

You are more likely to receive inspiration when you realize that you are continually accompanied by a force which is greater than you, the Divine. When you comprehend this, you are prone to feeling more powerful, even in the face of difficulties. You truly know that you are never left to your own devices. You understand that with the support of the Universe, you can do anything you desire, even things beyond your limited rationale. You can perform any of your activities with actual aplomb and determination. You can also face challenging circumstances without feeling defeated or hesitant.

You must always bear in mind that Divinity is on your side, willing to help you. Inspiration becomes only a proof of your lingering partnership with the Absolute. Remember that whenever you act based on inspiration, you actually team-play with Divinity and this team is totally invincible.

e) Effortlessness

You might be accustomed to planning your activities, like the rest of the people, by using some creative tools like brainstorming, lateral thinking, mind-mapping and others. These tools can be useful and bring about original outcomes but they all use the information held in your subconscious mind, which is essentially limiting.

Instead when you receive inspiration there is no need to use any of these instruments; the countless creative ideas pop out in your mind spontaneously, like bubbles in the water. In most cases, your inspiration comes unbidden, not as a consequence of an elaborative thinking process.

When you are inspired, you do not look for ideas, they come to you in a graceful manner. Your creative approaches seem to unfold effortlessly and in unencumbered manner. When you are inspired you become limitlessly prolific and productive, like an endless water fountain. You might even feel as if you were downloading prized information from the Divine Planes. It is as if you were converted into a channel for the messages from the Divine.

When you are truly inspired you access limitless valuable knowledge with no effort. In relation to this, Levenson states: *"Real knowledge lies just behind thought, which is relative knowledge, and relative knowledge is ignorance."*

335

f) Flow

> *Inspiration is available on tap. You only need to ask it and it is yours... For inspiration to flow freely you must let attachment fall away... Let go and Let God at the helm on your behalf, for this day at least.*
> – Stephanie King

When you are inspired, you are more likely to experience this state of flow. When you experience this state these is no contradiction in your actions which are aligned with your main purpose. Your goals seem to be feasible; your activities are performed effortlessly and joyfully. When you do things you are passionate about, you can easily enter into this state of flow.

You are more likely to experience the state of flow and in turn to be more prone to receive divine inspiration when you are fully focused on the now. However, whenever you think about the future (worries, expectations, projections) or the past (regrets, guilt, resentment) you are less susceptible to receive divine guidance.

2.5. Mission and inspiration

When you work on your mission you are more likely to receive more divine guidance than when you carry out other activities. For this reason, it is really important that you discover your mission in life, if you have not done so yet.

Your personal mission, also called dharma, is the main purpose that brought you into this world. It is your unique and meaningful contribution which adds distinct value to humanity, on a small or big scale.

When you discover your mission, you are committed to it because is the right thing to do. When you discover your mission, the message is not dubious. Warren states that by knowing your mission your life becomes more meaningful, simple, focused and motivating.

Your mission is generally something that you are delighted and motivated to do; activities you can perform with no effort. It is also related to actions through which you can apply your personal skills and talents. You tend to fulfil your mission, even if you are not paid for it.

When you perform activities focused on your mission you can also feel more expressive and authentic. At first, you might feel a bit fearful, doubtful or uncommitted; nonetheless as the time goes by, these negative states tend to subside naturally.

If you don't know your mission, the only way to find out about it is to look within yourself thoroughly. The main clues about your mission are concealed within yourself. It is important to not get distracted by other people's advice or, even worse, by the media conditioning.

You can obtain some hints about your mission with a very simple and well-known exercise. Write down three lists on a piece of paper. The first list is an enumeration of your main skills. The second list encloses great men and women in history you most admire. The third list is of activities which give you pleasure.

After this, you can ask yourself: *"What are the common factors of these lists?"*, *"What is the essence of these lists?"*, *"Which of all these pieces of information represents my mission?"* or *"Which of these things reflect my authentic nature?"* Your mission is surely hidden in all this information. You can also say the four Ho'oponopono phrases many times.

Another way to discover your mission is to ask your subconscious mind for details about it. Some masters suggest that you should ask Divinity for information about this. You can also recollect the things that made you feel gleeful when you were a little child; explore all dreams cast away or forgotten.

It is important to not jump into conclusions; it frequently takes a while to unveil your mission. When you do these exercises, wait for insights. The answers are provided in a very casual way, for example, through a book you read, a conversation you have or a seminar you take.

When you have a more accurate picture of your mission and take consequent action on it, you are more likely to receive divine inspiration supportive of it. Patanjali says:

When you are inspired by some great purpose... your thoughts break their bounds. Your mind transcends limitations, your thoughts expand in every direction and you find yourself in a new, great, wonderful world, you discover yourself to be a greater person by far than you ever dreamed yourself to be.

3. Practical tips on inspirational messages

Inspiration is the act of imparting Spirit into the physical word to cause effects.
– E. Bernard Jordan

When you receive inspiration, you don't need to think up any idea at all; directions are downloaded from the Higher Planes in a graceful fashion. Inspirational messages provide you with useful information to deal with your challenging life circumstances in a more effective manner. Divine guidance also helps you perform all your activities in a more meaningful way. You can find below some tips to harness the benefits from inspiration:

3.1. Inspirational messages come in different ways
Many inspirational messages are clear, straightforward and easy to understand. Others might seem, at first, unintelligible or blurred. You must be aware of the signals and clues you receive. You should avoid being shortsighted when you receive and interpret these signals. You should sense them with your whole being, not only with your physical senses.

In some cases you feel that the message you receive is just

right for you. You are also likely to feel more peaceful, relaxed and loving; sometimes, you might be also prompted to act on them immediately.

The inspirational messages can be conveyed in a very indirect manner, for example, opportunities you encounter, information you obtain, people who advise you on certain topics, among others. Remember, some metaphysical sages say that: *"When the student is ready the master appears."* You are more likely to receive inspiration when you offer no resistance to it. You should be always hopeful that the divine guidance will come to you.

3.2. Be serene
In their daily activities most people tend to be overstimulated by many sensory stimuli, such as TV, magazines, conversations with people, etc. For this reason, it is important to experience peacefulness whenever possible. Being in a quiet state makes you more prone to receive divine guidance.

You are more likely to receive inspiration when you are frequently in contact with your inner world. There are certain activities which help you reflect, such as yoga, meditation, tai chi, among others.

You can also be in silence for a while in order to let your thoughts pour out from your mind and pass by. Your analytical mind is disconnected temporarily; you reach a state of peacefulness and become more likely to hear the messages from the Divine.

3.3. Use affirmations and questions
You are more prone to receiving divine guidance when you use some meaningful sentences like:

– *Divinity, let me know the best way to direct my affairs.*
– *I am being taken care of by Divinity.*
– *I am always nurtured by divine guidance and everything goes well.*

– I am like a child bathed by divine wisdom.
– I am open to receive divine inspiration at all times. And it is done.
Thank you.

This list above is only indicative; you can also use other similar sentences. You must say these phrases, as frequently as possible. When you use these affirmations you must feel that you are being supported by the Higher Planes.

Some masters suggest that you should always trust that the Divine will resolve all your difficulties in the best way. In order to do so, you can use affirmations such as *"Divinity, I am always open to receive indications from you"* or *"Universe, just let me know what I have to know from you"*, *"Divine source, provide me with the best information to approach all my life affairs"* or *"Thank you, Divinity, because I know that you are dealing with all my difficulties and I truly feel you will resolve them in the best manner."*

You can also invite the Divine to express through you by using sentences like *"I am a channel for Divinity's unbounded expression"* or *"I am a conduit for the ideas from the Divine"* or *"I am the revelation of the message from the Higher Planes."*

Another way to be more prone to receiving inspiration is by communicating with the Higher Planes through specific questions, such as *"How could I deal with this situation?"* or *"What is the divine way to solve this?"*

The answers to these questions might come in the most unusual ways. If you don't get an immediate answer you should not despair. You must be faithful and wait for divine messages patiently. Divinity never leaves any questions unanswered.

Dr. Len suggests a very interesting way to get answers from the Divine. You must first clean the question that you want to pose to the Divine. In order to do so, you must say *"I love you"* and *"Thank you"* three times, and then pose the question to the Divine.

3.4. Be humble

When you have an unostentatious attitude, you are more likely to receive inspiration from the Divine Source. When you are humble you implicitly show willingness to follow directions from the superior planes. When you have a humble attitude, you don't believe that you have all the answers to your problems.

Instead whenever you behave arrogantly you express you do not need assistance from the Divine, which makes you less likely to receive inspiration. You must bear in mind that you are continually constrained by your past programming; your knowledge is always limited, if not trivial. Instead Divinity is all-knowing and almighty; its wisdom is limitless.

You should always have the attitude of a little child, who is innocent and curious at all times. A child does not pretend to know everything; he is open to receive new information in order to learn as much as possible.

Besides humility, other values which make you more prone to receiving inspirational messages are: compassion, wholeheartedness, passion, persistence, uprightness, generosity, equanimity and tolerance. The four qualities enclosed in the Ho'oponopono sentences (repentance, forgiveness, love and thankfulness) also make you more predisposed to receive inspiration.

3.5. Release the control

In order to receive inspiration, you must also release any control over future outcomes. Whenever you have expectations, you are trying to somehow control your future circumstances throughout your mind projections.

When you have expectations on how things should unfold, you actually hinder your connection to the Divine. You should always be open to the possibility that there are many other ways for things to happen besides the one that you prefer. The Divine can always help you deal with your life circumstances, in ways which are beyond your current level of reasoning.

Whenever you plan your activities you are also trying to control your future circumstances. For this reason, it is really important to get rid of your plans whenever possible. When you have no plans, you are more likely to receive divine directions on how to act, the best timing for your actions and the most appropriate resources to use.

Every time you surrender, by not having plans or expectations, you confide in Divinity. When you surrender, you also cast away any doubt or fear about the future. With this attitude, you realize that the Absolute only has loving intentions for you.

When you surrender you truly know that divine guidance is based on unconditional love and absolute truth. Ribot (cited by Geley) states that:

Inspiration reveals a power superior to the conscious individual, strange to him and though acting through him – a state which many inventors have described by saying of their work – I had not part in it.

3.6. Evoke times when you were inspired
In order to access more inspirational messages, you can also think about times you received inspiration in the past. Once you have identified those moments, you should ask yourself some questions such as:

– *How was the quality of the message received?*
– *What were the outcomes of having taken action on inspiration?*
– *What was I doing when I received inspiration?*
– *What was my prevalent mood when I got those inspirational messages?*
– *What might have happened if I had not followed those directions?*

You can use other similar questions. These questions can provide you with useful insights and make you more prone to receive inspiration.

3.7. Acknowledge your interconnection with all

In order to become more susceptible to receiving more inspiration in your life, you can do a very simple exercise on your own. Visualize that you are connected to the Higher Planes through a luminous thread of light. You should visualize a bright white or gold thread linking you to the Divine on a frequent basis.

You can also imagine being bathed by love light coming from the Divine. This type of visualization makes you more aware of your natural connection with Divinity.

Roman and Packer suggest a very interesting visualization exercise. You must sit down in a quiet and comfortable place with your eyes closed. Visualize a ray of light coming from the top of your head, like a bridge, which goes upwards and connects you with Divinity.

Then you must envision the divine energy filling all your body. See your mind as if it were a crystal-clear lake, which reflects the Divine Planes. Envision each and every cell of your body as if they were a reflection of energy from Divinity. You can also imagine that your solar plexus is connected to the Higher Planes.

During this exercise you can also picture the divine energy like a bright gold sphere of energy above your head which gradually pervades your body. You can also envision a blue flame inside or outside you which grows bigger and pervades all your body. This blue flame is your soul; and if you trust it, it will give you the guidance you need. Then you must also imagine that there is an antenna on the top of your head which connects you to your divine dimensions and allows you to receive inspiring messages.

Another way to be more ready to receive inspiration is by recognizing that you are connected not only to the Divine, but also to all that exists. The second chapter of this book explained the principle of wholeness. It is important that you reread that chapter to analyze the main aspects underpinning that principle.

You must always remember that there is a common thread of life force which unites everything that exists in the Universe. Steiner says that you should feel as a *"link in the wholeness of life."*

3.8. Take a notebook with you

Inspirational messages can be fleeting. So, in order to prevent the divine messages from evaporating, you must always carry a notebook and a pen with you wherever you go. You must grab the signals as soon as they appear.

Inspiration can come at any time and place. Thus, you have to be ready to write down the inspirational whispers whenever they pop up in your mind.

After taking notes, you should try to act on those messages without delay. You must remember that all inspirational messages come to you for a reason, so you must acknowledge them and avoid procrastinating.

3.9. Be welcoming

You are recognizing the importance of divine inspiration when you fully welcome it. So you must avoid overanalyzing the messages you receive from the Divine but act on them.

Sometimes you don't receive a complete and thorough sequence of steps on how you should act but the next step is obvious to take. You will notice that as soon as you take initial action you tend to gain momentum and everything becomes more effortless. If you do not to follow through with the idea which comes from inspiration, you might feel restless or fretful.

When you take inspired actions, subtle glee or explicit enthusiasm pervades your whole being. It does not feel like it was work, nor an obligation. Nonetheless, sometimes your inspired action might feel, at first, unfeasible, unrealistic, or unreasonable.

3.10 Other aspects

Every time you receive inspiration, you must be flexible with your thinking and actions. You must be open to approach things in a different way, as compared with your own ideas. Follow the divine guidance as abidingly as possible, avoiding getting stuck to your personal agenda. Avoid being sidetracked by negative comments from other people.

Every time Divinity guides you, you must be willing to do things in a non-traditional way, the inspired manner. Sometimes the inspirational messages prompt you to act against your most ingrained beliefs. It is important to not get stuck to your belief system, which is just your subconscious programming.

You are more likely to receive inspiration when you perform activities that have a real impact on your world. These activities can be also called love service. Some examples of these activities are: charity, mentoring, teaching, tithing, and donating, among others.

These activities naturally make you experience unconditional love, which renders you prone to receiving inspiration. The Divine is also more likely to provide you with guidance when you perform these activities because you can spread the benefits of inspirational messages over the people you assist.

Lastly, gratitude is another relevant requirement to receive inspiration. Besides, every time you are inspired you must be grateful because receiving divine guidance is a blessing. You must say *"Thank you"* as many times as possible.

You can also say like: *"Thank you, Divinity, for all the inspiration that you will provide me with"* or *"Thank you, Divinity, for all the directions I will receive from you."*

Chapter 14

Ho'oponopono Exercises

1. General aspects of the Ho'oponopono exercises

Over this book we saw that the main Ho'oponopono tool is the frequent use of the four sentences: *"I am sorry, Please forgive me, I love you, Thank you."* For example, with certain people who annoy you or criticize you, you can use these four sentences before, during or after meeting these people. You will notice that the energy in these relationships is transformed for better.

Some masters also suggest that you should frequently ask yourself: *"What is the actual meaning of these four sentences?"* and patiently wait for any insights into this question. It is very important to be open-minded when you ask these types of questions.

You will see below some other techniques that can support you during the process of removing your subconscious programs. Although some of these tools might look a bit wacky, you should give them a try, at least once. Do not overanalyze these tools, but experience their effects.

2. Using blue water

The blue water is also called solar water. The frequent use of this water helps you remove your subconscious programs. In order to prepare blue water, you should use a blue bottle made of glass, not plastic. If you don't have this glass bottle at home, you can buy this type of product on the Internet very easily. The bottle must also have a cork or a plastic top.

You have to fill up the bottle with tap water and stand it in the sunlight; choose a day which is not cloudy. The solar energy naturally purifies the water, converting it into blue water.

The water should be under the sun for at least one hour, albeit some masters recommend between two to six hours. On the safe side, try to rest the bottle under the sun as long as possible.

There is a second way to convert normal water into blue water. You should keep the blue bottle full of tap water under a lit light bulb up to one hour. You should not use fluorescent tubes.

You can also multiply the blue water in a very easy manner: you must pour a little bit of it into containers with normal water. When you do so, the water in the containers is converted into blue water.

Many sages recommend that you should drink blue water whenever possible. This water has natural purifying properties and cleans your subconscious programming in a progressive and effortless manner. Many masters say that the blue water is blessed by the universal forces.

You also can use this water for other purposes, such as washing your body, your clothes or your car, watering your plants and giving this water to your pets, among others. You can also apply blue water to the wounds on your skin because this water has curative properties. Some people also use this water for cooking activities, for example: boiling, steaming, or washing food.

Some masters say that you do not even need to prepare solar water to clean your subconscious memories but to visualize it in your mind. This has the same effects as if you were using blue water.

There is another way to purify water suggested by Ray. You should write the words *"I love, I bless you, thank you"* on a piece of paper and put it under a glass of common tap water and leave it there for a while to purify the water.

3. Practicing Ha respiration

A good respiration exercise provides you with more oxygen and strengthens your immune system. Respiring correctly also releases any stress symptoms from your body and mind and improves your overall health conditions.

The Ha respiration is a very well-known technique, which is also called square breathing. It is very well used in yoga and other relaxing disciplines. In order to use the technique of Ha respiration you should preferably be in a comfortable place.

When you practice this type of breathing you should keep yourself away from any distractions. Nonetheless, with enough practice, you will be able to apply this technique anywhere, at all times.

When you practice Ha respiration you should stand up on the floor with your back straight, or also rest on the floor or a bed. You can even sit on a comfortable chair with your back straight.

When you use this technique you should unite the tips of your forefingers and thumbs in each hand in order to form the shape of two circles interlocking with one another. In other words, your index fingers should be united with the respective thumbs in an OK gesture. Your thumb represents Divinity; your index finger is your being. When you link both, this represents your union with the Divine or infinity. You can also place your hands on your lap in order not to tire them. When you use this position, you should maintain your fingers this way during the entire exercise.

When you inhale you must count up to seven. Then you must hold the air in your lungs while you count up to seven again. After this, you exhale also counting up to seven once more. And then stay with the lungs empty while you count up to seven again. You should repeat the entire sequence in the same way for seven times, with no interruption.

Many masters state that this is a powerful way to remove your most ingrained subconscious memories. After this, you can also say the four Ho'oponopono sentences many times. You should practice this type of respiration frequently, at least once a day.

4. Having a grateful attitude

Chapter 11 thoroughly explained the Ho'oponopono sentence: *"Thank you."* Most people generally waste their time talking about things they dislike or don't want. Whenever you act this way, you are being unappreciative. With this attitude, you are focused on negative things in your life instead of concentrating on the positive ones. You are actually radiating very low vibratory energy which attracts more negative things in your life.

Instead, when you are appreciative and say *"Thank you"* to every single thing you experience you are emanating love energy. When you get used to talking about what you love, enjoy or like you radiate positive energy, which helps you manifest even more positive things into your life.

This powerful sentence is based on the value of thankfulness. It is important that you say these words as regularly as possible in order to be appreciative.

Many masters suggest that you should also keep a gratitude journal. You can use a notebook or your personal computer to take notes. You should include all the things, people, places and situations that you are grateful for.

Rosenberg recommends that you should also state the benefits which these things, people or situations brought into your life, the needs of yours they satisfied as well as the positive emotions you feel because of them. As you take note in this journal you will be generating positive energy which will bring about positive things into your life.

It is really important to keep records every day, either before going to bed or right after waking up. Read these notes frequently and bask in the good feelings they make you evoke.

When you are grateful, you show you have a prosperity mindset; you are implicitly relying on the Universe's abundant flow. A very good way to be grateful is by giving things away to others. From this perspective, not only can you give money to others, but also information, care, advice, company and affection, among others.

From the metaphysical point, receiving and giving are sides of the same coin; when you give more you tend to receive more. Some masters suggest that you should frequently give the very things you want to receive.

You don't have to be grateful only for the things you own and the experiences you enjoy, but also for all people involved previously who make all that available to you. For example, when you are grateful for having a pair of shoes, you should also be grateful for activities performed by the shoe shop, the shoe producer, the leather supplier, and so on. The same principle can be applied to people; you should be grateful for them but also for their forebears.

You can also keep a journal with all things that you give. The important tip is to give wholeheartedly, without any expectation of receiving anything in return. Every time you give you are in a good emotional state, which raises your vibratory rate. And this, in turn, will make you manifest more good things into your life.

There is a very interesting exercise suggested by Borysenko. This author says that when you are not appreciative of your body, it becomes weak or sick. You should sit in a meditative posture and be appreciative of each part of your body for their prized contribution to your life.

Tithing is another systematic way of giving but also an evident display of appreciation. Some suggest that you should tithe ten percent of your income. It said that whenever you tithe you are likely to attract good things into your life.

5. Eliminating negative remarks

Some masters say that every time you are judgmental you are acting against the essence of the Divine. Harsh criticism is also opposite to Ho'oponopono's philosophy. When you judge others or yourself, you replay memories held in your subconscious mind.

For this reason, you should always be a zealous guardian of your mouth and avoid any form of condemnation. Criticism always lowers your energy vibration, which attracts negative circumstances in your life.

Instead of criticizing, you should praise everything that you encounter to show your love and gratitude. Goddard says that: *"Praise expands the mind upward, while its contrary, condemnation, contracts and restricts."*

He added:

If one learns the simple method of praise, that alone will stimulate and increase his good… He lifts his consciousness to a higher realm and becomes a greater channel to receive the good that is ever waiting to come to him… Praise opens a little door in his mind that enables him to draw closer to God and to be attuned to the Divine forces within him…

Praising is the shortest way to manifest positive things in your life.

Moreover, when you praise you focus only on positive aspects of all things and people around you and dismiss their short-comings. Some masters also state that praising makes you more receptive to divine inspiration. From the Ho'oponopono perspective, every time you praise you do not activate any negative memories held in your subconscious mind.

You should look at your negative habits, such as judging everything around you. Sometimes these habits can be very subtle, for example moaning or patronizing others or yourself. You might also tend to see the negative side of every situation in an exaggerated manner, for example being catastrophic in relation to future circumstances.

Every time you catch yourself in any of these detrimental habits you should immediately focus on the positive aspects of the situation at hand. You can also say the four phrases *"I am sorry"*, *"Please forgive me"*, *"I love you"* and *"Thank you"* many times. The frequent use of these sentences will help you remove the subconscious memories underpinning this negative habit.

6. The mirror exercise

To do this well-known exercise you need a mirror, for example the little one generally found in your bathroom. You must stand up in front of a mirror, calm and at ease. If you are fretful, you can even take a deep breath to release any tension.

Then you must look at your eyes in the mirror. It is important that you see yourself beyond the physical aspects of your body, beyond the mask of appearances. The objective of this exercise is to discover your essential spiritual core.

You can focus on your eyes with undivided attention to perceive the presence of your soul. You should feel appreciative of your unpolluted essence. While you stare at your eyes in the mirror you must say the four Ho'oponopono sentences many times.

Be aware of your emotions, thoughts and sensations when you say these four phrases. You can also ask yourself: *"What is going on in my life?"* In that effect, you must gaze at your eyes deeply and then wait for answers to come.

There is a second way to do this exercise, which entails seeing yourself in the mirror in a compassionate manner. This means that you should forsake any negative way of labelling yourself. You must perceive your expression, your facial aspects and body movements from the perspective of love. Feel the love energy flowing from you and pouring onto the image in the mirror. You can also imagine that you embrace the image in the mirror with your heart, which is full of love.

You can apply this technique to people you know, which means encompassing them with loving energy coming from your heart. You can envision this either when you are with these people or when you are alone. You can also use photographs of these people. The frequent use of this simple exercise helps you overcome the apparent separateness between you and other people around you.

There is a third way regarding the mirror exercise, which can be used when it is difficult for you to see yourself through loving eyes. You can try to see yourself through the eyes of someone that honestly loves you. You can even imagine the loving comments that this person would make about you.

There is a fourth way to do the exercise with the mirror. You should observe your image in the mirror and imagine as if you were a little child. Then you should say to this child the four Ho'oponopono sentences as many times as possible. After this, you must promise this child that you will always care for him or her.

7. Saying "Aloha" to everyone

The Hawaiian word *aloha* has a very interesting meaning; the first part *a* means *"being present"* and *loha* means *"connection with Divinity."* From the Ho'oponopono perspective every time you say *"aloha"* you are in the presence of Divinity, which is the main source of life, powerfulness and universal love.

According to Martinez Tomás the term *aloha* entails harmony, affinity and cooperation with other people. From this viewpoint, you should concentrate more on commonalities you have with other people, instead of things which separate or differentiate you from others. We are all spiritual beings with physical experiences. Our appearance might look different, but in essence we are all divine beings.

We are all naturally interconnected. As a consequence, you can think of different ways of assisting others. When you have a cooperative attitude with people around you your energy levels tend to rise, which helps you attract more positive circumstances into your life.

DeNoyelles says that:

Aloha symbolically means to share breath and to be present with the essence of life, which is love. When we think or say the word aloha, we generate loving vibration and attune ourselves to the Divine or Spiritual power, what Hawaiians call mana.

The term *Aloha* helps you connect with the vital force which enlivens all that exists in the Universe.

According to Shook the word *aloha*:

expresses love and it is a greeting and a farewell. More subtly, it suggests the highly valued character of generosity, friendliness, patience and productivity. The spirit of aloha carries with it an understanding that the ability to soothe and prevent conflicts, shame and other disruptive occurrences is important, and that if the harmony has been disrupted, one should have the courage to ask for and give forgiveness.

For this reason, many people use the term *aloha* as a way of greeting others in a kind manner. This meaningful term creates a sense of communion and supportiveness which strengthens all your relationships.

You should use the term *aloha* as frequently as possible, for example every time you meet someone. With this simple word you wholeheartedly welcome the divine part of that person. With the regular use of the word *aloha* you will notice that you develop a more affectionate connection with all people. Sondra Ray says every time you say the word *aloha* to others, you acknowledge the bright light in them and also within yourself.

8. Using the power of water

Cabanillas suggests that you should place a glass of tap water nearby when you are working or sleeping. This glass should be three-quarters full of fresh tap water. You might see that, after a while, the water is filled with small bubbles, which means that this liquid is absorbing your limiting subconscious memories.

If the water is bubbling, you should empty the glass and fill it again with fresh tap water. You should empty and fill the glass as many times as necessary. In relation to this, Dr. Len recommends that you put a glass of water by the computer every time you connect to the Internet because the World Wide Web is full of negative memories. If you are facing any negative situations in your life, you should try this exercise as frequently as possible.

Cabanillas suggests that you should put a piece of paper under the glass with the name of the person with whom you are in conflict. You can also include a piece of paper with a brief description of the difficulties that you are going through. You will see over time that the negative issue will dissolve almost miraculously.

9. Connecting with your inner child

Some sages suggest this very well-known exercise which you can do when you are by yourself. Then you must be in a quiet and comfortable place; you can even light a candle or incense. Look for a picture from your childhood when you were on your own.

Look at the picture with undivided attention for several minutes. Observe any emotion and thoughts coming up during this process and say the four Ho'oponopono phrases many times. You can also visualize the Divine clearing out the subconscious programs affecting this little child in the photo. Make this imagery as vivid as possible.

There is a second version of this exercise suggested by Dr. Len. In this case, you don't need any picture. You have to be in a comfortable place, relaxed and with your eyes closed. Breathe slowly and deeply. You seek to improve the relationship between your conscious mind (called *the mother*) and your subconscious mind (known as *the child*). This is a paramount relationship in your life.

As previously seen, the subconscious mind is the place where all memories running your life are kept. Bear in mind that this little child (your subconscious) is a very pure part of your being. The child has a very spontaneous, naïve and playful essence.

The mother can decide to have either a loving relationship with the child or a dismissive one. You should visualize that you (the mother or your conscious mind) connect with your inner child (your subconscious mind).

In that effect, you must try to envision the face and body of this child clearly; you can even greet him or her. The child must be visualized with loving eyes. You (the mother) should look at the child's eyes and ask yourself: *"Is the child saddened?"*, *"Does the child look abandoned?"* and *"Is there any pain in the child's face?"* If you have difficulties envisioning the child you can look at a picture from your childhood; this might help you with this exercise.

Then you (the mother or your conscious mind) have to say loving words to the child (your subconscious mind). You can say to this child the words *"I love you"* or any similar ones. You should also say that you are truly sorry for all the pain you caused to him or her. You should apologize for having ignored him or her for a long time.

You can also say to the child that you are really sorry for having given umpteen wrong programs to him or her. Besides, you can even say that you appreciate this child is a relevant part of you.

Whenever you do this exercise, you are taking responsibility for having given the child these detrimental memories. You can also apologize to the child for having hurt and manipulated him or her.

You must also express that you want the child to have all his or her grievances removed. In order to do so, you can use the Ho'oponopono sentences many times. You can also ask the child for permission to hold his or her hands tenderly. You can even hold the child's shoulders in a loving way.

You should nurture the child with unconditional love. You can also thank the child for having been with you at all times. You can give the child a very gentle but warm hug. Then you kindly ask the child to release all past programming which he or she has been holding on tight to.

Once you teach the child to release the memories he or she will carry out the cleaning process on its own, without your guidance. You can also tell the child about other cleaning tools that you are using to remove your memories, such as blue water.

You can also ask the child to release the memories which create specific problems, for example, health conditions, financial difficulties, among others. You should not forget to tell the child that you will always care for him or her. You can also say to the child that you feel very well for having contacted him or her.

There is a second part of this exercise. Imagine that you are now the child (your subconscious mind) and you are observing your mother (your conscious mind) and your father (your super conscious mind) filling you with love. From this perspective, you must envision both parents caring for you, sending all their love and fully appreciating you.

In this part of the exercise, you are the child and from this perspective you hear the four Ho'oponopono sentences being said to you by the mother (conscious mind). After this, you can also do the Ha respiration, which was explained earlier in this chapter.

10. Managing mana

Mana is pure energy that brings about great spiritual power as well.
– JA Lee

Mana, also called prana, is the vital universal energy, life force and spiritual power permeating everything that exists in the Universe.

You can always harness this subtle energy to heal yourself or others. Besides you can use this energy to perform your projects more effectively and also improve your relationships.

When you experience any negative emotional states the access to this vital energy is hampered. Saradananda says that: *"if you imagine that your body is a factory, your prana is the person in charge."*

This energy is what enlivens all the air you respire. Sondra Ray suggests a type of breathing which helps you store mana; you must empty your lungs firstly and then inspire slowly while you press your lips. It is important that your lips are pursed as if you were whistling.

Then you should slowly but forcefully release all the air in your lungs. Pay close attention to whole breathing process and repeat this sequence many times. This type of breathing also acts like a propellant for prayers and requests to the Divine.

There are other subtle ways to obtain more mana. Lee says that you can naturally accumulate mana whenever you act humbly and when you are open to learning from your life experiences. From this particular perspective, you can also obtain this prized energy when you cast aside any judgmental or begrudging attitudes. As well as this, you can gather mana when you devote your time to a meaningful cause. You can even ask the subconscious part of your mind to download more mana for you.

According to Von Deck, there is another interesting exercise to gather prana; you must stand up with your attention focused inwardly and stretch your arms downwards, with your hands in prayer position. Imagine that you absorb the energy of the Earth through your hands. Then cup your hands over your chest and the rest of your body in order to impregnate your whole being with mana recently absorbed.

After this, you must do the same with the hands stretched forward; you absorb the energy of your surroundings. Again you must spread this mana all over your body with your hands.

Then you have to stretch your arms upwards, with your hands

in the prayer position. The purpose of this is to absorb the energy from heaven. When you do so, you must cup your hands and move them all over your body to spread the energy you gathered.

Lastly, you must stretch your arms sideways to absorb the energy from other planets and galaxies. After this you must spread that energy you absorbed all over your body with your palms cupped.

Saradananda suggests another version of the respiration to gather prana. You must start the exercise seated and with your eyes open and lips closed. Then you must breathe in as deeply as possible. While you inhale you must open your eyes, as widely as you can. In the inhalation you must imagine that you gather light energy, which represents prana. Visualize this energy entering the top of your head, filling your ears and your face and going into your lungs.

Once your lungs are filled, you must retain your breath for a while. Now with your eyes closed, you concentrate on your third eye, which is the point between your eyebrows. You must envision the energy that you inhale is forming a ball made of sparkling light situated in the middle of your forehead.

Then you must exhale while you imagine that this ball is transformed into an energetic shower which pervades all of your body, boosting its energy and rejuvenating it. You must go through this sequence at least ten times.

There is another variation of this exercise in which during the retention phase, instead of imagining the ball of light, you must envision the prana energy circulating flowingly throughout your entire body. Then when you exhale, you must envision that you expel any negative energy far away from your body.

Fontana suggests other ways to gather prana. Inhale with the lips pursed as if you were whistling, fill up your lungs and exhale slowly through the nose. Your exhale should last double the time that your inhale does.

Lastly, Lee suggests a mana prayer which says:

Thank you, Father, Mother, God, for all the blessings you have bestowed upon us. We accept and appreciate them and endeavor to pass them on to others less fortunate and in need. PAU (clap hands and raise arms heavenward). Our prayer takes flight. May the rain of blessings in the form of the high mana descend... Thank you very much.

You can use this prayer frequently. You will notice an increase in the vital energy that you harness.

11. Visualization exercise

This visualization exercise called Mystic Mountain is suggested by Jirsch and Cafferky. Look for a comfortable and quiet place; you can either be seated or laid down on a bed. Your breathing must be slow and deep.

With your eyes closed, start to visualize that you are climbing up a very high mountain; you should enjoy your stroll uphill. Once you have reached the summit of that mountain, you should observe the entire world below. Look below and appreciate every detail of the beautiful nature. Visualize that there are a lot of people below who love one another.

In the depth of your heart you feel that love energy pervades all that exists, neighborhoods, towns, cities, countries and planets. You must also feel that this energy permeates every single nook of your body.

12. Blessing everything around you

To love without passion is an impossibility.
– Soren Kierkegaard

There is a very well-known Hawaiian tradition that says that you must bless everything in your life. Every time you bless things, people, places or situations you are focusing on their positive attributes.

From the metaphysical perspective, whenever you bless something you use divine energy to transmute any fault in it. You send love energy to the objects of your blessings and recognize their sacred essence.

Some masters suggest that you should even bless your problems and mistakes. In some cases, these difficulties tend to disappear almost by magic. In other cases, you are more likely to discover the solution for them.

Additionally, Peale suggest that you should bless your conversations with people. When you do so, your relationships will tend to improve effortlessly. You can use words like *"I bless this conversation"*, or *"Divinity, please bless this chat"*, among others.

In relation to this, Roberts says that when you bless things on a regular basis you don't even need to be repentant for your wrongdoings. From this perspective, when you have a blessing attitude you don't have to ask for forgiveness for your mistakes because you purified them with love energy flowing through you.

Some say that blessing is just another form of appreciation. Every time that you bless something you are showing Divinity how thankful you are; you express that you have abundance in your life.

When you bless everything and everyone in your life you naturally radiate energy of a very high vibration. From the Ho'oponopono perspective whenever you bless you contribute to the removal of your subconscious programs. Moreover you can overtly bless your subconscious memories in order to remove them.

When you bless things on a frequent basis, you cancel out any negativity in your life. In this book it was commented that Dr. Emoto conducted an experiment in which people sent blessings to water. Then its structure was analyzed in a microscope and the crystals showed beautiful structures, only after the water was previously blessed.

The simple way of blessing anything is to say *"I bless this"* to anything you encounter. Everything can be blessed, for example your food. Blessing meals before eating is a very common ritual in many religions. You can repeatedly say *"I love you"* to the meal or *"I bless this food that I am about to eat"* many times.

From the Ho'oponopono perspective there is no such a thing as *bad food* or *good food*. From this viewpoint, what gives a negative meaning to certain types of food, such as junk food, is your subconscious memories. When you repeatedly say *"I love you"* to the food you are about to eat, you are removing all subconscious memories you have about it.

13. Harnessing the power of smile

Many studies confirm that sincere smiles improve your communication and rapport with other people. Furthermore, smiling is always a demonstration of friendliness, good intentions and lovingness. This in turn prompts you to be in a continuous good mood.

Whenever you smile your confidence is strengthened; smiling also boosts your overall levels of energy. Your smile represents the main cornerstones for glee, enthusiasm and any other positive emotional states you can experience.

From the metaphysical perspective, whenever you smile you radiate very positive energy, which makes you attract more positive circumstances into your life. Besides, smiling is one of the most effective nonverbal ways to share your positivity with others. Becker says that: *"Your smile reminds others that love is present."*

Your smile is like a beam of light that pervades everything around. You create a positive connection with everyone around you. Smiling is always contagious; people can easily attune with your smile and reciprocate, in most cases unwittingly. Fredrickson says that smiling not only illuminates the *"smiler"* and *"smilee"* but also the connection between both.

In order to harness all the benefits of smiling we mentioned above, you can find below some brief tips:

– *Honor everything with a smile:* Make a habit of smiling at anyone. In most cases, people will smile at you back because they cannot prevent it, like an automatic reflex. You should also try to smile more frequently to people you don't get on well with. Your relationship with these people tends to improve significantly over time. Some metaphysicians say that you should also smile at any physical objects to radiate positive energy to them.

– *Always show an honest smile:* Your smile must be authentic. The real smile involves the muscles of your entire face, especially your eyes. On the contrary, when a smile is fake or forced, only the lower part of the face is involved. You have probably recognized when people smiled at you in a feigned manner; their smiles looked mechanical and lifeless. People use fake smiles just as a sign of politeness or sociability, for example, most sellers at shops.

– *Smile with your body:* Some masters also suggest a very well-known exercise related to the discipline of Qigong. Get in a comfortable place and with your eyes closed; your breathing must be slow and deep. Visualize that you are smiling with every part of your body (organs, your cells, etc.). Feel as if every part of your body is expressing love, happiness and thankfulness. You should also visualize as if you were smiling with your body at people, especially when you hold conversations with them.

– Lastly it is important to highlight that there are some scientific studies which found that frequent smiling has very tangible positive effects on your overall well-being. Waynbaum, cited in Watson, states that smiles improve the blood flow in your brain and prompt you to experience more positive emotions. There are some disciplines like the so-called smiling therapy which is primarily focused on the therapeutic benefits of smiling.

14. Writing your autobiography

This is also an exercise widespread in many metaphysical circles. Sit on your own in a comfortable and quiet place and time block at least one hour for this exercise. On a piece of paper, write down the most relevant aspects of your personal story which come to your mind. Write down details about yourself without stopping; don't correct or edit. Then read each paragraph carefully.

When reading your notes, you are likely to experience thoughts, physical sensations or emotions, which are manifestations of your subconscious programs. Then you must ask yourself *"What is going on in me now that I am experiencing this?"* and listen attentively to any insights into this. Then say the four Ho'oponopono statements repeatedly.

15. Cleaning the places you visit

Some ancient traditions assert that everything is alive, even things that appear lifeless. From this perspective, every single thing also has a definite identity and radiates vital energy. As a consequence, you can talk to things as if you were holding a conversation with another person. If you do so, you must always talk to things around you in a kind and friendly manner.

Some oriental philosophies even assert that everything which exists has a soul. In accordance to this, Ewing says that: *"the land and rocks speak, if only we listen... all beings are related in the sacred cycle of life."*

From the metaphysical perspective, every single thing that exists has an energetic body which envelops its physical aspects. For example, whenever you enter a place, you can easily sense its particular vibe; you quickly know if its energy is heavy or light.

In the case that this energy is stagnant, the place is pervaded by negative vibrations. When the energy circulates flowingly the place is impregnated with positive energy.

If the place is charged with negative vibrations you will feel fretful and taut when you are there. If the place radiates positive energy, you will be comfortable, relaxed and at ease. When you try to sense the place's energy, you should not connect to the outer aspects of that location, which means its appearance or physical traits. Instead, you must always get attuned to its inner essence. Sense the energetic aspects of the place.

Many people think that sensing the energy of a place is an expert skill which only few people possess. However, everyone can tune into the vibratory rate of places. You surely recollect some places where you felt uncomfortable for no reason. You might also have some memories of places where you felt at ease and safe.

In order to distinguish the quality of energy of a specific place you must be absolutely tranquil and relaxed when you are there. Empty your mind from worries or any negative emotional state in order to concentrate only on the now. If this is the first time you visit that place you might have expectations regarding it. As you get rid of any presumption you will feel the place as it is.

When you are at the place, feel its different temperatures, textures and sensations. Let your feelings be your main guidance. Ewing recommends that, when you sense the energy of a place, you should always be grounded, which means that you must imagine you are connected to the Earth.

In order to feel grounded, visualize a beam of light that extends from the bottom of your backbone to the floor that goes further down deep into planet Earth. You must also envision yourself connected to the sun; this vision will make you feel more balanced. Some masters suggest that every time you enter a new place you should imagine a shield around you to protect you from potential negative vibrations inhabiting the place.

Some sages even say that places, as any other thing which exists, hold subconscious memories, which can be removed. From this perspective, you can delete the memories accrued in a specific location by saying the four Ho'oponopono sentences as many times as possible.

From this perspective, places are living beings; they are actually alive. As a consequence, every time you enter a place you can ask the place how it feels. You can even ask the place permission to stay there or perform any activity in it. From this viewpoint, you can also ask the place for advice to improve its own energy.

Whenever you communicate with the place you are at, you must always be respectful with it. When you are at the place you can ask yourself: *"How do I feel when I am at this place?"* or *"What is going on in me when I am at this location?"* to receive prized insights into the quality of the energy there.

After this, you can even say the four Ho'oponopono sentences. These phrases will help you remove any negative energy from the location where you currently are. You can also say another sentence like *"I am the peace of I."* Dr. Len states that you can also use the word *"Hawaii"* to clean the place; this term is another cleaning word.

When you are exploring the place, you can also ask yourself a question like *"How am I affecting this place and vice versa?"* With this type of question you become more sensitive in relation to different places you are. You can also ask questions to the different objects located there. Some examples are *"How are you?"* or *"Do you need anything?"* or *"May I stay here?"* Then repeat the four Ho'oponopono sentences many times.

16. The inner chamber exercise
This useful exercise is suggested by David and Kristin Morelli (who are cited by Shimoff and Kline). You must be in a comfortable and tranquil place. Close your eyes, breathe deeply

and concentrate in the area between your eyebrows called *the third eye* or sixth chakra.

Put aside any past memories or worries and concentrate on the now. Focus on a point in the center of your head. After this, visualize a pipe which links your head with your heart. Envision yourself sliding down through that pipe toward your heart. Once there, look for a door and open it. This door will lead you to the inner chamber where God resides.

After opening the door, you must enter this chamber and close the door behind you. You must carefully observe all the details inside the chamber. Imagine that you are connected with God's beam of light that comes from above. Next, cast away all aspects of your personality (name, physical appearance, nationality, temperament, occupation, etc.). From the Ho'oponopono all these aspects are just subconscious memories. When you strip yourself from all these personal traits, you can access the authentic you.

In the chamber you should also ask any important question you would like to know about, and wait for the answer. This answer can come either in a verbal or nonverbal manner. After you have received the answer, say *"Thank you."*

Slowly leave the chamber and close the door. Bring the answer with you and return to the central part of your head, where you started this exercise. Then you should appreciate any wise insights you obtained throughout the whole process.

17. Practicing the Golden Key

This tool was originally developed by Emmet Fox and it is really very simple to use. To put it simply, you must focus on God or the Divine, instead of concentrating on your problems. That is the complete exercise; you do not have to do anything else. It is important not to get deceived by the simplicity of this tool because it is very powerful. You must actually think about God's characteristics such as: wholeness, love, omniscience, omnipresence and powerfulness, among others.

You can also say *"I apply the Golden Key to... (and you name the problem once)."* After saying that, you must continue focusing on God. You should always be concentrated on God's features, even when you don't have any problem at all.

Whenever you think about the Divine, you are connected to the purest form of energy, which transmutes any negative life circumstance almost magically. There is a good way to test that you are using the tool correctly, which is to ask yourself: *"What am I thinking about now?"* If you are thinking about the problem then you are not thinking about God, and vice versa.

There is another version of this exercise that you can use. For example, you can also say some sentences such as *"I am pervaded by God's love"* or *"God is my continual guide."* These sentences reflect your connection with the most powerful energy that exists.

Whenever you use the Golden Key you leave your problem in the Divine's hands to be solved. This technique can be used for problems affecting various areas of your life, such as work, career and relationships, among others.

When you apply this technique, you truly rely on the divine limitless power to solve all your problems. The Divine is your best ally; you totally surrender your difficult circumstances to it.

18. Eliciting clues from your subconscious memories

You have many other ways to unearth information from your subconscious in order to remove this data. The sentences you frequently use in your daily conversation give you some clues about your subconscious memories.

It is said that underneath any question you ask using the word *"How?"* there is always a sensation of uneasiness. When you ask how-questions you can experience, for example, doubt, fear, guilt, fretfulness, among other states.

Let's have a look at the question: *"How will I get in healthier conditions?"* In this example you are implicitly stating you feel dissatisfied with your current situations. These negative emotional states are just subconscious memories popping up, which must be removed by doing Ho'oponopono. You can also ask yourself: *"What is going on in me that I am experiencing these emotions?"* after using this technique.

Audlin says that when you use questions that start with the words *"What if...?"* you are prone to experience a state of anxiety linked to imagined negative future scenarios. Worry and anxiety are negative states which beckon the existence of subconscious memories to be removed.

Some other expressions you regularly relate to states of inadequacy or powerlessness remind you that you have subconscious programs to remove. Some examples are *"I can't..."*, *"I will not be able..."*, or any other similar ones.

Another word you might frequently use is *wish*. When you use the word *wish* you are generally expecting things to be better, which implies the existence of subconscious memories to remove. The same applies to words like *want* or *desire*.

A similar expression is *"if only..."* which is generally related to guilt or regret. These negative emotions are prompted by the programs playing out in your subconscious mind.

Sometimes your subconscious memories are shown up in a more subtle way. For example, when you use any type of objections, including the word *but*. This type of sentence also entails negativity.

You must be aware of sentences enclosing the word *must*. The word *must* is generally related to obligations, which are things or activities you place resistance against. The frequent use of this word indicates that you have memories to be cleaned.

You should be careful when you use sentences starting with the words *"I am..."* When you use this powerful phrase you are asserting to the Universe what you deserve, either positive or negative. For example, you might also use sentences such as *"I am a fool."*

Whenever you use this type of negative sentence, even jokingly, you are reinforcing these messages in your subconscious as memories. The opposite is true too; when you use positive sentences about yourself (for example, *"I am intelligent"*) this also becomes imprinted in your subconscious mind as positive programming.

In all the previous cases, it is important to repeat the four Ho'oponopono phrases many times. You should try to use this cleaning technique as frequently as possible.

19. Keeping a diary of your night dreams

Some psychological schools of thought suggest that dreams you have when you are asleep are symbolic messages related to emotions or thoughts popping up subconsciously. These feelings and ideas are not likely to emerge in an overt manner when you are awake.

While you sleep, even though your conscious mind stops working, your subconscious still plays out its memories. Take note of the details of your dreams, right after you wake up. Keep a notebook and a pen by your bed. You should read these notes aloud many times and ask yourself: *"What is going on in me that I manifested these dreams?"* Let insights come to your mind and say the four Ho'oponopono sentences repeatedly.

Nightmares are clear indicators of subconscious programs which must be removed as soon as possible. A dream repeated many times is also a signal that there are messages to which you must pay close attention. Sometimes it might be advisable to analyze your dreams with the support of a psychologist. From the Ho'oponopono perspective, you can introspect through your dreams by yourself.

In relation to this, Dr. Len also recommends that when you have conflict with some people, you must say the sentences *"I love you"* and *"Thank you"* to the subconscious minds of people with whom you are at odds. You should say these words during a time when you suppose these people would be sleeping so that you can affect them more effectively. When you have conflicts with organizations, you can say these very phrases during a time outside their working hours.

20. Seeing yourself as a loving being

This exercise is suggested by Teck and Chapman. You must be in a comfortable and quiet place; think of a person who loves you in an honest and caring manner. See this person in front of you; then observe yourself from her or his perspective. Experience this person's love feelings toward you. Try to sense what this person likes most about you and the reasons for that.

If you have difficulties with this exercise, imagine that this person is in front of you. Then step out of your body and into this person's. You can guess this person's likely usual thoughts about you. Imagine all the loving words that this person would say to you, if in front of you. You can even imagine that you, in the body of this person, hug yourself in a loving manner. Bask in these positive feelings and sensations for a while.

Then imagine that you come back to your body and wallow in these loving feelings. As you do this exercise regularly, you will realize you are loved and that you will always be.

21. Connecting with your radiant sun

This exercise was adapted from one suggested by Villoldo. You can do this exercise on your own in a quiet place. Place your hand in prayer's posture in the center of your chest, at the heart's height, and imagine that over the top of your head there is a radiant sun with refulgent rays. Feel its energy and temperature and vibration, and visualize its beaming radiance bathing the top of your head, which represents your connection with the Divine Source.

Then slowly move your hands (still in prayer's pose) upward just above the top of your head. When you do this, you must sense that the bright sun opens up to you. Then open your hands sideward and downward, as if you were a peacock showing your fan boastingly.

Take a minute to appreciate the energy of the radiant sun; feel a peaceful sensation pervading your whole being. Then imagine that the sun's energy cleanses every single part of you, even the memories stored in your subconscious mind. See the sunlight removing these programs completely.

Lastly, move your outstretched arms upwards to the top of your head and place your hands in prayer position above it. Then move your hands back to the area of your heart, while still keeping them in prayer position.

22. Reading a letter from the Divine

This is a very interesting exercise suggested by Kok. Every week you should write yourself a love letter as if it were written by the Divine. In this letter, the Divine expresses how much you are loved by the Higher Planes.

The text for this letter can have any format; below find one example of a letter that you can use. Feel free to amend it to make it more personal.

Dear... (your name)
I want to tell you are always covered in love. Always remember that your life is pure love and everything you create is also made of love. Love is what actually sets you free from bondage of the past. Always be at ease because all apparent negativity within you is being dissolved into love, which also spreads all over your mind and body. Bear in mind that love is the most important gift in your life.
　　I love you
　　The Divine

You should read this letter many times, if possible aloud. After this, say the four Ho'oponopono sentences repeatedly.

23. Talking to your body

You can use this technique especially when you suffer from any type of illness. You can do this exercise on your own in your spare time. You should talk to the part of your body which is ill and say: *"I am sorry, please forgive me, I love you, thank you"* as many times as possible. Then say: *"Sorry for having manipulated, misused and abused you."*

Try to befriend that part of your body in order to improve its health conditions. When you say these sentences, you should treat your body in a loving manner. You can also visualize that this part of your body is covered with loving light. You can even apply this tool to intrusive thoughts and disturbing emotions affecting you.

When you are affected by any disease you can also observe your body, as if you were an external witness. Visualize that love energy is circulating throughout your body. Do not judge what you feel or see but repeat the Ho'oponopono sentences.

24. Asking your subconscious mind questions

You can ask questions to your subconscious level such as *"Subconscious mind, what should I know about...?"* It is better to pose this type of question before going to sleep. You might receive some related insights during your sleep time or later on. Take note of them and say the four Ho'oponopono sentences repeatedly.

You can also use a pendulum to ask questions to your subconscious. A pendulum can be bought in any new age shop. This technique helps you access the past programming stored in your subconscious mind. In order to use the pendulum, you must previously agree on the codes you will use to communicate with your subconscious mind.

The pendulum generally moves in four different ways: a) clockwise; b) counterclockwise; c) backward and forward; and d) sideward. You must know the meaning of these four directions before using the pendulum. These directions will have specific meanings which are *"no"*, *"yes"*, *"I don't want to answer that"* and *"I don't know yet."*

You should hold the pendulum and ask: *"Which oscillation means 'no'?"* and the pendulum will show you so. Then you must ask for the rest of the meanings. Then you can ask your subconscious mind questions about topics you want to know about and it will provide answers through the movement of the pendulum.

You must hold the pendulum taking its cord with your thumb and index fingers. Its heavy part must be dangling downwards in a tranquil way. You should never move the pendulum; it has to move by itself right after you ask a specific question.

When you use the pendulum you can ask questions to your subconscious mind about beliefs you would like to replace. For example, you can ask questions such as: *"Can I change this belief... in this way...?"* or *"Is this the right way to change this specific belief?"*

According to Satyam you can also ask your subconscious mind: *"Am I one hundred percent responsible?"* In case your subconscious mind (your inner child) happens to say *"No!"* you must explain to it that you are now being totally responsible. Then you can ask the child the same question again to check if it truly believes you.

25. The Furba Clearing Process

This ancient energy technique is proposed by Joe Vitale. You have to choose only one problem affecting you a lot, which could be financial difficulties, relationship challenges, or any other one. Think about the problem; you will realize that you can feel it in different parts of your body.

Scan your body to see in which part of it the problem is reflected on; the area you can feel its energy. Embrace these sensations and feelings; do not suppress or deny them. The energy related to your problem is trapped in your body-mind system.

Once you identify where the problem is located in your body

on an energy level, you must mentally place this energy mass in front of you. See its shape, color and texture, and ask yourself: *"What is the lesson I have to learn regarding this problem?"* Then wait for insights.

Then you must visualize that you grab a sharp object like a sword, dagger, knife or even a Furba, which is a Tibetan knife commonly used for rituals. Dr. Vitale suggests that you can even imagine using your own personal business card with its sharp edges.

With this object you must slice the energy field related to the problem into small pieces, until it is totally dissolved. See how the energy field of the problem is broken down into minute bits until it disappears in front of you.

Once the energy field of the problem has disappeared from your sight, ask yourself: *"What is going on inside me now?"* Wait for any insights; your energy is likely to be clearer and lighter. You might even feel more at ease and relaxed. Depending on the type of problem you might have to repeat this exercise many times. From the Ho'oponopono perspective, this exercise helps you clear the subconscious programs which originate your problems.

26. Other exercises

There are other short exercises which can be very useful to eliminating your subconscious negative memories. Do not to be tricked by the simplicity of these tools; try these techniques for a while to test their effectiveness.

a) Consuming certain food products

You should frequently eat some products which help you clean your past subconscious memories such as: sugar cane liquid, ginger biscuits, vanilla ice cream, hot chocolate, strawberries, jelly beans, gingerbread and blueberries. You can have them at any time.

In relation to the jelly beans, Dr. Len suggests that you should tell your inner child (your subconscious mind) that you have this food for him or her. You can even ask this inner child if there is any opposition to this type of food or also visualize this child eating this food.

b) Using the rubber eraser to clean

Perez suggests that you should use a rubber eraser on the things that you want to clean. For example, you can rub things that you want to purify such as documents or any other belongings of value. As you rub these things with the eraser on a frequent basis, you remove negative subconscious memories contained in these objects. Use this tool with any critical documents such as traffic fines, tax inspection documentation, contracts and loan debt notifications, among others.

You can buy a pencil with a rubber eraser on one of its tips. Dr. Len states that in order to activate the pencil you must say the word "dewdrop" to it and touch or tap the rubber eraser on any object you want to remove subconscious memories from. You can also imagine that you touch the object with the pencil.

You can also write a brief description of your current problems with a pencil on a small piece of paper. After this, you must erase what you have just written, slowly but completely. As you do so, the memories related to these problems are being erased too.

Lastly, some suggest that you should keep an eraser with you at all times, for example in your pocket. By carrying this object the cleaning process of your subconscious memories is done automatically while you do your daily tasks.

c) Hugging yourself for while

Satyam suggests a very interesting exercise you can do when you go to bed. You must lay down on the right part of your body and caress with your right arm your left arm, as if you were pampering a little baby. The left side of your body represents your subconscious level (the child), and the right side your conscious mind (the mother).

Symbolically speaking, when you do this exercise, the mother is hugging the child where all your past memories reside. While you do this exercise you should repeat the four Ho'oponopono phrases. When your right side embraces your left side you can also say that you (the mother) will take care of the child.

d) Using sticky notes

This is another simple but interesting exercise you can do whenever possible. You can place many sticky notes in your workplace and at home with the four sentences *"I am sorry, please forgive me, I love you, thank you."* Use bright colors to grab your attention. These notes will remind you of the cleaning process every time you see them.

The positive energetic vibration of those written words also contributes to the purification of your own subconscious memories. You can also carry these sticky notes wherever you go, in your pocket, notebook, wallet or briefcase. Look at the notes on a frequent basis and say the four sentences accordingly.

e) Taking note of your daily activities

This exercise is explained by Perez. This author suggests that every day, early in the morning, you must take note of the activities you have to perform that day. After taking note of these affairs, you must tap the cover of the notebook with your fingers (or a rubber eraser) and ask divinity to clean them. In this way all subconscious programs hindering these activities are being removed.

When you take note of these activities, you might feel fear (or any other negative emotional state); if so, do not resist that feeling. If you suppress or repress it, it will become more embedded in your subconscious. You can also say the four Ho'oponopono sentences many times.

f) Writing your eulogy

This is an adaptation of an exercise suggested by Pattakos. You should write down your imaginary obituary to be read during your funeral. In that eulogy other people will say how loving, forgiving and thankful you were over your life.

An example of the text for this obituary can be:

> *We are together to say goodbye to... (your name), a person that (describe your positive traits)... when (state the moments when you showed those traits overtly). The world is better because of... (comment about specific positive contributions of yours)...*

You must read the obituary many times loudly; give your full attention to these words and try to feel them. After this, you should say the four Ho'oponopono sentences many times.

g) Making fists

Dr. Len suggests a very interesting and simple way to let go of your subconscious memories. Clench both fists tightly as your arms are extended forward and parallel to the floor. You must clench both fists at the same time; then you should open them as much as possible. You must go through this sequence many times.

When you clench your fists you are actually squashing your subconscious programs, and when you open your fists you let go of these memories. You can even visualize that your subconscious memories go away for good. You can also say the four Ho'oponopono sentences or *"Whatever is going on in me, I am sorry, please forgive me, I love you, thank you"* repeatedly.

h) Expressing your love through art

Holden states that when you do artistic activities, such as theatre, painting, sculpting and others, you are actually displaying your love energy. It is advisable to perform artistic activities frequently to connect to love energy. As you know, this energy helps you remove your subconscious programs.

Some psychologists use a very well-known exercise; they request patients to make some drawings freely on a piece of paper. By looking at the drawings these professionals can deduce important aspects of patients' feelings. You can do this exercise on your own; scribble freely on a piece of paper for a while.

Look at your drawings and ask yourself: *"What is going on in me in relation to this?"* You will receive some insights in relation to these scribbles, which are just reflections of your subconscious mind. Then say the four Ho'oponopono sentences many times.

i) Miscellaneous exercises

There are other Ho'oponopono exercises you can do whenever possible, as follows:

– When you go to a natural place, you must touch every tree or plant and say: *"Eyes blue."* According to Dr. Len, trees and plants give you a treatment to remove your subconscious programs.

– You should carry a green maple leaf in your pocket. If you feel despondent, uncared for, unloved, or weak-willed, this leaf will clean all your subconscious memories related to these negative states.

– You must put a little of Arrowhead blue corn meal in a cup or in your food. It is said that this product is very useful in deleting genetic memories or ill curses.

– Some suggest that you should use pillows filled with duck feathers when sleeping. As you lay your head on the pillow your subconscious memories are automatically deleted.

– Dr. Len said that you can repeat the four Ho'oponopono sentences to clean your car or house. You can even ask your car or house if they can help you with the cleaning of your subconscious memories. First you teach them how to clean so that they can do the cleaning process on their own.

Chapter 15

Presence and Ho'oponopono

When, by means of meditation, a man rises to union with the spirit, he brings to life the eternal in him, which is limited by neither birth nor death.
— *Rudolf Steiner*

1. Cultivating your presence

1.1. Being in the now

Your subconscious memories do not allow you to be fully concentrated on the now, the only moment that really exists. Many sages over centuries have asserted that there is only a continuous present moment; past and future are just meaningless illusions. Unless you give power to them they are naturally powerless. Your past is just a bunch of memories and recollections; and your future is only made up of mental projections based on your subconscious programming.

Different philosophies state you should honor the present moment because it is all that you have; it is your most important point of power; all the rest is just an imaginary game. Past and future are never actually in reach; they do not really exist but in your mind.

If you are like most people, you might have the natural tendency to focus on the future or past, instead of being fully integrated in the present moment. This happens especially when you do not like what is currently in your life. It is important to understand that things can only exist and occur at present; it is the only time you can actually benefit from them. You can actually achieve true personal development in the now.

When your mind is centered in the present moment you are

prone to perform more productive actions. You can experience the state of *flow* also called *the zone*. You can harness your unbounded power because you are truly connected to your pure essence.

From the Ho'oponopono perspective, being fully present is utterly liberating; you are less likely to be snared by your past memories. Your actions tend to be more creative and spontaneous. You are also more susceptible to receiving inspiration from the Divine. You might also feel more connected to everything that exists. Liberman and Liberman say that: *"the more present we become, the more life communicates through us."*

When you are completely present you are likely to feel more at ease and still. You magically dissolve any negative emotional state and you are more willing to forgive yourself and others. Your mind is clearer and your energy more vibrant. There are some clear signs that you are not concentrated in the present moment, such as:

- *Blaming others or yourself for your problems*
- *Moaning about your difficulties*
- *Wishing things were better*
- *Waiting for things to change*
- *Avoiding your responsibility*
- *Daydreaming*
- *Being anxious or nervous*
- *Judging anything as good or bad*
- *Using any other categories to label reality*
- *Dwelling in the possible outcomes instead of the experiences*
- *Being taking over by recollections of any type*
- *Feeling regretful or guilty about past situations*
- *Worrying about future circumstances*
- *Making plans or setting goals*
- *Being tense or contracted*
- *Feeling distracted or out of focus*

– Imagining what people might think about you
– Having expectations on future outcomes
– Envying what others have

Instead, whenever you are in the now, your energy levels rise automatically. All your negativity, which is produced by your subconscious memories, is drained away. You tend to perform your activities almost effortlessly. Your perception of time and space seems to disappear.

1.2. Tips to be more centered on the now

You can find below some tips to harness the benefits of the present moment:

(a) Befriend the present moment; never go against it. Embrace all your situations, even the negative ones. Accepting what is occurring at present is a very important starting point to transform it.

(b) Never wish things were different but accept your full responsibility for everything around you. Avoid criticizing, judging or overanalyzing things.

(c) When you practice Ho'oponopono you focus on the present moment. Avoid distractions when you utter the four sentences. However, some masters state that the cleaning process is effectively performed at all times, even when you are not focused on the present moment.

(d) Avoid judging yourself or your environment in a positive or negative manner. When you label different aspects of your reality you are affected by your past subconscious memories. Every time you classify things, you are not being fully present. Your environment tends to lose its natural freshness. Get accustomed to using your senses without any judgment at all.

(e) You must center on each of your five senses: sight,

hearing, touch, smell and taste, one at a time. For example, concentrate only on what you hear from second to second. The same applies to the rest of your senses.

(f) Concentrate on one task at a time, even mundane or ordinary ones. Be fully engaged and integrated with the activity at hand, completely present. Multitasking makes you unproductive, decreases your IQ, and your attention gets scattered. There is a saying which goes *"When I eat, I only eat"* which implies being fully attentive to the task at hand. Block some time devoted to that activity, without allowing any distraction to interfere.

(g) Concentrate on your breathing; be aware of the air entering your nostrils filling your lungs when you exhale. Feel your lungs being emptied as the air goes out through your nostrils. When you exhale you must feel the air flicking your upper lip. You can also scan your body and focus on every part of your body, one at a time.

(h) Tolle provides some other ideas to be present in the now, for example focusing on the energy circulating inside your body. Another tip suggested by this author is observing your thoughts as if you were an external witness without any judgment on them.

In the following point we will discuss the main aspects of meditation, which will help you be more centered on the now.

2. Meditation and Ho'oponopono

2.1. General aspects of meditation

Meditation, then, is bringing the mind home... To bring your mind home means to bring the mind into the state of Calm Abiding through the practice of mindfulness.
– Sogyal Rinpoche

Meditation is a complementary tool to the Ho'oponopono cleaning technique. It is a very important energy-shifting exercise. Many people tend to associate meditation with devotional and holy activities even though this practice actually has no relation to any specific set of religious beliefs.

If your life is quite chaotic or hectic, at first you might find this practice a bit difficult but beneficial. You can escape the turbulent influences of your environment in order to feel more at ease with your inner being.

Meditation is considered as a way of being, which helps you connect to your true essence. You can reach an overall state of harmony and also linger in it. When you meditate, you are mentally unaffected by external stimuli; you temporarily put your worries aside. It also helps you go beyond a rational under-standing of situations affecting you. When you meditate your full focus is inside you, not your environment. Some masters define meditation as the digestive process for your mind; you can unclog the memories cluttered in your mind more easily.

During meditation you can observe the messages broadcast by your subconscious mind in a dispassionate manner. Many stray thoughts and emotions are likely to pop out spontaneously when you meditate. Your rational mental processes become neutral or tend to slow down, which facilitates the emergence of these subconscious messages.

Meditation helps you release any physiological tension and spinning emotions. There are some studies which confirm that meditation strengthens your immune system, and lowers your heart rate and brainwaves; it also hastens the recovery from diseases. Meditation also improves your creative and problem-solving skills, and makes you less reactive to stimuli from your environment.

The right way to meditate is, in fact, very simple: you must be in a quiet place, seated on a chair or laid down on a bed. Wear comfortable clothes; you can have your eyes closed or open, as you like. If you meditate with your eyes open focus on one single object with undivided attention for a while.

A very important factor when you practice meditation is your breathing, which continually affects your body systems. According to Saradananda:

Your breath is your most intimate company on your journey through life... Your breath is the interface between your body and mind.

Some masters say that your breathing is the connective breeze between your inner part and the outer environment.

During meditation you must be mindfully aware of your breathing. You can use a rhythmical and deep respiration called rebirthing; your inhale must be flowingly linked to your exhale and vice versa, like a full circle.

It is advisable to use only abdominal breathing also called diaphragmatic. It tends to be more calming and deeper than thoracic breathing, which is your normal respiration. You are breathing abdominally if that area expands and contracts like a balloon.

When you meditate you should respire in a rhythmical fashion; you can also count the inhalations and exhalations mindfully. For example, you can count up 1, 2, 3, 4 when you inhale and again 1, 2, 3, 4 when you exhale. You should always respire slowly and deeply; you can also visualize your breathing going in and out.

You can even envision that you breathe in pure love light, which is radiant energy, and breathe out negativity, which is produced by your past memories. You can also concentrate on a single point, for example your nostrils while being brushed by the air inhaled and exhaled.

Some masters suggest that you should breathe naturally without structuring your respiration. Irrespective of the type of respiration you choose, you must always be fully absorbed in the process.

As you concentrate on your breathing some masters suggest that you should also use mantras such as *"Ohm"*, *"Love"* or *"One."* As was explained, mantras are key words repeated in a rhythmical manner to obtain a more disciplined and undivided concentration.

From the Ho'oponopono perspective, you can use as mantras the four sentences *"I am sorry"*, *"Please forgive me"*, *"I love you"*, *"Thank you"* during the meditation process. You can also practice meditation without using any mantra.

When you say the mantras you should feel the modulation and intonation of the words; repeat these sentences in a mindful and ceaseless fashion. You can also use visual mantras when you meditate; for example, focus your attention on a candle or a bright light in an uninterrupted manner. To improve your concentration during meditation, you can also imagine a smile in the area between your eyebrows called the *third eye*.

2.2. Thoughts, emotions and sensations during meditation

A regular practice of meditation helps you wipe away the muddy thoughts that prevent your wisdom from getting a clear view on where you are and in what direction you are headed.
– Mindy Audlin

When you enter the meditative state, images, voices, sensations and feelings are likely to emerge. These messages are just subconscious memories surfacing spontaneously. Observe them in a detached manner, as if you were a neutral outsider; never become reactive to what you experience.

You can imagine that these thoughts, feelings and sensations are like clouds passing by in the sky. You should never push them away because it is counterproductive; they will come back to you more intensely.

From the Ho'oponopono perspective, whatever you experience

in your mind or body during the meditative process must be cleaned. For this reason, you must use the four Ho'oponopono sentences during meditation.

In relation to this, remember Joe Vitale's "whiteboard" exercise. You can practice this exercise either when you meditate or outside the meditative state. When you do this exercise during meditation, some thoughts, sensations, or feelings come up. They are in fact subconscious memories of yours. Remember that you are not your thoughts, feelings or sensations; your untainted divine essence is beyond all this.

According to Vitale you must visualize these emotions, thoughts and sensations covering a whiteboard in front of you. Then imagine that you delete these from the board with an eraser, leaving nothing written on it.

The objective of this exercise is to keep the whiteboard totally clean, with no thoughts, feelings and emotions on it. This clean whiteboard represents that divine nature called zero point or zero state, where you are memory-free.

2.3. Mindfulness and meditation

As you saw before, you can circumvent the thoughts, feelings and sensations appearing during the meditation just by taking mental note of them. You must always surrender to their passing appearance.

When you surrender, you will experience a drifting state, like dreaminess. According to oriental philosophies, this quiet and peaceful state of mind is called mindfulness. Goleman says that: *"mindfulness is the attitude of paying external stimuli the barest attention."*

When you are truly mindful you can eliminate automatic behavior to concentrate on the task at hand (in this case, meditation). When you are mindful you are not judgmental, but fully integrated in the present moment; you feel your experiences more intensely and lively.

Wallin states that mindfulness is a liberating self-observant state, which frees you from grievance and pain. He also says that mindfulness is a nonverbal state because:

> *the experience of mindfulness cannot be captured in words, because awareness occurs before words arise in the mind.*

Besides, when you are mindful you are not distracted by external stimuli, and purge bothering thoughts or superfluous desires. You are less likely to react to any thoughts, emotions or sensations coming up. Mindfulness is a state of receptivity and increased awareness. Moreover you can access your innermost wisdom, usually stifled by your mental noise.

For this reason, the frequent practice of meditation can help you tap into your innermost resources. You are also more likely to receive divine directions. During meditation you can ask yourself questions about relevant topics in order to obtain useful insights. You can pose some questions, as follows:

– *What is going on in me now?*
– *What is the meaning of love (repentance, forgiveness or thankfulness, choose one of these values at a time)?*
– *Who am I?*
– *Am I taking full responsibility for everything around me?*
– *Am I connected to all that exists?*

You should always let any insights come up into your mind without forcing them. Listen to any responses that appear in your mind in a detached manner. You can also ask yourself questions right after you finish meditation, for example: *"What was going on in me during meditation?"* Take thorough notes of any insights in a personal notebook or journal. You must repeat the four sentences (*"I am sorry"*, *"Please forgive me"*, *"I love you"* and *"Thank you"*) as many times as possible.

2.4. Other aspects of meditation

In the reflective meditation you pose a topic before entering in the meditative state. You tend to actively reflect on the different perspectives of the chosen subject, but in a calm and relaxed manner. This type of meditation can be useful to solve difficult problems.

Nonetheless the most common way of meditating is the receptive one, in which you allow thoughts, emotions and sensations to come on their own; without you pushing them actively to come or go away.

When you practice meditation on a frequent basis, you will notice that you tend to perform your activities more mindfully. This means that you are less likely to be taken over by your subconscious programming, because your awareness is more enhanced.

Meditation is one of the most powerful ways to connect to the Divine. In relation to this, Jirsch and Cafferky state that:

meditation is a key tool that connects you directly to the universal force – Cosmic Energy – by taking you into an altered state of awareness.

Many people admit that after practicing meditation for a while they became more spiritual.

When you are frequently devoted to meditation, your life becomes more joyful; you will enjoy every little thing in your life. You are able to embrace every single life experience more authentically. With the frequent practice of meditation, your concentration on the tasks at hand is also improved.

2.5. Benefits of meditation

When life becomes our meditation, we experience heaven on earth.
– Jacob Liberman and Erik Liberman

When you practice meditation on a continuous basis, you will experience countless accumulative wonderful benefits. In that regard, some of the advantageous effects of meditation are:

- *It allows you to be secluded from the busyness of your daily activities.*
- *It helps you raise your awareness.*
- *It produces a permanent emotional betterment.*
- *It quiets the constant inner chattering of your mind.*
- *It makes you feel more relaxed.*
- *It makes you feel more peaceful and harmonious.*
- *It provides you with more clarity and discernment.*
- *It increases your intuitive skills.*
- *It improves your concentration on your daily activities.*
- *It provides you with more creativity to solve problems.*
- *It makes the different parts of your brain work more in harmony.*
- *It improves the functioning of your immune system.*
- *It has a restorative and healing effect on your mind and body.*
- *It connects you to your unbounded divine part.*
- *It makes you more prone to receiving inspiration from the Divine.*
- *It unleashes your unlimited power.*
- *It helps you access your inner knowingness.*
- *It makes you experience pure love.*
- *It allows you to be more forgiving and compassionate.*
- *It prompts you to focus on the now, instead of your past or future.*

2.6. Tips to practice meditation

Meditation is an inner mental action, a deliberate use of thought to fulfil a specific purpose. This process acts on deep levels of our being, giving us a quality that can cause major positive transformations to occur within our lives.
– Edith Stauffer

You can find below some tips to improve your experience during the meditative process.

– During the state of meditation, your mind tends to be in a state of surrender or non-resistance. For this reason, you can ask yourself some questions like: *"What is going on in me that I am manifesting my current life circumstances?"* or *"What memories am I holding right now?"* among others. When you meditate, you are more likely to receive prized insights regarding the memories held on your subconscious level.

– You can imagine as if you cast away the different layers of your personality, for example your name, nationality, gender, occupation, etc. You must visualize yourself getting rid of all the traits of your ego to access your core authentic being.

– You should be mindful not only when you meditate, but at all times. Be aware of what you are doing in the present moment; never consider your activities as a means to an end. Any trivial activity such as strolling in a park can be converted into a session of meditation if you focus your attention on it fully. Be mindful of your movements, internal sensations, thoughts and feelings.

– While you practice meditation, you can repeat the words *"I love you"* or any other of the Ho'oponopono sentences. You can say these sentences during, before or after the meditation process. During the meditative state, you can also imagine that love energy pervades all of your body.

– Bear in mind that meditation not only makes you feel more at ease, but also raises your energy levels. Dr. Hawkins says that peacefulness is one of the most powerful energetic states a human being can experience. Jayne states that: *"the reasons for meditation are that of moving towards a quieter mind you are better to attune to the higher self and the source of spiritual energy."*

– Before you practice meditation, you can set objectives to be fulfilled during the meditative process. For example, you can set the goal to receive some insights on the values of repentance, forgiveness, love and thankfulness. During the meditative process, you should be open to receiving any insights about these values. After meditating, take note of any insights you received and repeat the Ho'oponopono sentences.

You can also do a very well-known visualization exercise while you practice meditation. You must visualize all the most important inhibitors in your life: for example fear, hatred, etc. It does not really matter if these blockages are repetitive or sporadic. Sometimes these blocks are reflected in your body as tension or physical pain.

During the meditative process you must realize that these blockages are memories replaying in your subconscious mind. Once you acknowledge these hindrances you must say the four Ho'oponopono statements repeatedly.

There is another version of this exercise. After practicing meditation you can write down these blockages on a piece of paper. Then you can ask yourself: *"What is going on in me in relation to this?"* Wait for insights and say the four sentences several times.

Section IV

Appendices

This section includes several appendices related to different topics regarding Ho'oponopono.

Miracles

Miracles are not contrary to nature, but only contrary to what we know about nature.
– Saint Augustine

1. Main aspects of miracles

Many people refer to miracles as a synonym of good luck and fortune. From a wider perspective, life itself is a miracle, for example the internal intricacies and complexities of the functioning of your own body. You can perceive that there are hidden harmonious forces underpinning every single thing that exists. You can easily realize the miraculous essence of everything that exists in the Universe.

From a narrower viewpoint, a miracle is a phenomenon which is unexplainable according to the latest parameters of scientific disciplines; something that happens against all odds. Garlow and Wall say that: *"Miracles supersede nature's basic known laws."*

Science provides explanations about various phenomena. These scientific laws are a set of beliefs validated over time in different ways. These scientific laws are limited by nature and tend to evolve over time. Throughout history scientific disciplines changed their paradigms (which are specific perspectives on the world). Miracles cannot be explained by the current scientific knowledge; however, it does not mean that they do not exist at all.

Some say that miracles are prompted by the Divine. In other words, miracles are always under the Divine's lead. Thus miracles are not likely to be explained from a rational perspective. It is important to highlight that miracles are spontaneous; they cannot be manufactured on demand by people.

Miracles cannot be prompted or requested either. Garlow and Wall say that:

We can't merit miracles. We can't win them, warrant them or work for them. Miracles are given because of who God is, not because of who we are. They are granted because of God's mercy and grace.

When you are willing to receive miraculous gifts in your life miracles tend to show up more frequently. Miracles are more likely to appear in your life when you rely on the universal forces. However, the timing and ways of manifestation of miracles are always the domain of the Divine. Divinity always knows the best way for all things to occur, and this includes miracles.

The main purpose of miracles is to infuse your life with unconditional love. The alchemic power of divine love transforms any type of situation, even negative ones, almost instantaneously.

Many masters say miracles compress time; they go beyond linear time as you know it. Overall situations can be changed almost instantaneously. Divine has no time; everything is eternal.

Most people perceive themselves as limited beings. However, from the Divine's perspective, nothing seems to be impossible; extraordinary things can happen in life when the Divine intervenes.

Schambach states that: *"our God is a miracle-working God."* This author also states that:

God is looking for the believer to take up his or her responsibility – to be obedient to His voice and help release God's miracle power.

2. Other characteristics of miracles

Miracles are not the little stuff of myth and legend, they're an everyday occurrence from ordinary to quite profound. They are not

things of magic but more life's own helping hand, to put in place what comes to pass for the highest good... Miracles are not new, they have always been part of your life...
– Stephanie King

The text *A Course in Miracles* states that a miracle is just a change in your perception. From this perspective, when you see all your circumstances through the lens of love and forgiveness (and not from the viewpoint of fear) you can live a miraculous life.

Quantum Physics asserts that when you modify your way of observing things they change. This implies that your thoughts are intrinsically creative. In relation to this, this book also says that:

Miracles occur naturally as expressions of love. The real miracle is the love that inspires them. In that sense, everything that comes from love is a miracle.

Some other characteristics of miracles are:

– Miracles have a very important purpose, which is the wondrous manifestation of Divinity's unbounded love.
– Miracles always embody a natural sense of omnipotence, which challenges all limits set by your rational mind.
– Miracles cannot be understood scientifically. In most cases, they occur against scientific laws.
– All miraculous circumstances tend to occur in a graceful fashion; things seem to unfold effortlessly.
– Miracles are never random or unpredictable, even though they might seem this way. They are relevant components of the Divine's master plan.

3. Tips related to miracles

– *Practice Ho'oponopono on a frequent basis:* With the frequent use of the four sentences you become a channel or conduit for the Divine's love energy, which makes you more prone to becoming a miracle-worker.

– *Be a loving person with yourself and others:* It is important to bear in mind that love is one of the purest forms of energy. When you express love you are closely linked to the Divine, which is the source of all miracles. Williamson says that when people behave in a loving way they naturally become *"open vessels through which God expresses."* Likewise, Roman and Packer state: *"Miracles come from love, are created by love, and are magnetized through you by love... A miracle is a demonstration from the universe and your soul of their love to you."*

– *Follow your mission:* You must do things to which you can apply your distinct skills and add value. When you follow your mission, also called dharma, you deeply love what you do, even if you are not paid for it. As a consequence of this, you are more likely to be benefited by miraculous gifts from the Divine.

– *Be grateful at all times:* Gratitude is a very important factor to attract miracles into your life. When you have a thankful attitude your overall energy is uplifted, which makes you more susceptible to receiving miracles from Divinity.

– *Be concentrated on the present moment:* You must be focused on the now; miracles only occur in the current moment; not in the past or future. When you are not constantly attached to your past (through guilt, resentment, etc.) or your future (through plans, expectations, worries, etc.) you are more likely to experience miracles.

– *Be open to receiving miracles in your life:* A positive but serene expectancy of miracles can favor their occurrence. On the contrary, when you are anxious or fretful you are less likely to experience miracles in your life.

– *Be faithful in the Divine's assistance:* You must truly know the Divine will always support you, even in your difficult circumstances. You only have to give Divinity permission to come into your life. Schambach says that: *"God always has a miracle waiting for us if we'll just step out in faith and do what He's calling us to do."*

Appendix B

Great Masters of Ho'oponopono

1. Morrnah Nalamaku Simeona

This lady was a priestess and healer, also called kahuna in the Hawaiian language. She was formally considered *"a living treasure"* by the Hawaiian state. Morrnah was also a renowned international speaker and spiritual teacher. She even worked for some prestigious bodies, such as the United Nations.

The updated version of the Ho'oponopono technique was entirely created by this lady. She founded a non-profit organization which introduced this simplified perspective on the Ho'oponopono cleaning technique called Self I-Dentity through Ho'oponopono. As a consequence of its revamped version, this tool became known worldwide.

She adapted the traditional version of this tool, which was originally used for solving problems among group members. The modern version of this technique is fundamentally centered on the individual and it is used to clean memories held in the subconscious mind.

In Metaphysics there is the principle called the Law of Causality, which states that every cause has an effect. In accordance to this principle, Morrnah always believed that the programs you hold in your subconscious mind (cause) create all your life circumstances (effect).

2. Dr. Ihaleakala Hew Len

This psychologist attended Morrnah's seminars and later on he became her most prized disciple and administrative assistant. In the past, Dr. Len appeared in the news because of his unconventional healing technique. This very interesting anecdote related to Dr. Len was mentioned in the preface of this book.

As explained, in a mental hospital in Hawaii, Dr. Len cured most inmates held in the wards without even seeing them personally. He only did Ho'oponopono on a regular basis for months. Most of the prisoners became cured because of his particular healing technique.

Nowadays he is considered one of the most renowned authorities on Ho'oponopono. He travels all over the world delivering seminars and giving talks on this cleaning tool.

3. Other luminaries related to Ho'oponopono

Mary Abigail Kawena Wiggin Pukui was a very well-known Hawaiian historian who wrote many studies about Hawaiian traditions, including healing practices such as Ho'oponopono. Professor Max Freedom Long researched Hawaiian traditions and published several studies related to this topic from his particular perspective; his viewpoint was called Huna.

Dr. Joe Vitale is a renowned pundit who is specialized in many disciplines such as Metaphysics, Hypnotism and Marketing. He penned a book with Dr. Len, about Ho'oponopono, which became a bestseller worldwide.

Appendix C

Main Aspects of Traditional Ho'oponopono

1. Foundations of the traditional Ho'oponopono technique

The Ho'oponopono tool is from Hawaiian origin; however, there are several old records of similar techniques over different islands of the Polynesian area. The Ho'oponopono tool explained throughout this book is the modern version called Self I-Dentity through Ho'oponopono. Ho'oponopono has been used by Hawaiian communities for a long time but in a different way, called the traditional version of Ho'oponopono.

There are many values and beliefs which within ancient Hawaiian older generations have been passed onto newer ones. For example, some Hawaiian people fervently believe that all illnesses (or, in general, any states of imbalance) people experience are natural consequences of their own errors. To be cured, people have to atone for their faults. This expiation must be performed in the presence of a guide, generally a healer or a religious minister.

When people ask for forgiveness from God, it is believed they have been completely healed. In other words, when they confess their mistakes and ask for forgiveness, their natural balance is restored and they become healed. On the contrary, when people do not acknowledge their past errors, the healing process is delayed or even prevented.

In many ancient cultures in the Pacific Ocean, there is a widespread belief that all unacknowledged faults not only affect the people who made the mistakes; these faults are also passed onto future generations. In addition, all natural disasters (like earthquakes, tsunamis, etc.) are consequences of people's unacknowledged mistakes. These cultures also recognize their direct connection to the source of life, their forebears and all living beings existing on Earth.

Hawaiian communities tend to value the development of interpersonal relationships. If any conflict arises within a group this is considered as a disruption in the natural harmonious relationship among the group members; family is considered the main group and it is perceived as a system, in which all its components interact and affect one another. They are necessary parts to maintain the family's harmony. Any problem of a member affects the rest.

Shook states that the typical Hawaiian family implies a:

sense of unity, shared involvement and shared responsibility. It is mutual interdependence and mutual help. It is emotional support given and received. It is solidarity and cohesiveness. It is love – often it is loyalty – always... Elders... are respected for their wisdom and experience... Generosity, hospitality, sharing and reciprocity are also valued.

2. Application of the traditional version of this tool

Communities tend to use the traditional version of Ho'oponopono to solve problems arising among their members. This technique helps these groups maintain strong ties among their members. In the past, all members of a family used to live in the same place, so conflicts among family members were very frequent. Family members even believe that every time group members become ill it is because of conflicts affecting the group.

The traditional version of Ho'oponopono is both corrective and preventive. It helps eradicate the transgressions occurred among family members and prevents conflictive family issues from becoming more virulent.

In order to use the traditional version of Ho'oponopono, family members agree to hold several meetings to solve their conflicts. There are various requirements for these meetings such as:

(a) All members must be totally committed and willing to solve all problems affecting them.

(b) All family members agree to overtly convey their particular views of the problems and also their emotions during their meetings.

(c) All group members affected by conflicts decide to meet at a specific place as many times as necessary in order to solve their conflictive issues.

(d) All family members must explicitly promise to deal with troublesome issues in the most honest and responsible manner.

(e) The communication among members must always be transparent.

(f) There must be an atmosphere of understanding, benevolence and cordiality during the meetings.

(g) All group members guarantee that all topics discussed will be kept confidential.

(h) All meetings are conducted by a leader who is in charge of safeguarding the whole process. This leader acts as a facilitator or a mediator and monitors the interactions. The meetings are generally led by the wisest elder person of the familial group.

Main aspects of the Ho'oponopono traditional version

At the beginning of each meeting, family members pray together for a while, before dealing with the problematic issues. After this, each member describes the problems affecting them from their own perspective, so that all participants can discuss it.

None of the participants must use any recriminating or blaming remarks toward the others. Every family member must be heard by the others in a very attentive and kind manner.

One of the main purposes of these meetings is that all attendees can admit their own participation and responsibility for the conflicts affecting them. Every attendee provides additional information to others in relation to their own perspectives of the problem.

If any of the family members experiences negative emotions during the meeting, there can be a cooling-off break time, in which the family members reflect on the situation on their own to calm down.

During the meetings, members ask for and grant forgiveness to one another. In this way, all parties are released from any negative emotional ties regarding their conflicts.

Sometimes restitution is also possible, which means immediate compensation to the people directly affected by the problems discussed. The immediacy of the compensation is justified because all the agreements among the family members are verbal, not written.

The person who guides these sessions always looks for the reconciliation of the family members in conflict, which means an amicable solution. After the family members have granted and received mutual apologies the leader invites them to celebrate the solution of their differences. The leader can also summarize the main aspects of the meeting.

The problematic issues must not be mentioned any longer in the future. The session can end with an expression of gratitude and a prayer to strengthen the family ties even more.

The problems among family members are not necessarily solved in one session, especially conflicts with many facets. When the family members are affected by several problematic issues, it is usual to deal with one problem at a time. Ho'oponopono traditional procedure is like peeling the layers of an onion; firstly members approach the superficial issues and later go through the core ones.

3. Traditional and updated versions of Ho'oponopono
For some people, this ancient approach on Ho'oponopono seems complicated and structured. For this reason, this tool was

updated for our era. This new approach is called Self I-Dentity through Ho'oponopono. Morrnah Simeona streamlined the Ho'oponopono procedure adapting it for modern times.

As a consequence of this, the modern version became more simple to use and more widespread. Some of the differences of the modern Ho'oponopono technique as compared with the traditional one are:

(a) In the modern version of Ho'oponopono there is no need for a mediator or guide to use this tool. An individual can use this tool by himself or herself in total solitude. The modernized version of this tool can also be used for problems outside the familial environment, for example money difficulties, health conditions, among others.

(b) With this new perspective on the tool, you are even responsible for any single circumstance around you, for example, problems affecting strangers. This extended principle of responsibility is not applied in the traditional version, albeit members of the community do recognize their interconnection with all that exists.

(c) The modern version of Ho'oponopono implies the use of the four sentences (*"I am sorry"*, *"Please forgive me"*, *"I love you"* and *"Thank you"*) for the healing process. These four phrases are not used in the traditional version of this tool.

(d) As we have seen, when you practice Ho'oponopono you are requesting assistance from the Divine for the removal of your subconscious programming. In the traditional version, it is the guide who accompanies the family during the problem-solving process; however, the conflicts are solved by the family members themselves.

Appendix D

Ho'oponopono Prayers

You can find below some examples of prayers which will help you remove your subconscious memories.

Morrnah Simeona suggests a beautiful prayer to purify your memories. This prayer goes:

> *Divine creator, father, mother and child in union. Forgive me for all accumulated offensive thoughts, emotions, actions or words created up to the present moment by me, my family, relatives or forebears. Purify and let go of any negative memories, free us from our erroneous perceptions and transmute all blocking and negative energy, transforming it into pure light. And it is done.*

You can adapt this prayer according to your preference but include words of repentance and forgiveness in it.

Another interesting short prayer that you can use to remove your subconscious programs is:

> *Divine presence, please delete any inharmonious memory affecting me. Eliminate any limitation and lack of love in me forever.*

Dr. Len suggests that you should use this prayer:

> *Peace be with you, all my peace, the peace that is I. The peace that is I am. The peace for always, now, forever and ever more. My peace I give to you, my peace I leave with you. Not only the world's peace but my peace. The peace of I.*

He also suggests another prayer which says:

I am the I. I come forth from the void into light. I am the breath that nurtures life. I am that emptiness, that hallowness beyond all consciousness.

There is a specific prayer that can help you clean the ties that link you to your ancestors suggested by Martinez Tomás:

Divine Creator, Father, Mother and Son. All in one. If I, my family and forebears have offended, in thoughts, words, deeds or actions, since the beginning of our creation up to the present, we ask for forgiveness. Divine presence, allow us now to clean this and purify it and free it. Cut all the memories, blockages, energies and negative vibrations, transmute all these undesirable energies into pure light and it is done.

Similar words have been suggested by Morrnah Simeona.

Dr. Len suggests another prayer like:

Spirit, Superconscious, please locate the origin of my feelings, thoughts of... Take each and every level, layer, area, and aspect of my being to this origin. Analyze it and resolve it perfectly with God's truth. Come through generations of time and eternity, healing every incident and its appendages based on the origin. Please do it according to God's will until I am at the present filled with light and truth, God's peace and love, forgiveness of myself for my incorrect perceptions. Forgiveness of every person, place, circumstance, and event which contributed to this, these feelings and thoughts.

In order to express your limitless love, Méndez suggests these words:

My soul is filled with Divine Love. I am surrounded by Divine Love.

I radiate Love and Peace to the entire world. I am conscious of Divine Love. God is Love and all that exists is God's creation. All human beings are expressions of Divine Love, so I can only find expressions of Divine Love. All things that happen in my life are expressions of Divine Love. This is the Truth now.

Appendix E

Other Aspects of Introspection

As seen, the introspection process allows you to obtain useful insights about your subconscious memories through questions, such as *"What is going on in me now?"* Once you receive the insights, you can ask for further details about them by posing other questions like *"What is the meaning of all this?" "What is this related to?" "What are the specific aspects of this?"* or *"What else is going on in me in relation to this?"*

According to the discipline called Neuro Linguistic Programming (NLP), the language you regularly use in your sentences is full of omissions, generalization and distortions; you never convey your experiences or their detailed meaning but simplify them for practical conversational purposes.

Every time you convey a message you only express the superficial part of it, but not its deep structure, which is the complete idea you seek to communicate generally hidden behind your words.

NLP has a tool called the Meta model of language, which seeks to unveil the hidden bits of your messages to have a more complete picture of what you communicate. This tool can be also used during the introspection process, especially when the answers you receive to your question *"What is going on in me now?"* are too vague, short, or meaningless. When you use this Meta model, your introspective insights will become clearer.

For example, when you ask yourself the original question *"What is going on in me now?"* you can provide answers which are too general or vague, like *"I am tired."* In order to elicit more information about this, you can use a meta-model question like *"Tired specifically about what?"* to know more about the causes of your tiredness.

In some cases, your answer to the question *"What is going on in me now?"* might appear of general application, for example, *"I am always tired."* In this case, you can use the meta-model questions: *"Always?"* or *"Are there any exceptions to this?"* The same type of question applies to answers including words such as *everyone* and *everywhere* and others.

In other cases, when you ask the question *"What is going on in me now?"* you can give answers with unclear verbs, for example: *"I work too much."* To obtain more details you can ask: *"In which way am I working too much?"* to be as specific as possible.

You can also give answers with undefined pronouns such as *it, that* or *this* among others. For instance, to the question *"What is going on in me now?"* you can answer: *"It's exhausting."* So you can pose a more specific question like *"What is exhausting?"* to have more detailed insights.

In some answers you can state that other people are affecting you in some way, which is called mind reading. For example, you ask yourself *"What is going on in me now?"* and your answer is *"I feel tired because people don't recognize me."* You can re-ask this way: *"How do I know that I am not recognized?"* With this additional question you are likely to obtain more specific details justifying that assertion.

There are some answers which might appear self-limiting albeit that you do not state your own limitations. For example, when you ask yourself *"What is going on in me now?"* you can answer this way: *"I cannot do anything."* These terms *"I cannot"* imply a limitation enunciated in an unspecific fashion. To have more details you can ask: *"What is preventing me from doing anything?"* to know more about these hidden limitations.

Some answers might include nominalizations, which are words related to intangible things. These words represent things which cannot be perceived by your senses, such as peace, justice and rest, etc. When you ask yourself the question *"What is going on in me now?"* your answer can be *"I need a rest."* In this case, *"rest"* represents different things to different people, for example sleeping, taking a holiday, etc. So you can re-ask: *"What do I specifically mean by a rest?"* to obtain more insights into this.

In other cases your insight can include a cause and effect. These types of answers generally tend to be incomplete because they do not exhibit the obvious link between cause and effect. An example of this is: *"I feel tired because I have a lot of problems."* In that case, you can re-ask this way: *"How is that having a lot of problems makes me feel tired?"* to find details of the link between cause (having a lot of problems) and effect (feeling tired).

In NLP there is a second approach on introspection called the Milton model. This approach is based on many principles set by a famous hypnotherapist called Milton Erickson. Some of the main aspects of this approach are described as follows:

– During the introspection process, it is important to ask questions in an intentionally vague manner to have better insights into your subconscious memories. In order to make your introspective questions as unspecific as possible you must reverse the rules previously explained for the Meta model. For example, you must deliberately omit relevant words (nouns, verbs, etc.) to make your questions much vaguer than usual, for example, *"What is going on in my subconscious mind, now?"*

– You can use questions including verbs like *feel*, *understand* and *sense*, which are called unspecified verbs. They prompt you to make sense of your thoughts, feelings and sensations in a more thorough manner. An example of this is *"What are you sensing now?"*

– In the Milton model, you can also pose questions in a more subtle and indirect manner. Some examples are: *"I would like to know what is going on in me now?"* or *"I think that my subconscious mind could tell me what is going on now"* or *"I am sure that you could tell me what is going on now."* These statements have implicit interrogative words embedded in them.

Appendix F

Other Types of Love

Perfect Love is perfect Wisdom. The man who loves all is the man who knows all. Love illuminates the intellect; without it the intellect is blind and cold and lifeless... Love is the supreme reality in the universe, and as such it contains all Truth.
– James Allen

1. Classical types of love

When one has once fully entered the realm of Love, the world – no matter how imperfect – becomes rich and beautiful; it consists solely of opportunities for Love.
– Soren Kierkegaard

You can find below several well-known classes of love. This specific classification is based on many widespread psychological and spiritual schools of thought. Among others, two important authors taken into account in this classification are Erich Fromm and John Lee.

1.1. Self-love

This is the type of love you feel toward yourself. It is can be unconditional, when you love yourself regardless of your thoughts and actions. It can also be conditional, when you feel love for yourself only when you think or act correctly.

Most psychologists say that self-love is related to the concept of self-esteem. When you have a very low self-esteem it is difficult to experience self-love. When you love yourself you are not so dependent on others. Unmani Liza Hyde says that:

if you recognize the Love that you are, then you know the Love never needs any other person or situation in order to be Love.

1.2. Erotic love

This type of love is only limited to the members of the relationship; it is not extended to outsiders. Erotic love entails deep fusion between the lovers, which sometimes yearn to eliminate all boundaries between them to become one. It is characterized by intense sensuality.

Another type of love related to this is sentimental or romantic love, which is the stereotypical and idealistic way of love shown in romantic comedies and books. It is depicted as a way to find intimacy, enjoyment, sensual attraction, affection and completeness in a partner.

A type of love related to erotic love is called ludic or playful love. In this type of love, partners can relate to many other people because they do not have an exclusive bond with one another.

1.3. Maternal love

This is a very intimate form of love, related to the bond between a mother and her children, which is unconditional, protective and caring. It is different from pure unconditional love because the mother only experiences it with her children.

It is more intense when the children are very young because the mother tends to altruistically support them as they look defenseless. The main objective of the mother's help is that the children can finally rely on their own resources.

In relation to this, Erich Fromm states that the mother when experiencing maternal love feels as if her children are an intrinsic part of her, as main factors for her transcendence in life.

1.4. Fraternal love

Also called brotherly, it is not limited to specific people, but extended to your fellow men. Fraternal love is based on values such as assistance, respect, care, cooperation, companionship, compassion and solidarity.

Its starting premise is that all people need help and you can always make a true difference to them. When you express brotherly love, you tend to focus on the core essence of people and not their external appearance, also called persona. Erich Fromm states this type of love is more centered on commonalities between people. Some authors consider fraternal love as synonymous with unconditional love.

1.5. Idolatrous love

Fromm said that this type of love is likely to be experienced by people who have an underdeveloped sense of identity. He mentioned that the person tends *"to lose himself in the loved one, instead of finding himself"*; you tend to venerate the person or object of your love.

It is fanatical by nature; the person who experiences it tends to naturally dismiss any negative aspects of the object of love, which can be people, and also tangible and intangible things.

1.6. Manipulative love

This is also known as conditional love and it is experienced by people who are controlling and selfish. It is never given freely but subject to certain conditions. It is never expressed without any reason but expecting something in return.

1.7. Need-love and gift-love

From this perspective, some authors like Lewis make the distinction between need-love and gift-love. In that effect need-love is self-centered, selfishly satisfied and also attention-demanding; you tend to experience states of loneliness and helplessness.

Gift-love tends to be pure, noble, willing to serve, selfless and, in some way, godly. An example is God's unconditional love.

1.8. Other classifications

There are other types of love, such as:

– *Unrequited love:* One of the participants expresses love without receiving anything in return. Sometimes there can be a blatant rejection to the lover. The person who expresses his love has intense expectations of receiving a reciprocal loving treatment from the object of love, which never happens.

– *Pragmatic love:* The person who experiences pragmatic love tends to feel that others are just a means to an end, which is to achieve the lover's own goals.

– *Obsessive love:* When you experience this type of love you naturally tend to have strong and intense attachments and uncontrollable compulsion toward the object of love. The lover also craves reciprocation from the recipient of his love. It resembles idolatrous love.

– *Platonic love:* The lover does not experience any sensual attraction toward the object of love, but spiritual things.

Bibliography

Abd-Ru-Shin (1993) *In the Light of Truth: The Grail Message*. Stiftung Gralsbotschaft Publishing Co: Stuttgart

Alatalo, Jerry (2012) *Unconditional Love for Humanity*. The New Earth: Jerry Alatalo

Allen, James (1902) *As a Man Thinketh*. GP Putman's Sons: New York

Allen, James (1903) *All These Things Added*. http://james-allen.in1woord.nl/

Allen, James (1904) *Byways to Blessedness*. http://james-allen.in1woord.nl/

Allen, James (1915) *The Shining Gateway*. http://james-allen.in1woord.nl/

Allen, James (1911) *Man: King of Mind, Body and Circumstance*. http://james-allen.in1woord.nl/

Anthony, Robert (2007) *Beyond Positive Thinking: A No-Nonsense Formula For Getting The Results You Want*. Morgan James: New York

Anthony, Robert (1996) *How to Make the Impossible Possible*. Berkley Books: New York

Arewa, Caroline Shola (2010) *Energy 4 Life: High Energy, Conscious Living*. O-Books: UK

Arylo, Christine (2012) *Madly in Love with Me: The Daring Adventure of Becoming Your Own Best Friend*. New World Library: California

Assagioli, Roberto (1974) *The Act of Will*. Penguin Books: USA

Atkinson, William Walker (1906) *Thought Vibration: The Law of Attraction in the Thought World*. The Library Shelf: Chicago

Atkinson, William Walker (1908) *Mind Power: The Secret of Mental Magic*. The Progress Company: London

Audlin, Mindy (2010) *What If All Goes Right? Creating a New World of Peace, Prosperity & Possibility*. Morgan James: New

York

Augustine, Saint (2003) *The City of God*. Penguin Classics: UK

Ayne, Blythe (2009) *Love Is The Answer*. Emerson and Tilman Publishers: USA

Baer, Greg (2005) *Real Love: The Truth about Finding Unconditional Love & Fulfilling Relationships*. Gotham Books: USA

Bailes, Frederick (2004) *Basic Principles of the Science of Mind*. DeVorss Publications: California

Bailey, Becky A. (2000) *I Love You Rituals*. William Morrow: New York

Baird, David (2000) *A Thousands Paths to Tranquility*. MQ Publications Limited: London

Barkai, John (no date) *Ho'oponopono*. William S. Richardson School of Law, University of Hawaii at Manoa

Baron, Robert A. and Michael J. Kalsher (2001) *Essentials of Psychology*. Allyn and Bacon: USA

Barthes, Roland (2001) *A Lover's Discourse: Fragments*. Hill and Wang: New York

Bauman, Zygmunt (2003) *Liquid Love: On the Frailty of Human Bonds*. Polity: Cambridge

Bavister, Steve and Amanda Vickers (2010) *Essential NLP*. Hodder Education: UK

Bavister, Steve and Amanda Vickers (2008) *NLP*. Hodder Headline: London

Becker, Harold W. (2010) *Inspiring Unconditional Love: Reflections from the Heart*. White Fire Publishing: Tampa, Florida

Becker, Harold W. (2007) *Unconditional Love: An Unlimited Way of Being*. White Fire Publishing: USA

Belton, Aine (2012) *The Amazing Powers of Gratitude*. www.globalloveproject.com

Benner, David G. (2003) *Surrender to Love: Discovering the Heart of Christian Spirituality*. IVP Books

Berg, Yehuda (2005) *Life Rules: How kabbalah can turn your life from a problem into a solution*. Kabbalah Centre International: Los

Angeles

Berne, Eric (1973) *What Do You Say After You Say Hello?* Corgi: UK

Berney, Charlotte (2000) *Fundamentals of Hawaiian Mysticism.* Crossing Press: Santa Cruz, CA

Bernstein, Gabrielle (2013) *May Cause Miracles: A 6-Week Kick-Start to Unlimited Happiness.* Hay House: UK

Bird, John (2006) *How to Change Your Life in 7 Steps.* Vermilion: London

Blackmore, Susan (2004) *Consciousness: An Introduction.* Oxford University Press: New York

Borysenko, Joan (1994) *Pocketful of Miracles: Prayers, Meditations, and Affirmations to Nurture Your Spirit Every Day of the Year.* Grand Central Publishing: USA

Braden, Gregg (2007) *The Divine Matrix: Bridging Time, Space, Miracles, and Belief.* Hay House: UK

Branch, Rhena and Rob Willson (2010) *Cognitive Behavioural Therapy for Dummies.* Wiley: England

Brandon, Diane (2013) *Intuition for Beginners: Easy Ways to Awaken Your Natural Abilities.* Llewellyn Publications: Minnesota

Breakwell, Glynis M. (1980) *Interviewing (Problems in Practice).* Routledge: UK

Brett, Regina (2012) *Be the Miracle: 50 Lessons for Making the Impossible Possible.* Grand Central Publishing: USA

Bridges, William (2013) *Managing Transitions: Making the Most of Change.* Nicholas Brealey: London

Bristol, Claude (1948) *The Magic of Believing.* Princeton Licensing Group: USA

Bruce, Philena (2010) *Know That You are Loved: Self-Healing Techniques for Everyone.* O-Books: UK

Buckingham, Dwayne K. (2009) *Unconditional Love: What Every Woman and Man Desires in a Relationship.* R.E.A.L. Horizon Consulting Service: USA

Burns, David D. (1980) *Feeling Good: The New Mood Therapy.*

Harper: USA

Buscaglia, Leo (2006) *Living, Loving and Learning.* SLACK Incorporated: USA

Buscaglia, Leo (1972) *Love: What life is all about...* Fawcett Columbine: New York

Butler-Bowdon, Tom (2007) *50 Psychology Classics.* Nicholas Brealey: London

Buzan, Tony and James Harrison (2010) *Use Your Head: How to unleash the power of your mind.* Pearson: UK

Byrne, Rhonda (2012) *The Magic.* Simon and Schuster: UK

Byrne, Rhonda (2010) *The Power.* Simon and Schuster: UK

Cabanillas, Maria Jose (2012) *Ho'oponopono. Conéctate con los milagros.* EDAF: Madrid

Cameron, Julia (2002) *The Artist's Way. A Spiritual Path to High Creativity.* Tarcher Putnam: New York

Canfield, Jack (2015) *The Success Principles: How to Get from Where You Are to Where You Want to Be.* William Morrow and Company: USA

Carnegie, Dale (1998) *How to Stop Worrying and Start Living.* Vermilion: London

Casarjian, Robin (2012) *Perdonar: Una decisión valiente que nos traerá paz interior.* Urano: Espana

Cathcart, Jim (1999) *The Acorn Principle.* St. Martin's Press: New York

Chabris, Christopher F. and Daniel J. Simmons (2010) *The Invisible Gorilla: And Other Ways Our Intuition Deceives Us.* Crown Publishers: USA

Chan, Jason and Jan Rogers (2012) *Infinite Abundance: Becoming a Spiritual Millionaire.* Light Foundation: UK

Childre, Doc; Howard Martin and Donna Beech (2000) *The HeartMath Solution.* HarperCollins: USA

Chopra, Deepak (1997) *Las Siete Leyes Espirituales del Exito.* Norma: Argentina

Chopra, Deepak and Rudolph E. Tanzi (2013) *Super Brain:*

Unleashing the Explosive Power of Your Mind. Rider: UK

Claxton, Guy (2005) *The Wayward Mind: An Intimate History of the Subconscious.* Abacus: London

Clifford, Lorenza (2006) *Interview Others: How to spot the perfect candidate.* A & C Black Publishers: UK

Csikszentmihályi, Mihály (2008) *Flow: The Psychology of Optimal Experience.* Harper Perennial: USA

Currey, Mason (2013) *Daily Rituals: How Great Minds Make Time, Find Inspiration, and Get to Work.* Picador: UK

Dainow, Sheila (2007) *Be Your Own Counsellor: A step-by-step guide to understanding yourself better.* Piatkus: London

Davis, Audrey Craft (1996) *Metaphysical Techniques That Really Work.* Blue Dolphin Publishing: USA

Davis, Martha; Robbins Eshelman, Elizabeth and McKay, Matthew (2008) *The Relaxation and Stress Reduction Book.* New Harbinger Publications: USA

Dawson, WJ (1906) *The Forgotten Secret.* Fleming H. Revell Company: New York

de Bono, Edward (1995) *Teach Yourself to Think: Five easy steps to direct, productive thinking.* Penguin Books: England

de Botton, Alain (1993) *Essays in Love.* Picador: UK

DeNoyelles, Alaya (2012) *The Sovereignty of Love: Coming Home with Ho'oponopono.* Vesica Publishing: Hawaii

De Saint-Exupery, Antoine (1993) *The Little Prince.* Wordsworth: UK

Dobelli, Rolf (2013) *The Art of Thinking Clearly.* Sceptre: London

Dossey, Larry (1994) *Healing Words: The Power of Prayer and the Practice of Medicine.* HarperOne: USA

Douglas, Mark (2000) *Trading in the Zone: Master the Market with Confidence, Discipline, and a Winning Attitude.* New York Institute of Finance: USA

Dowrick, Stephanie (1997) *Forgiveness and Other Acts of Love: Finding true value in your life.* Penguin: UK

D'Souza, Steven and Diana Renner (2014) *Not Knowing: The art of turning uncertainty into opportunity.* LID Publishing: London

Dugan, Susan (2011) *Extraordinary Ordinary Forgiveness.* O-Books: UK

Duprée, Ulrich (2012) *Ho'oponopono: The Hawaiian forgiveness ritual as the key to your life's fulfillment.* Earthdancer: UK

Duprée, Ulrich (2013) *Ho'oponopono. Un sencillo sistema de cuatro pasos para recuperar la unidad, la armonía y la paz interior.* Ediciones Obelisco: Barcelona

Dwoskin, Hale (2000) *The Sedona Method Course.* Sedona Training Associates: USA

Dwoskin, Hale and Lester Levenson (2001) *Happiness Is Free: And It's Easier Than You Think!* Sedona Training Associates: USA

Dyer, Wayne (1978) *Tus zonas erróneas.* Grijalbo: Barcelona

Dyer, Wayne W. (1992) *Tus zonas mágicas.* Grijalbo: Barcelona

Dyer, Wayne (1998) *Manifest Your Destiny: The Nine Spiritual Principles for Getting Everything You Want.* Harper Perennial: New York

Dyer, Wayne (2004) *The Power of Intention.* Hay House: USA

Dyer, Wayne (2006) *Inspiration: Your Ultimate Calling.* Hay House: London

Elrod, Hal (2012) *The Miracle Morning: The Not-So-Obvious Secret Guaranteed to Transform Your Life (Before 8AM).* Hal Elrod International: USA

Eisenstein, Charles (2011) *Sacred Economics: Money, Gift, and Society in the Age of Transition.* Evolver: Berkeley, CA

Emmons, RA and ME McCullough (2003) "Counting blessings versus burdens: An experimental investigation of gratitude and subjective well-being in daily life." *Journal of Personality and Social Psychology*, 84, pages 377–389

Emoto, Masaru (2004) *The Hidden Messages in Water.* Beyond Words Publishing: Hillsboro, OR

Ewing, Jim Pathfinder (2006) *Clearing: A Guide to Liberating Energies Trapped in Buildings and Lands.* Findhorn Press: USA

Farhi, Donna (1996) *The Breathing Book: Good Health and Vitality*

Through Essential Breath Work. St. Martin's Griffin: New York

Ferrini, Paul (1991) *The 12 Steps of Forgiveness: A Practical Manual for Moving from Fear to Love.* Heartways Press: USA

Ferrini, Paul (2003) *Love Without Conditions: Reflections of the Christ Mind.* Heartways Press: USA

Field, Lynda (2012) *The Self-Esteem Coach: 10 days to a confident new you.* Watkins Publishing: London

Flippen, Flip (2007) *The Flip Side: Break Free of the Behaviors That Hold You Back.* Springboard Press: USA

Fontana, David (1992) *The Meditator's Handbook: A Complete Guide to Eastern and Western Techniques.* Thorsons: London, UK

Ford, Debbie (1998) *The Dark Side of the Light Chasers.* Riverhead Books: New York

Foucault, Michel (2002) *The Order of Things: An archaeology of the human sciences.* Routledge Classics: London

Foundation for Inner Peace (2007) *A Course in Miracles: Combined Volume.* Foundation for Inner Peace: USA

Fox, Emmet (2006) *The Mental Equivalent.* Kessinger Publishing: USA

Fox, Emmet (2011) *The Golden Key.* Literary Licensing LLC: USA

Fox, Emmet (2005) *Power Through Constructive Thinking.* http://self-improvement-ebooks.com/

Frankl, Viktor (1992) *Man's Search for Meaning.* Beacon Press: Boston

Fredrickson, Barbara L. (2013) *Love 2.0: How Our Supreme Emotion Affects Everything We Feel, Think, Do, and Become.* Hudson Street Press: USA

Fremantle, Francesca (2001) *Luminous Emptiness: Understanding the Tibetan Book of Death.* Shambhala Publications: USA

Freud, Anna (1993) *The Ego and The Mechanisms of Defence.* Karnac Books: UK

Fromm, Erich (1956) *The Art of Loving.* Harper & Row: New York

Fromm, Erich (2002) *The Sane Society.* Routledge Classics: UK

Fromm, Erich (2011) *The Fear of Freedom.* Routledge: UK

Gardner, Howard (2011) *Frames of Mind: The Theory of Multiple Intelligences*. Basic Books: USA

Gardner, Steve (2011) *Your Superpowers*. Inglestone Publishing: USA

Garlow, James L. and Keith Wall (2011) *Miracles Are For Real: What Happens When Heaven Touches Earth*. Bethany House Publishers: USA

Geley, Gustave (1920) *From the Unconscious to the Conscious*. William Collins Sons and Co: Glasgow

George, Mike (2010) *The 7 Myths about Love... Actually! The Journey from your Head to the Heart of your Soul*. O-Books: UK

Gerstung, Wilhelm and Jens Mehlhase (2000) *The Complete Feng Shui Health Handbook*. Lotus Press – Shangri La: USA

Gide, Andre (1973) *The Counterfeiters*. Vintage Books: USA

Gladwell, Malcolm (2000) *The Tipping Point: How Little Things Can Make a Big Difference*. Little, Brown and Company: USA

Glenn, Richard (2003) *Transform*. Providence House Publishers: USA

Goddard, Neville (1961) *The Law and the Promise*. G and J Publishing: Los Angeles, CA

Goddard, Neville (1990) *The Miracle of Imagination*. Canterbury House: Ottawa

Goleman, Daniel (1988) *The Meditative Mind*. GP Putnam and Sons: New York

Greene, Brian (2000) *The Elegant Universe: Superstrings, Hidden Dimensions and the Quest for the Ultimate Theory*. Vintage: UK

Grout, Pam (2013) *E-Squared: Nine Do-It-Yourself Energy Experiments That Prove Your Thoughts Create Your Reality*. Hay House: UK

Gutowski, Lisa Marie (2008) *Beyond Techniques: The 2012 Shift: Evolving from Lightworker to Light*. iUniverse Inc: USA

Haanel, Charles (1916) *The Master Key System*. Psychology Publishing: Saint Louis

Hale-Evans, Ron (2006) *Mind Performance Hacks*. O'Reilly: USA

Hanley, Jesse Lynn and Nancy Deville (2001) *Tired of Being Tired*. Penguin Books: England

Hartong, Leo (2007) *Awakening to the Dream*. Non-Duality Press: UK

Hawkins, David R. (2002) *Power vs. Force: The Hidden Determinants of Human Behavior*. Hay House: USA

Hendrix, Harville (2008) *Getting the Love You Want: A Guide for Couples*. St Martin's Griffin: New York

Herrick, Robert (1898) *The Hesperides and Noble Numbers*. Lawrence and Bullen: London

Hicks, Esther and Jerry (2004) *Ask and It Is Given: Learning to Manifest Your Desires*. Hay House: USA

Hill, Napoleon and W. Clement Stone (1990) *Success Through a Positive Mental Attitude: Discover the Secret of Making Your Dreams Come True*. Thorsons: London

Hill, Napoleon (2003) *The Laws of Success*. Ralston University Press: USA

Hill, Napoleon (1960) *Think and Grow Rich*. Fawcett Crest: New York

Holden, Robert (2005) *Success Intelligence: Essential Lessons and Practices from the World's Leading Coaching Program on Authentic Success*. Hay House: UK

Holden, Robert (2013) *Loveability: Knowing How to Love and Be Loved*. Hay House: UK

Holliwell, Raymond (2009) *Working with the Law*. http://self-improvement-ebooks.com/

Howard, Pierce (2006) *The Owner's Manual for the Brain: The Ultimate Guide to Peak Mental Performance at All Ages*. William Morrow: USA

Hunt, Valerie V. (1996) *Infinite Mind: Science of the Human Vibrations of Consciousness*. Malibu Publishing Co: Malibu, CA

Hurtado-Graciet, Maria Elisa (2013) *Cuaderno de ejercicios para practicar Ho'oponopono*. Terapias Verdes: Barcelona

Hyde, Unmani Liza (2011) *Die to Love*. O-Books: UK

Hyde, Unmani Liza. "Not Knowing" (article) www.not-knowing.com

Irvine, William B. (2006) *On Desire: Why We Want What We Want.* Oxford University Press: USA

Jampolsky, Gerald G. and Diane V. Cirincione (1990) *Love is the Answer: Creating Positive Relationships.* Bantam Books: USA

Jayne, Nicola (2013) *The 5 Points of Power and Wisdom: A Guide to Intuitive Living.* 6th Books: UK

Jeffers, Susan (1991) *Feel the Fear and Do It Anyway: How to Turn Your Fear and Indecision into Confidence and Action.* Arrow Books: UK

Jirsch, Anne and Monica Cafferky (2009) *Cosmic Energy: How to harness the invisible power around you to transform your life.* Piatkus: London

John-Roger and Peter McWilliams (1992) *Do it! Let's Get Off Our Buts.* Prelude Press: USA

Johnson, Bill (2005) *The Supernatural Power of a Transformed Mind: Access to a Life of Miracles.* Destiny Image Publishing Inc: USA

Jordan, Bishop E. Bernard (2012) *The Laws of Thinking: 20 Secrets to Using the Divine Power of Your Mind to Manifest Prosperity.* Hay House: USA

Katin, Ken (2011) *In the Presence of Unconditional Love: Understanding the Near Death Experience.* Booklocker.com, Inc: USA

Katz, Mabel (2009) *The Easiest Way: Solve your problems and take the road to love, happiness, wealth and the life of your dreams.* Your Business: USA

Katz, Mabel (2014) *Mis reflexiones sobre Ho'oponopono.* Editorial Sirio: Malaga

Keller, Gary and Jay Papasan (2014) *The One Thing: The surprisingly simple truth behind extraordinary results.* John Murray Learning: UK

Kerins, Patricia Iris (2012) *Love.* 6th Books: UK

Kierkegaard, Soren (1847) *Works of Love: Some Christian Reflections in the Form of Discourses.* Harper & Row: London

King, Stephanie J. (2013) *Divine Guidance: The answers you need to make miracles.* 6th Books: UK

Kok, Elsa (2002) *A Woman Who Hurts, a God Who Heals.* New Hope Publishers: USA

Laing, RD (1990) *The Politics of Experience and The Birds of Paradise.* Penguin Books: UK

Lake, Gina (2011) *What about Love? Reminders for Being Loving.* Endless Satsang Foundation: USA

Lama, The Dalai and Victor Chan (2004) *The Wisdom of Forgiveness: Intimate Conversations and Journeys.* Hodder and Stoughton: UK

Lama, The Dalai (2001) *An Open Heart: Practicing Compassion in Everyday Life.* Little, Brown, and Company: Boston

Leboff, Gary (2006) *Dare: Take Your Life on and Win.* Hodder and Stoughton: London

LeDoux, Joseph (2003) *The Emotional Brain: The Mysterious Underpinnings of Emotional Life.* Phoenix: London

Lee, JA (1973) *Colours of love: An exploration of the ways of loving.* New Press: Toronto

Lee, Pali Jae (2007) *Ho'opono: The Hawaiian Way to Put Things Back into Balance.* IM Publishing Ltd: USA

Len, Hew. Interview with Dr. Hew Len, Parts 1 to 9:
Part 1: http://www.youtube.com/watch?v=OL972JihAmg
Part 2: http://www.youtube.com/watch?v=bG6b6NzTBv8
Part 3: http://www.youtube.com/watch?v=DqiiUuY7WoE
Part 4: http://www.youtube.com/watch?v=n9cqsnZJd7w
Part 5: http://www.youtube.com/watch?v=Ka5w8gAL0eM
Part 6: http://www.youtube.com/watch?v=jxjpi_artxc
Part 7: http://www.youtube.com/watch?v=1OZ8YxCx0DE
Part 8: http://www.youtube.com/watch?v=q80hDYKf3SU
Part 9: http://www.youtube.com/watch?v=mSDkm7XLQjQ

Len, Hew. Dr. Len Hew Interview, Parts 1 and 2:
Part 1: http://www.youtube.com/watch?v=3xCmvZZFQI0

Part 2: http://www.youtube.com/watch?v=dVUqtZb78N4

Leonard, George (1992) *Mastery: The Key to Success and Long-term Fulfillment*. Plume: USA

Lerner, Michael (2000) *Spirit Matters*. Hampton Roads Publishing Company: USA

Levenson, Lester (1993) *Keys to the Ultimate Freedom: Thoughts and Talks on Personal Transformation*. Sedona Institute: USA

Lewis, CS (1988) *The Four Loves*. Harcourt Brace and Company: USA

Liberman, Jacob and Erik Liberman (2001) *Wisdom from an Empty Mind*. Empty Mind Publications: USA

Libet, Benjamin (2005) *Mind Time: The Temporal Factor in Consciousness*. Harvard University Press: London

Lipton, Bruce (2008) *The Biology of Belief: Unleashing the Power of Consciousness, Matter & Miracles*. Hay House: USA

Liquorman, Wayne, ed. (1992) *Consciousness Speaks: Conversations with Ramesh S. Balsekar*. Advaita Press: California

Locke, John (2014) *The Reasonableness of Christianity, as Delivered in the Scriptures*. First Rate Publishers

Long, Max Freedom (2009) *The Secret Science Behind Miracles: Huna Magic and Ho'Opono, Ho'Oponopono Instant Healing*. Amazon.co.uk Ltd: England

Losier, Michael (2008) *Law of Attraction: The Secret Behind the Secret*. Hodder Mobius: UK

Love, Lisa (2007) *Beyond the Secret: Spiritual Power and the Law of Attraction*. Hampton Roads: Canada

Loyd, Alexander (2011) *The Success Codes*. Dr. Alex Loyd Services LLC: USA

Luskin, Fred (2002) *Forgive for Good*. HarperSanFrancisco: USA

Lynch, James J. (1986) *The Language of the Heart: The Body's Response to Human Dialogue*. Basic Books: USA

Lytle, Larry (2007) *Energy Transcendence: A Guide for Living Beyond the Ordinary Range of Perception*. AuthorHouse: USA

Manby, Joel (2012) *Love Works: Seven Timeless Principles for*

Effective Leaders. Zondervan: USA

Mandino, Og (1975) *The Greatest Miracle in the World*. Bantam Books: USA and Canada

Marion, Susan Ann (2010) *Freeing Unconditional Love: Unchaining Your True Self*. ClearView Press Inc: USA

Martinez Tomás, Maria Carmen (2012) *Ho'oponopono: lo siento, perdóname, te amo*. Oceano Ambar: Espana

Maturana, Humberto and Pille Bunnell. "The Biology of Business: Love Expands Intelligence." Society for Organizational Learning. www.sol-ne.org/res/wp/maturana/

McKenna, Eugene (2012) *Business Psychology and Organizational Behaviour*. Psychology Press: East Sussex

McKenna, Paul (2004) *Change Your Life in 7 Days*. Transworld: UK

McRaney, David (2011) *You Are Not So Smart*. Gotham Books: UK

McTaggart, Lynne (2008) *The Intention Experiment: Use Your Thoughts to Change the World*. HarperElement: UK

Méndez, Conny (1991) *Metafisica 4 en 1*. Bienes Lacónica CA: Venezuela

Méndez, Conny (1994) *Metafisica 4 en 1*. Bienes Lacónica CA: Venezuela

Metafisica XII (1993) CZ Ediciones. Argentina

Metafisica X (1993) CZ Ediciones. Argentina

Mills, Derek (2012) *The 10-Second Philosophy: A Practical Guide to Releasing Your Inner Genius*. Hay House: London

Mohr, Barbel (2009) *Cosmic Ordering: The Next Step*. Hay House: UK

Mohr, Barbel (2011) *The 21 Golden Rules of Cosmic Ordering*. Hay House: UK

Money Mind Fest Sessions:
http://www.moneymindfestevent.com/

Morris, Henry M. (2004) *Miracles: Do They Still Happen? Why We Believe in Them*. Master Books: USA

Mulford, Prentice (2009) *Thoughts are Things*. Seeds of Life Publishing: USA

Murphy, Joseph (1963) *The Power of Your Subconscious Mind.* Prentice Hall Inc: USA

Murphy, Joseph (2010) *Love is Freedom.* Willing Publishing Company: California

Naisbitt, John (2006) *Mind Set! Reset Your Thinking and See the Future.* HarperCollins: USA

Neill, Michael (2013) *The Inside-Out Revolution: The Only Thing You Need To Know To Change Your Life Forever.* Hay House: UK

Nepo, Mark (2012) *Seven Thousand Ways to Listen: Staying Close to What is Sacred.* Simon & Schuster: New York

Nightingale, Earl (2012) *The Strangest Secret of Succeeding in the World Today.* Nightingale Conant: USA

Norretranders, Tor (1996) *The User Illusion: Cutting Consciousness Down to Size.* Penguin Books: England

Olson, Jeff (2005) *The Slight Edge.* Success Books: USA

Osho (2011) *Book of Nothing: Hsin Hsin Ming.* Osho Media International: New York

Osho (2004) *Freedom: The Courage to Be Yourself.* St. Martin's Press: New York

Parish, Angela (2012) *The Christian Ho'oponopono Forgiveness Practice: Forgiving Yourself and Forgiving Others, and Accepting the Love and Blessings of Our Lord and Savior Jesus Christ.* Amazon.com Ltd: Great Britain

Patent, Arnold (2005) *Money.* Celebration Publishing: Arizona

Pattakos, Alex (2004) *Prisoners of Our Thoughts: Viktor Frankl's Principles for Discovering Meaning in Life and Work.* Berrett-Koehler: San Francisco

Peale, Norman Vincent (2013) *The Power of Positive Thinking.* Fireside: New York

Peale, Norman Vincent (1981) "How to Have a Good Day Every Day." *Guideposts Outreach*: USA

Peel, Malcolm (2004) *Readymade Interview Questions.* Kogan Page: London

Perez, Adolfo (2012) *Ho'oponopono.* Ediciones Masters: Madrid

Persaud, Raj (2006) *Simply Irresistible: The Psychology of Seduction.* Bantam Press: London

Pert, Candace B. (1999) *Molecules of Emotion: The Science Behind Mind-Body Medicine.* Simon & Schuster: New York

Petroff, Mark (2011) *Being Love: 26 Keys to Experiencing Unconditional Love.* iUniverse Inc: Bloomington, Indiana, USA

Ponder, Catherine (2010) *Open Your Mind to Receive.* Princeton Licensing Group: USA

Ponder, Catherine (1966) *The Dynamic Laws of Healing.* DeVorss Publications: Camarilla, CA

Pope, Alexander (2012) *Pope's Essay on Criticism.* Forgotten Books: UK

Powell, John (1978) *Unconditional Love: Love without Limits.* Tabor Publishing: Texas

Prabhupada, AC Bhaktivedanta Swami (2011) *Chant and Be Happy: The Power of Mantra Meditation.* The Bhaktivedanta Book Trust: UK

Ray, Robert F. (2012) *Return to Zeropoint II: Ho'oponopono for a better reality.* Balboa Press: USA

Ray, Sondra (2012) *Kahuna y Ho'oponopono: Secretos de los Maestros Hawaianos y de la Vida Eterna.* Arkano Books: Madrid

Ray, Sondra (2005) *Pele's Wish: Secrets of the Hawaiian Masters and Eternal Life.* New World Library: California

Renard, Gary R. (2004) *The Disappearance of the Universe: Straight Talk About Illusions, Past Lives, Religion, Sex, Politics and the Miracles of Forgiveness.* Hay House: USA

Resnick, Stella (1998) *Reencontrar el placer.* Urano: Barcelona

Richardson, Diana and Michael Richardson (2010) *Tantric Love: Feeling vs Emotion: Golden rules to make love easy.* O-Books: UK

Rinpoche, Sogyal (2008) *The Tibetan Book of Living and Dying.* Rider: UK

Robbins, Anthony (1997) *Mensaje a un amigo.* Grijalbo Mondadori: Barcelona

Roberts, Jane (1970) *The Seth Material: The Spiritual Teacher That*

Launched the New Age. Buccaneer Books: New York

Robertson, Ian (2002) *The Mind's Eye: The essential guide to boosting your mental, emotional and physical powers.* Bantam Books

Robinson, Ken (2009) *The Element: How Finding Your Passion Changes Everything.* Penguin Books: England

Robinson, Lynn (2013) *Divine Intuition: Your Inner Guide to Purpose, Peace and Prosperity.* Jossey-Bass: USA

Rogers, Carl (1961) *On Becoming a Person: A therapist's view of psychotherapy.* Houghton Mifflin Company: USA

Roman, Sanaya and Duane Packer (1988) *Creating Money: Keys to Abundance.* HJ Kramer Inc: Tiburon, CA

Rosenberg, Marshall B. (2003) *Nonviolent Communication: A Language of Life.* PuddleDancer Press: USA

Ruiz, Don Miguel (1997) *The Four Agreements.* Amber-Allen Publishing: California

Samuels, Michael (2011) *Just Ask the Universe: A No-Nonsense Guide to Manifesting Your Dreams.* Amazon Digital Services Inc

Saradananda, Swami (2009) *The Power of Breath: The Art of Breathing Well For Harmony, Happiness and Health.* Duncan Baird Publishers: London

Satyam, Shri Khaishvara (2009) *El Otro Secreto: Liberación emocional con Ho'oponopono.* Fundación Krodhedharma

Schambach, RW (2009) *Miracles.* Destiny Image Publishers: USA

Schucman, Helen (2007) *A Course in Miracles.* Foundation for Inner Peace: UK

Schwartz, David J. (2007) *The Magic of Thinking Big.* Fireside/Simon and Schuster: New York

Schwartz, Jeffrey M. and Sharon Begley (2003) *The Mind & The Brain: Neuroplasticity and the Power of Mental Force.* ReganBooks: USA

Seife, Charles (2000) *Zero: The Biography of a Dangerous Idea.* Souvenir Press: London

Shakespeare, William (2009) *The Sonnets and the Lover's Complaint.* (Clothbound Classics) Penguin Classics: England

Shakespeare, William (1993) *The Merchant of Venice*. Wordsworth Classics: Great Britain

Sha, Zhi Gang (2006) *Soul Mind Body Medicine: A Complete Soul Healing System for Optimum Health and Vitality*. New World Library: California

Sha, Zhi Gang (2009) *The Power of Soul: The Way to Heal, Rejuvenate, Transform, and Enlighten All Life*. Atria Books: USA

Shaw, Peter (2008) *Making Difficult Decisions: How to be Decisive and Get the Business Done*. Capstone Publishing: UK

Shearer, Caroline A. (2011) *Love Like God: Embracing Unconditional Love*. Absolute Love Publishing: USA

Shimoff, Marci and Carol Kline (2010) *Love for No Reason: 7 Steps to Creating a Life of Unconditional Love*. Free Press: New York

Shinn, Florence Scovel (2012) *The Game of Life and How to Play It*. Start Publishing LLC: USA

Shook, E. Victoria (2002) *Ho'oponopono: Contemporary Uses of a Hawaiian Problem-Solving Process*. University of Hawaii Press: Honolulu

Siegel, Bernie (1986) *Love, Medicine and Miracles*. Rider: UK

Siegel, Bernie S. (2005) *101 Exercise for the Soul: Simple Practices for a Healthy Body, Mind & Spirit*. New World Library: California

Siegel, Bernie S. (2011) *A Book of Miracles: Inspiring True Stories of Healing, Gratitude, and Love*. New World Library: California

Silva, Jose and Burt Goldman (1989) *Dinamica del Metodo Silva de Control Mental*. Vergara Diana: Buenos Aires

Skomal, Lenore (2006) *LifeLessons: Gratitude*. Cider Mill Press: Kennebunkport, Maine

Slatter, Jean (2003) *Hiring the Heavens: A Practical Guide to Developing Working Relationships with the Spirits of Creation*. New World Library: Novato, CA

Smith, Marilyn (2010) *Gratitude: A Key to Happiness*. Heaven's Library: Canada

Starzynski, Father Stefan and Chris Grzasko (2010) *Miracles: Healing for a Broken World*. Our Sunday Visitor Publishing

Division: USA

Stauffer, Edith R. (1987) *Unconditional Love and Forgiveness.* Triangle Publishers: California

Stein, Steven J. (2009) *Emotional Intelligence for Dummies.* Wiley: Canada

Steiner, Rudolf (2014) *Knowledge of the Higher Worlds: How Is It Achieved?* Rudolf Steiner Press: UK

Steiner, Rudolf (1986) *The Philosophy of Spiritual Activity.* Anthroposophic Press

Sunyatananda, Khenpo Gurudas (2011) *Sunyata: The Transformative Power of Emptiness in Esoteric Buddhism, New Thought and the Ancient Hawaiian Spiritual Tradition.* Vajra Sky Media and Publishing: USA

Taylor, Sandra Anne (2009) *Quantum Success: The Astounding Science of Wealth and Happiness.* Hay House: UK

Teck, Dan and Jodi Chapman (2011) *Transitions: 50 Prompts to Help Guide You Through Life's Changes.* www.souljournals.com

Tennov, Dorothy (1999) *Love and Limerence: The Experience of Being in Love.* Scarborough House: New York

Theodore, John (2011) *Lessons from the Life of a Salesman.* Books of Africa: UK

Tolle, Eckhart (2001) *A New Earth: Create a Better Life.* Penguin Books: USA

Tolle, Eckhart (1999) *The Power of Now: A Guide to Spiritual Enlightenment.* Hodder & Stoughton: UK

Tolle, Eckhart (2002) *Practicing the Power of Now: Essential Teachings, Meditations, and Exercises from the Power of Now.* Hodder Mobius: USA

Trent, John and Gary Smalley (1986) *The Blessing: Giving the Gift of Unconditional Love and Acceptance.* Thomas Nelson: USA

Ulanov, Ann and Barry (1983) *Primary Speech: A psychology of prayer.* Westminster John Knox Press: USA

Villani, Elizabeth (2011) *Love: A Guide to Advancing Your Soul.* O-Books

Villoldo, Alberto and Stanley Krippner (1987) *Healing States.* Simon and Schuster: New York

Villoldo, Alberto (2001) *Shaman, Healer, Sage: How to Heal Yourself and Others with the Energy Medicine of the Americas.* Great Britain

Villoldo, Alberto (2005) *Mending the Past and Healing the Future with Soul Retrieval.* Hay House: USA

Vitale, Joe and Ihaleakala Hew Len (2007) *Zero Limits: The Secret Hawaiian System for Wealth, Health, Peace, and More.* John Wiley & Sons, Inc

Vitale, Joe (2006) *O Fator atraccao.* Lua de papel: Portugal

Vitale, Joe (2013) *The Miracles Manual: The Secret Coaching Sessions, Volume 1.* Hypnotic Marketing Inc: USA

Vitale, Joe (2013) *Faith.* Trumedia: USA

Vitale Joe, Healing with Ho'oponopono (Parts 1–6): http://www.youtube.com/watch?v=ZTViougNWKo

Vitale, Joe (2013) *At Zero: The Quest for Miracles Through Ho'oponopono.* Wiley: New Jersey

Von Deck, Tom (2011) *Oceanic Mind: The Deeper Meditation Training Course.* www.deepermeditation.net

Von Harrison, Grant (2006) *Drawing on the Powers of Heaven.* Sounds of Zion: USA

Wallin, David J. (2007) *Attachment in Psychotherapy.* The Guilford Press: New York

Warren, Rick (2002) *The Purpose Driven Life: What On Earth Am I Here For?* Zondervan: Michigan

Watson, Donald (1995) *A Dictionary of Mind & Body.* Andre Deutsch: London

Wattles, Wallace (2009) *How to Get What You Want.* The Princeton Licensing Group: USA

Wattles, Wallace (1910) *The Science of Getting Rich.* Elizabeth Towne Publishing: New York

Wicherink, Jan (2005) *Souls of Distortion Awakening: A convergence of science and spirituality.* www.soulsofdistortion.nl

Wilde, Stuart (2007) *Miracles*. Hay House: USA

Williams, Cissi (2013) *Supercharge Your Dreams Into Being: By Trusting Your Soul's Inner Guidance*. O-Books: UK

Williamson, Marianne (1996) *A Return to Love: Reflections on the Principles of A Course in Miracles*. Thorsons: London

Wilson, Timothy D. (2002) *Strangers to Ourselves: Discovering the Adaptive Unconscious*. The Belknap Press of Harvard University Press: Cambridge

Wolhorn, Herman (1977) *Emmet Fox's Golden Keys to Successful Living and Reminiscences*. Harper & Row: New York

Zagrans, Maura Poston (2010) *Miracles Every Day*. Doubleday Religion: USA

Zero Limits. DVD 1 to 6

Websites

http://www.businessbyyou.com
http://www.vitalesecrets.com/campaigns/tsm/download.php
http://www.self-i-dentity-through-hooponopono.com/
http://www.intentionallyclean.com
http://www.intentionallytreasure.com

The Author

Dr. Bruno Roque Cignacco (PhD) studied Metaphysics for more than 15 Years.

He is the author of the book *How to Manifest Money Effortlessly: Techniques to be more prosperous*. This book was published by O-Books (John Hunt Publishing) in 2013. The rights for this book were sold to Italy, Korea and India.

He is also the author of a business book called *Techniques of International Negotiation* published by Macchi Publishers in 2014 and *International Marketing: Fundamentals for SMES* in 2010 (Atlantic Publishers), published in Spanish and Portuguese. He also wrote a novel called *El niño errante (The Wandering Child)*, Bergerac Ediciones (2010).

The author is a University Professor both at undergraduate and postgraduate level in business subjects in the UK, and an international speaker and advisor on International Business and metaphysical topics. He is also a certified master life coach and certified NLP practitioner.

How to Manifest Money Effortlessly:
Techniques to be more prosperous

Dr. Bruno R. Cignacco (O-Books, 2013)

This book is primarily focused on the most relevant techniques to manifest money effortlessly. This text pinpoints the main metaphysical principles related to the creation of wealth. It also sets out wrong assumptions about money and replaces them with positive connotations about it. The book goes on to highlight the main requirements to attract more abundance. This text describes an overarching series of strategies to attract more prosperity, such as visualization, meditation, affirmations, Feng Shui, emotional release, objective setting, playfulness, generosity perspective, gratitude, intuitive insights, de-cluttering, positive thinking, chakra cleansing and energy management, among others. All these techniques are explained in detail, accompanied with easy practical exercises.

ISBN 978-1-78279-082-2

O-BOOKS

SPIRITUALITY

O is a symbol of the world, of oneness and unity; this eye
represents knowledge and insight. We publish titles on general
spirituality and living a spiritual life. We aim to inform and help
you on your own journey in this life.
If you have enjoyed this book, why not tell other readers by
posting a review on your preferred book site?

Recent bestsellers from O-Books are:

Heart of Tantric Sex
Diana Richardson
Revealing Eastern secrets of deep love and intimacy to
Western couples.
Paperback: 978-1-90381-637-0 ebook: 978-1-84694-637-0

Crystal Prescriptions
The A-Z guide to over 1,200 symptoms and their healing crystals
Judy Hall
The first in the popular series of eight books, this handy little
guide is packed as tight as a pill-bottle with crystal remedies
for ailments.
Paperback: 978-1-90504-740-6 ebook: 978-1-84694-629-5

Take Me To Truth
Undoing the Ego
Nouk Sanchez, Tomas Vieira
The best-selling step-by-step book on shedding the Ego, using
the teachings of *A Course In Miracles*.
Paperback: 978-1-84694-050-7 ebook: 978-1-84694-654-7

The 7 Myths about Love...Actually!
The Journey from your HEAD to the HEART of your SOUL
Mike George
Smashes all the myths about LOVE.
Paperback: 978-1-84694-288-4 ebook: 978-1-84694-682-0

The Holy Spirit's Interpretation of the New Testament
A Course in Understanding and Acceptance
Regina Dawn Akers
Following on from the strength of *A Course In Miracles*, NTI
teaches us how to experience the love and oneness of God.
Paperback: 978-1-84694-085-9 ebook: 978-1-78099-083-5

The Message of A Course In Miracles
A translation of the Text in plain language
Elizabeth A. Cronkhite
A translation of *A Course in Miracles* into plain, everyday
language for anyone seeking inner peace. The companion
volume, *Practicing A Course In Miracles*, offers practical lessons
and mentoring.
Paperback: 978-1-84694-319-5 ebook: 978-1-84694-642-4

Your Simple Path
Find Happiness in every step
Ian Tucker
A guide to helping us reconnect with what is really important in
our lives.
Paperback: 978-1-78279-349-6 ebook: 978-1-78279-348-9

365 Days of Wisdom
Daily Messages To Inspire You Through The Year
Dadi Janki
Daily messages which cool the mind, warm the heart and guide
you along your journey.
Paperback: 978-1-84694-863-3 ebook: 978-1-84694-864-0

Body of Wisdom
Women's Spiritual Power and How it Serves
Hilary Hart
Bringing together the dreams and experiences of women across the world with today's most visionary spiritual teachers.
Paperback: 978-1-78099-696-7 ebook: 978-1-78099-695-0

Dying to Be Free
From Enforced Secrecy to Near Death to True Transformation
Hannah Robinson
After an unexpected accident and near-death experience, Hannah Robinson found herself radically transforming her life, while a remarkable new insight altered her relationship with her father, a practising Catholic priest.
Paperback: 978-1-78535-254-6 ebook: 978-1-78535-255-3

The Ecology of the Soul
A Manual of Peace, Power and Personal Growth for Real People in the Real World
Aidan Walker
Balance your own inner Ecology of the Soul to regain your natural state of peace, power and wellbeing.
Paperback: 978-1-78279-850-7 ebook: 978-1-78279-849-1

Not I, Not other than I
The Life and Teachings of Russel Williams
Steve Taylor, Russel Williams
The miraculous life and inspiring teachings of one of the World's greatest living Sages.
Paperback: 978-1-78279-729-6 ebook: 978-1-78279-728-9

On the Other Side of Love
A woman's unconventional journey towards wisdom
Muriel Maufroy
When life has lost all meaning, what do you do?
Paperback: 978-1-78535-281-2 ebook: 978-1-78535-282-9

Practicing A Course In Miracles
A translation of the Workbook in plain language, with
mentor's notes
Elizabeth A. Cronkhite
The practical second and third volumes of The Plain-Language
A Course In Miracles.
Paperback: 978-1-84694-403-1 ebook: 978-1-78099-072-9

Quantum Bliss
The Quantum Mechanics of Happiness, Abundance, and Health
George S. Mentz
Quantum Bliss is the breakthrough summary of success and
spirituality secrets that customers have been waiting for.
Paperback: 978-1-78535-203-4 ebook: 978-1-78535-204-1

The Upside Down Mountain
Mags MacKean
A must-read for anyone weary of chasing success and happiness
– one woman's inspirational journey swapping the uphill slog
for the downhill slope.
Paperback: 978-1-78535-171-6 ebook: 978-1-78535-172-3

Your Personal Tuning Fork
The Endocrine System
Deborah Bates
Discover your body's health secret, the endocrine system, and 'twang' your way to sustainable health!
Paperback: 978-1-84694-503-8 ebook: 978-1-78099-697-4

Readers of ebooks can buy or view any of these bestsellers by clicking on the live link in the title. Most titles are published in paperback and as an ebook. Paperbacks are available in traditional bookshops. Both print and ebook formats are available online.
Find more titles and sign up to our readers' newsletter at
http://www.johnhuntpublishing.com/mind-body-spirit
Follow us on Facebook at https://www.facebook.com/OBooks/
and Twitter at https://twitter.com/obooks